*How To Think About Arms Control and Disarmament*

# HOW TO THINK about ARMS CONTROL and DISARMAMENT

by

James E. Dougherty

Published for
National Strategy Information Center, Inc.

Crane, Russak & Company, New York

*The National Strategy Information Center is a nonpartisan, tax-exempt institution organized in 1962 to conduct educational programs in national defense.*

*The Center is privately supported and espouses no political causes. Its funds derive from foundations, corporations and individuals. It has no government contracts, nor does it operate with government funds. It is not associated with the defense industry.*

*NSIC's Directors and Officers represent a wide spectrum of responsible political opinion from liberal to conservative. What unites them, however, is the conviction that neither isolationism nor pacifism provides realistic solutions to the challenge of 20th century totalitarianism.*

*NSIC exists to encourage civil-military partnership on the grounds that, in a democracy, informed public opinion is necessary to a viable U.S. defense system capable of protecting the nation's vital interests and assisting other free nations which aspire to independence and self-fulfillment.*



Published in the United States by
Crane, Russak & Company Inc.,
52 Vanderbilt Avenue
New York, New York 10017



ISBN 0-8448-0219-0

Library of Congress Catalog Card Number 73-76898

*Printed in the United States of America*

Strategy Papers No. 17

**To Maria**

# Table of Contents

# Preface

From earliest times, mankind has sought to mitigate the horrors of war through measures for the limitation and control of armaments and war. In more recent periods, the increasing destructiveness of weapons has lent urgency to the quest; and since the nineteenth century, disarmament has been a frequent theme of political discourse and action.

Down to World War II, however, not much substantive progress had been made, as the unlimited character of that conflict bore tragic witness. The catastrophic consequences of World War II did serve, however, to revitalize the movement for arms limitation and control; and the immediacy of the task was magnified by the introduction of nuclear weapons into the arsenals of the nations, and by the worldwide ideological split between the Soviet bloc of Communist countries and the Free World coalition led by the United States.

The present study by Dr. James E. Dougherty provides a remarkably lucid introduction to the whole complex subject of arms control and disarmament. Introductory chapters summarize the causes of war (and identify arms as primarily a symptom, rather than a fundamental cause, of human conflict); distinguish among various kinds of disarmament and arms control; and trace the historical record of disarmament negotiations down to World War II. The policies of the major powers in this field are then examined in some detail; and this is followed by a perceptive analysis of the problem of general disarmament, which the author concludes is simply not practical politics in the present historical epoch.

Dr. Dougherty then turns to more limited forms of arms control. It is in this field that some striking progress has been made in the postwar period, as evidenced by such landmarks as the "Hot Line" Agreement between the US and USSR, the Partial Nuclear Test Ban Treaty, the Nuclear Nonproliferation Treaty, and agreements for the prohibition of biological and chemical weapons. But while these and other steps represent a substantial achievement, they have not resulted in any significant reduction of arms levels, nor have they addressed the central problem of the control and limitation of strategic nuclear weapons.

The Strategic Arms Limitation Talks (SALT), on the other hand, are concerned with this overriding dilemma of the nuclear age. Dr. Dougherty reviews in detail the several years of SALT Phase I negotiations at Helsinki and Vienna that culminated in the 1972 Moscow Agreements on the interim limitation of strategic arms and the ABM Treaty permanently restricting antiballistic missile defense systems. His analysis of the strategic concepts underlying these agreements is especially useful; and while he cautiously applauds the Moscow Agreements as a promising first step, the author also points out that they hold great potential hazards for the United States. Much will depend on the outcome of SALT Phase II, already in progress, the negotiations for Mutual Balanced Force Reductions in Europe (MBFR) and for a European Security Conference, and other efforts to deal effectively with the continuing dilemmas of arms limitation and control in the nuclear age.

Dr. Dougherty is a leading authority in this field. He received his bachelor's degree from Saint Joseph's College, an M.A. in Political Theory from Fordham University, and his Ph.D. in International Relations from the University of Pennsylvania. Dr. Dougherty is now Professor of Politics and International Relations at Saint Joseph's College, and holds concurrent appointment as Executive Vice President of the College. He has also served as Professor of Political Affairs at the National War College, and has lectured frequently at the Foreign Service Institute, the Inter-American Defense College, and at many colleges and universities throughout the United States and Western Europe. He is the author or coauthor of several books in the field, including *Arms Control and Disarmament: The Critical Issues*, and of numerous articles on problems of foreign policy and defense strategy.

The present monograph is the seventeenth to be published by the National Strategy Information Center in its Strategy Papers series. This series has been designed primarily to assist the informed layman seriously interested in international affairs, as well as teachers and students at the college level, in analyzing and understanding some of the more complex issues of US foreign and national defense policy.

Frank R. Barnett, *President*
National Strategy Information Center, Inc.

May 1973

# 1

## Introduction

Probably there has never been an age in which at least some men failed to wonder why nations cannot live at peace with one another, and why they must maintain arms and armies in order to guarantee their own security. Nearly all the great world civilizations have produced poets, philosophers, and prophets who have pondered what man has made of man, and who have warned rulers to avoid relying too heavily upon might as distinct from right. The ancient Jewish Prophet Isaiah had a famous and oft-recalled vision: "And they shall turn their swords into ploughshares, and their spears into sickles: nation shall not lift up sword against nation, neither shall they be exercised any more to war."[1]

Yet in spite of recurring dreams of lasting peace in a disarmed environment, actual disarmament has been an extremely rare phenomenon in the history of the world. Even the philosophers who have warned against the destructiveness and unpredictability of war have acknowledged the need for defense preparedness. Take, for example, the case of ancient China. On the whole, this was among the most peaceful and least militarist of all the great civilizations, perhaps because of its cultural stability and homogeneity, as well as its isolation and tendency to be inward-looking. It is commonly held that the

[1] *Isaiah*, 2: 4.

Chinese reserved their highest esteem for the scholar, and often viewed the military with suspicion. Nevertheless the Chinese did maintain armies, and in Sun Tsu they produced one of the masterful strategists of all times. Although they had a distinctive attitude toward war, they were by no means pacifist. Confucius, the greatest of the Chinese teachers, regarded war as an evil; but he insisted that when it comes, it should be waged vigorously. Generally speaking, the ancient Chinese stressed the importance of human above material factors in war, just as Mao Tse-tung has done in this century; but this is a far cry from the advocacy of disarmament.[2]

No matter which civilization we look toward—ancient Egypt, Persia, India, Israel, Greece, or Rome; Islam, the Arabs, the Ottoman Empire, or feudal Christendom in Europe; modern England, Germany, France, the United States, the Soviet Union, Japan, or China —the underlying pattern is similar: the rhetoric is often of peace, but the social reality reflects a general tendency to prepare for war, to expect war and, in the terminology of the anthropologists, to institutionalize the expectation of war in the form of military establishments. Even where the problem of maintaining security against the danger of external attack is not seen as acute (as in the Latin American state system), the perpetuation of military forces and armaments is a deeply rooted "instinct" in society. Certainly some civilizations and states have been more aggressively militarist than others, but at one time or other virtually all political communities in history have behaved as if they believed in the classical maxim: *Si vis pacem, para bellum*, "If you want peace, prepare for war."

The idea of a disarmed, peaceful world undoubtedly has a universal human appeal. It has exercised a peculiarly powerful attraction upon the Western mind. Several factors in the Western cultural and intellectual tradition help to explain this. Modern Western civilization is a product of many confluent streams of thought—Greek rationalism, Roman legalism, Judaeo-Christian religious revelation, medieval romanticism and idealism, Renaissance utopianism, Enlightment paci-

[2] Mao Tse-tung wrote: "We see not only weapons, but also the power of man. Weapons are an important factor in war but not the decisive one; it is man and not material that counts." "On the Protracted War," in *Selected Works of Mao Tse-tung* (London: Foreign Language Press, 1954), vol. 2, p. 54. The same Mao, of course, is famous for a different axiom: "Political power grows out of the barrel of a gun."

fism, utilitarian internationalism, Marxist socialism, and modern anarchism. Each of these streams has contributed something to our longing for disarmament and a surcease to conflict in a new and as-yet-unknown unity of international peace. Here we can only touch lightly upon a few of these historic influences which, like the inner layers of an onion, comprise the hidden core of our minds on this subject.

The rationalism of the ancient Greeks led them to seek ways of resolving disputes among themselves by such peaceful means as arbitration and, if war came, of limiting its destructive effects. The Delphic Amphictyony, for example, outlawed taking Greeks as slaves in war, burning Greek cities, and cutting off a city's water supply. The greatest of the Greek political philosophers—Plato and Aristotle—were much more interested in cultivating the "good life" inside the city than in the problems of war outside. The Romans borrowed much from the Greeks. They, too, believed—at least in theory, if not in practice—that no greater force should ever be used in war to accomplish a military objective than was required by "legitimate necessity." The Romans were also inclined to think rather optimistically that matters of war, from its causes to the modes of waging it, were subject to analysis by reason and to regulation by law. Twentieth-century intellectuals frequently scoff at the notion that war can be controlled either by reason or by law; but they often seem to believe that the decision to go to war can be banned by reason and the implements of war abolished by law. Both Greek rationalism and Roman legalism have played a significant part in the shaping of Western ideals concerning what is possible in international relations.

The various religious-theological convictions that spring from the Jewish and Christian Scriptures constitute another important influence upon Western attitudes toward war, peace, and disarmament. The books of revelation abound with passages implying that war is the result of sinfulness, and that peace is to be equated with the reward of the virtuous or the condition of the blessed. It is true that both the Jewish and Christian traditions provide for the possibility of the "just war," or even of war waged at Divine command. But even the "good war" is never presented as an ideal; rather it is, in the words of Saint Augustine, a "sad necessity" for turning back evil.

Throughout Christian history, a radical pacifist minority has taken the position that all war is intrinsically evil, no matter for what cause it is fought. Convinced that the Christian must always turn the other cheek regardless of the consequences for the state, many members of the "peace churches" in recent centuries have refused to perform military service for reasons of conscience. Some pacifists distinguish between pacifism as an individual choice and pacifism as public policy, while others hope that the dictates of their private consciences will eventually become a governmental policy of military self-abnegation. Throughout the greater part of Western history, the more orthodox and dominant Christian position has been different. Even though the individual Christian should renounce resort to force when his own private rights are violated, nevertheless the organized political community is responsible for safeguarding the common good, the public order of justice, and must be prepared to defend it by force as the prudent, reasonable statesman, after weighing the likely consequences of alternative policies, deems the threat or use of force necessary.[3] But given the nature of modern total war, and especially of nuclear war, increasing numbers of "orthodox" religious thinkers have questioned whether the classical conditions of just war can any longer be fulfilled, and whether the wholesale obliteration of urban populations by nuclear-tipped ICBMs can ever be justified by any rational political objective. No one can deny that the religious roots of Western thinking about the arms problem have laid some of the foundations of the modern yearning for disarmament.

Western man is descended from a medieval European culture in which efforts were constantly made to impose authoritative, verbal controls upon the conduct of warfare. The Church specified times when fighting could not be carried on, sites where battle was prohibited, types of weapons that could not legitimately be employed, and classes of persons that were immune as targets of military action. The codes of chivalry and the rules of civilized warfare did not hold up very well in conflicts between diverse cultures (for example, Christian Europe and Islam), or hostile religious ideologies (Catholicism and Protestantism in the first hundred years after the Reformation).

[3] For a description of the "just war" theory, see James E. Dougherty and Robert L. Pfaltzgraff, Jr., *Contending Theories of International Relations* (Philadelphia: Lippincott, 1971), pp. 150-154 and 167-171. See also Paul Ramsey, *The Just War: Force and Political Responsibility* (New York: Scribner, 1968).

But religious and humanitarian limitations on fighting were often observed with surprising fidelity in the tournament-like wars of the feudal period, and later in the "drawing-room" wars of the interval between the Peace of Westphalia and the French Revolution. Even in the twentieth century, often branded as the era of total war, we can perceive vestiges of our medieval origins in such concepts as "open cities" in World War II, Christmas and New Year truces in Vietnam, the loathing we experience at the thought of using nuclear or biological weapons, or upon hearing of the bombing of hospitals, orphanages, schools, and churches.

From Dante down to our own day, Western thinkers have recurringly called for some form of international government able to prevent war by effectively guaranteeing the peaceful settlement of disputes. The Renaissance and Enlightenment periods have bequeathed to the West an influential school of pacifist thought combining religious idealism, humanitarianism, and bourgeois internationalism. Despite Marxist-Leninist charges that the capitalist bourgeoisie produced new economic causes of international conflict, actually the rise of bourgeois culture has operated in history to buttress pacifist more than militarist sentiments. Most businessmen do not want war, but rather an orderly world in which trade and profits are predictable. The middle class is normally interested in raising its level of material comfort, not sustaining the rigors and sacrifices of war.

Many of Europe's most prominent intellectual figures—Erasmus, Thomas More, Voltaire, Rousseau, Kant, and Bentham—have helped to impress deeply on the Western consciousness such concepts as the futility of war, the superiority of the useful life of the merchant over the destructive life of the soldier, and the urgency of bringing about a disarmed world. Our civilization has produced an abundance of plans for abolishing war and establishing perpetual peace. At various times in history, our rationalist ancestors have been convinced that the movement from monarchies to democratic republics would foster a new spirit of peaceful behavior; that science, education, and the benign power of public opinion would inevitably triumph over the historic curses of ignorance, poverty, disease, and war; that nations would accept a reduction of armaments if only they would give freedom to their colonial possessions overseas; and that war would quickly become obsolete once its economic unprofitableness had been recognized. One has to admire the abiding optimism of the Western intellectual: his faith in the power of logical reason to reorder the social universe, to make all things right, has never been shaken for long—not by the rise of nationalism, not by the temper of violent revolution, not by the appearance of totalitarian ideologies, nor by the tragedy of two world wars in this century.

What have all these old cultural ideas to do with the contemporary issues of disarmament and arms control? They are germane, for they comprise the warp and woof of our attitudes toward these issues. Western publics, especially in England and the United States, tend to posit an antithesis between power and morality, between the soldier and civilization, between "evil" expenditures for military defense and "good" expenditures for economic development and welfare. In some otherwise sophisticated quarters, there still lurk the vestiges of Marxist-Leninist theory in its crudest, most vulgar form—the "devil" theory of war, which explains wars as caused by bad men for motives of profit. The "devil" theory has long since been discredited by virtually all social scientists, but it keeps cropping up—a current version being the proposition, espoused by many teachers, students, and mass media pundits, that the chief obstacle to disarmament and world peace is the American "military-industrial" complex, including the "military mind," "Service lobbying," and the defense contract system headquartered in the Pentagon. Although widespread, this simplistic explanation hardly qualifies as serious thinking about the dilemma of arms confronting man today.

The twentieth century has witnessed the emergence of disarmament and arms control as a permanent theme in the foreign policies of major governments. The advent of nuclear, chemical, and biological weapons, as well as intercontinental delivery systems which can rain destruction on cities all over the globe in a matter of minutes, has made general disarmament appear to many a more desirable goal than ever before in history. Even proponents of a nuclear deterrence policy often say that theirs is a policy of temporary insurance until disarmament can be negotiated. Yet the same advanced military technology which makes disarmament so imperative also makes it the more difficult to achieve in a world of profound cultural differences, ideological divisions, and fundamental political disagreements over the way in which the international system is to be organized. As technology develops, the anxiety of nation-states over their own security increases rather than decreases. Most of the nation-states which are really free to pursue policies of their own choosing still prefer to base their security on some form of deterrence or power balance than on the expectation of disarmament and effective international peacekeeping. Perhaps this will strike many as illogical. But the realm of international politics is governed by more than logic, and often by less. When we think about national armaments, we have to think not only about how we would like nations to behave—based on the ethical and rational ideals of Western civilization—but also about how nations do in fact behave.

# 2

# Arms and the Causes of Conflict

A crucial question to be dealt with at the outset is whether the existence of armaments is in itself the cause of international war, or whether national armaments can make for peace through deterrence by preparedness. This question has been posed recurringly since the latter part of the nineteenth century. Obviously, the question has never been answered to the satisfaction of most intelligent men, for it keeps being asked. The author is not so presumptuous as to pretend that he will answer it once for all. Do arms cause war, or are armed establishments the symptoms and effects of conflict between societies? Perhaps, in the form posed, the query really cannot be answered with definiteness and finality, simply because it is ambiguous. But if in this crude, ambiguous form, a preliminary reply is needed, the author is inclined to agree with the analysis of such scholars as Frederick L. Schuman and Hans J. Morgenthau. Schuman, noting that peace advocates have long believed that arms lead to war and disarmament to peace, wrote: "In reality, the reverse is more nearly true: war machines are reduced only when peace seems probable, the expectation of conflict leads to competition in armaments, and armaments spring from war and from the anticipation of war."[1] Morgenthau gave this terse opinion: "Men do not fight because they have arms. They have arms because they deem it necessary to fight."[2]

[1] Frederick L. Schuman, *International Politics*, fifth edition (New York: McGraw-Hill, 1953), p. 230.
[2] Hans J. Morgenthau, *Politics Among Nations: The Struggle for Power and Peace*, fourth edition (New York: Knopf, 1967), p. 392.

But to be fair and objective, we have to refine the question. "The contention that arms are the fruits rather than the seeds of war," notes Charles P. Schleicher, "was probably nearer the truth in a simpler age than at present."[3] He goes on to argue that strategists in the nuclear age attach so much importance to the advantages to be gained from a first strike that the dangers of preemptive war are great enough to be tension-producing. Thus we must ask whether the "arms race," as conducted with nuclear-tipped intercontinental missiles (ICBM), along with technological developments in respect to antimissile defense (ABM), multiple warheads (MIRV), and antisubmarine warfare (ASW), is of such a nature as to be more conducive to the outbreak of war than to the continuation of deterrence.

Obviously those who advocate a strategic policy of nuclear deterrence hope that the existence of a massive, up-to-date arsenal of nuclear weapons will keep a surprise attack "unthinkable" as a deliberate option available to responsible, intelligent leaders who can foresee the consequences of their decisions. But there is a fear among some analysts of international relations that a policy of arming for defensive and deterrent purposes may eventually prove disastrously counterproductive. According to this school of thought, the mere act of adding a new generation of sophisticated weapons to a nation's forces, even if carried out with the purest of defensive intentions, might serve to arouse the fears and suspicions of the adversary that preparations are being made for attack. The adversary then embarks upon his own countermeasures, seen as equally defensive by himself but threatening to the other country. In such an action-reaction process, every acquisition of a new defensive capability by one side tends to confirm the conviction of the other that its rival is developing an aggressive intention. Thus we are brought rather quickly to the conclusion that virtually every increment of military technology serves to exacerbate an "unbridled arms race" which will lead ineluctably to the outbreak of war through a variety of mechanisms—the "mirror image," the mutual self-fulfilling prophecy, the spiraling of tensions and hostility, combined with some deep, irrational desire to escape from the intolerability of ambiguity, anxiety, and so forth.[4] (One

---

[3] Charles P. Schleicher, *International Relations: Cooperation and Conflict* (Englewood Cliffs, N. J.: Prentice-Hall, 1965), p. 413.

[4] See, for example, Charles E. Osgood, "Questioning Some Unquestioned Assumptions about National Defense," *Journal of Arms Control,* vol. 1 (January 1963), pp. 2-13.

occasionally feels himself swept along more by the power of the rhetoric than by the scientific accuracy of the analysis.)

The man of political intelligence is one who tries valiantly to tread his way between the distorted views of extremists at opposite ends of the spectrum—whether those rabid anti-Communists on the one hand who think that every new weapons deployment on the Soviet side constitutes proof of sinister designs, while every proposed new US deployment is necessarily good; or those overly ardent peaceniks, on the other hand, who condemn out of hand anyone seriously interested in US defense requirements as a minion of the "military-industrial complex," and who apparently proceed on the assumption that all concessions in international arms negotiations must come from the United States because they regard American capitalism as morally inferior to Soviet socialism. If many of the former extremists have subordinated their freedom of mind to patriotism, many of the latter have, wittingly or not, shifted their political allegiance to a foreign power and subordinated their freedom of mind to it.

In our analysis, we should put aside propaganda shibboleths of all sorts and strive instead to think the problem through with as much semblance of political-scientific logic as the contemporary propaganda-ridden mind can muster in an increasingly polarized society. No social scientist of any repute has asserted as demonstrable that arms in and by themselves are a primary cause of international war, or that the elimination of arms at any given time would permanently remove either the underlying sources of international political conflict or the danger of cataclysmic war. Nearly all prudent analysts concede that there is an intimate, almost circular relationship between armaments competition and political conflict. But the problem, as John G. Stoessinger has pointed out, is to determine the point at which we can intervene most effectively in the vicious circle:[5]

> Those who see arms races as a basic cause of war assert the primacy of international order-building through disarmament. They maintain that halting the arms race will lead to a reduction

[5] John G. Stoessinger, *The Might of Nations: World Politics in Our Time*, third edition (New York: Random House, 1969), p. 337.

in political tensions, which will likely result in an even further scrapping of weapons. On the other hand, a growing number of observers are defending the view that disarmament efforts are bound to fail unless they are preceded by more fundamental political accommodation. The way to disarm, according to this latter view, is not to begin by disarming but to concentrate instead on the settlement of political differences.

It is not possible here to discuss all the scientific theories of social conflict and international war that have been advanced in modern times. But a few summary observations about the "causes of war" will serve to demonstrate that the effort to understand and explain, as well as to control and prevent, war is extremely complex and difficult. There is no single theory that can do the job. Social scientists are not agreed as to whether the problem of war should be approached from the "micro" or the "macro" perspective—that is, whether the origins of large-scale, organized conflict should be sought primarily within the biological-psychological structure of man ("human nature"), or within the larger political, economic, and cultural institutions and structural configurations of human society. Nor are social scientists agreed as to whether conflict is basically irrational or rational. Most American psychologists, for example, look upon conflict as dysfunctional and disruptive, even pathological, whereas most European and a growing number of American sociologists (post-Parsonian) regard conflict as healthy, functional, and socially constructive, at least potentially. A certain amount of conflict seems to be inevitable in human affairs; its continuation has to be expected. Man's principal objective must be not to eliminate *all* conflict, but to direct conflict whenever possible into constructive, nonviolent channels which lead to human social development, while at the same time trying to limit such violent conflict as may occur beyond his ability to prevent.

Contemporary behavorial and social scientists are keenly concerned with why men behave aggressively and why nations wage wars. These two questions are related, but they are not the same. The former pertains to the inner springs of action within the psychological and biological structure of individual human beings. The second question pertains to the political decisionmaking processes of governments.

How should we explain why men fight wars? By focusing on the conscious, rational, verbalizable reasons and motives which governments give? Or by delving into the dark, unconscious forces and impulses which lurk in man and in society? Scientists divide on this as on other issues. Biologists, psychologists, and social psychologists tend to emphasize the part played by underlying irrational factors in human aggression. But most social scientists—in the fields of politics, sociology, history, anthropology, and communications—while acknowledging the importance of the unconscious and the emotional in society, are more apt to pay attention to the part played by the conscious, by words, symbols, and values, by motives for conflict which can be articulated, and by the way groups express their perceptions of the larger social situation, including threats to their security.

Between what men feel inside themselves and what national governments decide to do in the external international arena, there is a considerable distance, punctuated by several different levels of social action. Psychological states alone (such as fear, anxiety, hostility) can never adequately explain social-political behavior, nor can social-political conditions alone explain individual behavior. War does not occur merely because large numbers of people in one nation feel hostile toward another nation, or are afraid of it. Fear, resentment, or hostility may be widespread among the population, and yet the government can avert war. Under other circumstances, a people may want peace, detente, and cooperation, but the government is able to choose war when it deems war necessary in the national interest. War results not from the uncontrollability of popular emotional attitudes, but from a carefully calculated decision by governments—a decision taken by professional politicians. (This was not always true in history, of course, but it becomes an observation of increasing validity in the nuclear age.) War and the threat of war are political acts, undertaken or used for political reasons which make sense to bureaucratic experts and political decisionmakers.[6]

---

[6] See the trenchant analysis by Werner Levi, who argues that war results from a calculated decision by governments, regardless of the inner psychic states of citizens. "On the Causes of War and the Conditions of Peace," *Journal of Conflict Resolution*, vol. 4 (December 1960), pp. 411-420. See also the editor's "Introduction" in Herbert C. Kelman, ed., *International Behavior: A Social-Psychological Analysis* (New York: Holt, Rinehart and Winston, 1965), pp. 5-6.

From the modern scientific disciplines that have studied conflict and aggression, we learn that there is a wide variety of factors—both "inside" man, and "outside" man in his social structures—which might be associated with the phenomenon of individual or group fighting. The biologists remind us of population density and the effects of overcrowding; food supply and hunger; sexual and mating drives; bond-family patterns and the protection of the young; the desire to establish dominance-submission relationships; the "territorial imperative;" physical changes in the brain or chemical changes in the body of the organism; innate behavior and learning experience; the ritualization of aggression and the development of aggression-inhibitors in some species for self-preservation purposes.[7] Biologists are cautious about explaining war among humans. But they expect those who study the problems of war and peace not to forget that, however noble a creature man may be, he is also a biological creature who has inherited certain deeprooted behavioral characteristics not to be lightly thrown off.

Psychologists in recent decades have rejected Sigmund Freud's theory of the "death instinct" as the cause of recurring war among humans. Most psychologists today tend to explain individual aggressiveness within the framework of the frustration-aggression hypothesis. Briefly, it runs this way. Whatever interferes with goal-oriented behavior—and a great many things in every society do—frustrates the individual and gives rise to an aggressive impulse. The immediate frustrating agent (parent, sibling, teacher, husband, wife, boss, colleague) is the preferred target of aggression; but the very process of socialization is designed to render this infeasible in most cases, and to attenuate conflict in intimate social relationships by displacing the accumulated aggressiveness to more remote collective targets, whether to intranational scapegoat groups or to foreign nations. (Why it should be directed to certain nations—usually one or a few—and not to most foreign countries is a matter for sociologists, anthropologists, and political scientists, not psychologists.) People in one country, say the psychologists, suffer from perceptual distortion in receiv-

[7] See Peter A. Corning, "The Biological Basis of Behavior and Some Implications for Political Science," *World Politics*, vol. 23 (April 1971), pp. 321-370; Elton B. McNeil, "The Nature of Aggression," in McNeil, ed., *The Nature of Human Conflict* (Englewood Cliffs, N. J.: Prentice-Hall, 1965), pp. 14-41; and Konrad Lorenz, *On Aggression* (New York: Harcourt, Brace, 1966).

ing information about the enemy nation. They develop biases, prejudices, and stereotyped attitudes. Under certain circumstances, especially in times of international crisis, there may arise among aware publics (and this is a function of communications media) a sense of indignation, anger, desire to punish, or a sense of threat, anxiety, or fear.

Psychologists call attention to other factors which might have a bearing on the war problem. The perceptions and personality characteristics of leadership must be considered under conditions of stress. The presence of collective neurotic tendencies within the population—such as the growth of an authoritarian personality, which culminates in the adulation of a dictatorial leader—may enable the leaders to indoctrinate the masses with militarist, chauvinist attitudes. But we must reiterate a fundamental point made earlier. The final decision to go to war is one that is taken by governments for political reasons. It cannot emerge automatically from the psychic states of citizens, no matter how numerous. Furthermore, when armies engage in hostilities, they do so because they are trained to do so, not because they are frustrated or angry. Most psychologists are careful to exclude learned aggression from the frustration-aggressive hypothesis.[8] Biologists and psychologists agree that conflict arises from a combination of innate factors and learning based on experience and, in man's case, on culture.

It is to the "macro" scientists of human society that we must turn to complete our survey of the causes of war. Economists point to patterns of trade and investment that call for governmental protection; sources of essential raw materials; economic growth rates and the allocation of national resources as between internal and external objectives; the cost of defense technology and military operations, and so forth. (The Marxist-Leninists, of course, in their theory of capitalist-inspired imperialism emphasize the economic causation of

[8] The reader interested in pursuing psychological themes of conflict and aggression is referred to the following: Kelman, *op. cit.;* John Dollard and others, *Frustration and Aggression* (New Haven: Yale, 1939); Ross Stagner, "The Psychology of Human Conflict," and Stephen Withey and Daniel Katz, "The Social Psychology of Human Conflict," in McNeil, ed., *op. cit.*; Leonard Berkowitz, *Aggression: A Social Psychological Analysis* (New York: McGraw-Hill, 1962); J. K. Zawodny, ed., *Man and International Relations, Volume I: Conflict* (San Francisco: Chandler, 1966); and Jerome D. Frank, *Sanity and Survival: Psychological Aspects of War and Peace* (New York: Random House Vintage Books, 1968), especially ch. 5 to 9.

war to the virtual exclusion of all other factors.) Students of geography and its political implications have long expounded on the differences between the attitudes of land powers and sea powers toward foreign policy, defense, and war and the part played by geographic influences in the formation of friend-foe relationships as well as strategic doctrines.

Sociologists and anthropologists have cast light upon the significance of conflict for the internal cohesiveness and value structure of social groups, and vice versa. They suggest that through conflict in one form or another, whether external or internal (and these two modes of conflict seem to be inversely related), societies develop their sense of self-identity. At any given time, some national societies may be more "pacifist" or more "violence-prone" than others. Within any given society, various strata of elites and other classes may manifest quite varied dispositions toward issues of war and peace. Societies often perceive salient differences in the religious, cultural, ethnic, ideological, and political characteristics of other societies, particularly when the different values are combined with military power, as threats to their own security which must be reduced. Educational, family, communications, and other social institutions and systems are of central significance in transmitting from one generation to another the expectation of war. The role of the military institution within society requires careful attention. (Unfortunately, few domestic critics of the US military have any knowledge of the Soviet military.) In sum, until quite recently, preparation for war has been a deeprooted cultural phenomenon which, with some isolated exceptions (as in the case of the Eskimos and some Pacific islanders), has been ubiquitous among human societies.[9] What is more, its necessity has usually been taken for granted and seldom questioned with any political seriousness. Only in modern Western liberal-scientific culture has any large-scale intellectual effort been made to find alternatives to war, or what William James sixty years ago called " a moral equivalent of war."

---

[9] See Morton Fried and others, *War: The Anthropology of Armed Conflict and Aggression* (Garden City: Natural History Press, 1968); Robert C. Angell, "The Sociology of Human Conflict," and Margaret Mead and Rhoda Metraux, "The Anthropology of Human Conflict," in McNeil, ed., *op. cit.*; Lewis A. Coser, *The Functions of Social Conflict* (New York: Free Press, 1956); Leon Bramson and George W. Goethals, eds., *War: Studies from Psychology, Sociology, Anthropology*, revised edition (New York: Basic Books, 1968).

Political scientists and authorities in the field of international politics have identified numerous "conscious causes" or reasons for which governments in the modern nation-state era have opted for war: to vindicate an affront to the nation's honor; to protect the lives and property of citizens abroad; to maintain the national prestige against collapse; to retaliate against an attack on the nation's forces, or to defend against invasion; to preserve something called the "balance of power," or to restore it after it has been disturbed; to "fill a power vacuum," or to prevent it from being filled by another government; to intervene in another country either to support a friendly government or to topple an unfriendly one; to gain territory deemed vital to national security; to aid an ally and prevent the erosion of an alliance; to achieve political unity within the state and avert domestic conflict by embarking upon a popular foreign war; to obtain or subdue colonies abroad; to throw off the colonial yoke, or to put an end to what is perceived as foreign economic exploitation; to fight a preventive war before a rival gains a "decisive advantage," real or imagined; or to engage in a collective security "police" action to punish aggression or deny the aggressor his objectives, and thus to discourage similar aggression in the future. Other motives could be cited, but these will suffice.[10]

Governments are far from infallible. Clearly they often make mistakes when they decide to go to war, and fail to attain their objectives. (Witness Germany and Japan in World War II, or Britain and France in the Suez invasion.) But even in the nuclear age, at least some governments and organized political movements find it appropriate to resort to the threatened or actual use of military force to achieve desirable political ends. (Recent examples are the Soviet Union in Hungary and Czechoslovakia; France in Algeria and Britain in Malaya; China in Korea, the Quemoy Straits, Tibet, and along the Indian and Soviet borders; Israel in the Sinai Peninsula; India in Goa and East Pakistan; Greece and Turkey in Cyprus; West Pakistan in East Pakistan; North Vietnam in South Vietnam, Laos, and Cambodia, along with the Viet Cong and the Pathet Lao; the United

[10] See Dean G. Pruitt and Richard C. Snyder, eds., *Theory and Research on the Causes of War* (Englewood Cliffs, N. J.: Prentice-Hall, 1969); as well as the classic work by Quincy Wright, *A Study of War* (Chicago: University of Chicago, 1942), especially "The Political Utility of War" in vol. 2, pp. 853-860.

States in Korea, Lebanon, Berlin, Cuba, the Dominican Republic, and Southeast Asia.) So long as some governments find military force useful, most governments will look upon it as a necessary guarantor of their security, territorial integrity, and political independence. The virtually unanimous conclusion of political analysts is that, so long as the nation-state system endures in its present historic form, characterized by the longlasting condition of "international anarchy" in which there exists no reliable international peacekeeping organization, the normal behavioral tendency of governments, arising out of political unavoidability, will be for them to base their foreign and security policies on some form of manipulating and equilibrating political-military power in its several modalities. Each government will continue to define for itself both the quality and quantity of military capabilities which it requires in its own total situation as perceived by itself.

In none of the foregoing examples of international conflict would any government admit that the mere existence of armaments had been the primary cause of the hostilities. A scientific purist might well argue that the existence of weapons is a necessary condition of modern warfare, since in their total and permanent absence war could not possibly be waged. But the purist is also compelled to add that the existence of arms can seldom if ever be shown to be the sufficient cause of war. Our very sketchy review above of the myriad perspectives which the various scientific disciplines cast upon the problem of war would indicate that there must be a confluence of several forces and factors making for war before a government takes a deliberate decision for war.

It is impossible to prove scientifically that an "arms race" has ever been the primary cause of an international war in the modern era. The most famous instance prior to the nuclear missile era where this was alleged to be so was the case of the arms buildup in Europe in the years before World War I, and especially the naval rivalry between England and Germany. But the coming of the war in 1914 must also be traced to the interaction of the European alliance systems; nationalism and irredentism; the imperialistic rivalry of the powers in Asia and Africa; the antipathies and suspicions that prevailed among contrasting political systems (especially English and

French democracy, on the one hand, and German authoritarianism on the other); the role of the press; the impact of individual personalities and decisions; and other factors.[11]

But we would be unwise to carry too far the notion that armaments are not a cause of war. Arms import races have heightened regional political tensions and contributed to conflict in the Middle East, on the Indian subcontinent, and elsewhere in recent years.[12] The ready availability of conventional arms appears to have been an important contributing factor in the increased incidence and magnitude of guerrilla revolutionary warfare in the Third World during the past two decades. This factor, of course, must be weighed in the larger political context of contemporary revolutionary movements, including Communist doctrines of "wars of national liberation" or "people's war," the readiness of outside powers to intervene in internal wars, and the indigenous economic, social, psychological, and political matrix out of which violent revolution arises. But before a revolutionary leader decides to take to the hills and start applying the strategy and tactics of protracted insurgency against the incumbent regime, he requires some assurance that he will be able to obtain a steady flow of weapons, either by stealing them from government forces or by procuring them from external sources.

Furthermore, a frantic arms race between two technologically advanced powers could certainly exacerbate the political tensions and the psychological fears and hostility marking their relations. It is conceivable that a decision by one side to rush the deployment of a major new weapons system which would substantially alter the strategic equation might tempt the second power to consider a preventive first strike if this could be executed with relative impunity, that is, without running the risk of a retaliatory blow likely to inflict a catastrophic level of damage. But this is a highly abstract hypothetical situation. It leads us immediately to ask whether the United States and the Soviet Union are really involved in that kind of dangerously unstable "arms race."

[11] See Sidney B. Fay, *Origins of the World War* (New York: Macmillan, 1928).
[12] Geoffrey Kemp, "Dilemmas of the Arms Traffic," *Foreign Affairs*, vol. 48 (January 1970); Lincoln P. Bloomfield and Amelia C. Leiss, "Arms Transfers and Arms Control," in J. C. Hurewitz, ed., *Soviet-American Rivalry in the Middle East* (New York: Proceedings of the Academy of Political Science, Columbia University, 1969).

The facts of strategic mutual deterrence in the last ten years make it reasonable to conclude that the two superpowers, far from being engaged in an "unbridled arms race," have been carrying on a restrained, sophisticated, and unhurried arms competition, with each side constantly analyzing its own requirements in the light of developing scientific knowledge and technological feasibility, and making whatever quantitative and qualitative adjustments it deems necessary for the maintenance of the deterrent. (The debate in the United States over deploying our antimissile defense, for example, began in 1960. More than ten years later, partial deployment of the Safeguard system had scarcely begun. This was not exactly what one could call a feverish arms race.) The two superpowers, recognizing nuclear embroilment as a mutual-suicide encounter, are committed in their direct relations with each other to a policy of war-avoidance. Most strategic analysts are convinced that the motivations on either side to launch a deliberate surprise attack against the other's territory are infinitesimally low. Military theoreticians responsible for studying national security problems have to worry about the worst possible cases of "technological breakthrough" by the adversary. But the political leaders who make governmental decisions in Moscow and Washington, regardless of the intentions they may attribute to the adversary in their public statements, do not normally behave as if they are really afraid that the other side is planning or working for a first strike. When they see the other side trying to improve its military forces, political leaders are more likely to trace this to a desire to strengthen the deterrent which supports foreign policy than to any design for a deliberately chosen first strike. If one side were to remain absolutely stationary in its military posture for a long period (say, ten years or more), and make no changes in its weapons technology regardless of what its opponent did, then a truly dangerous instability might well set in. But that has not been the characterisic of the moderately paced weapons interaction process in which the United States and the Soviet Union have confronted each other—much alarmist literature to the contrary notwithstanding.

This is not to say that the present international military-strategic situation contains no cause for worry. It does. Human rationality can break down under some circumstances; technical accidents can happen; men might misinterpret warning signals and act precipitously;

conflicts thought controllable at the outset might escalate to the level of a nuclear confrontation; as nuclear weapons technology is diffused, a third party might be tempted to "catalyze" a nuclear exchange between the superpowers. For more than a decade, a conservative bureaucratic rationality within the governments of the two superpowers has pursued both unilateral and bilateral policies calculated to minimize the dangers of unintended nuclear war. (These efforts will be treated below, in Chapter 9, which deals with specific arms control steps.) Deterrence theory merely says that so long as governments behave rationally (and thus with some predictability), nuclear war can be averted. Deterrence theory provides no assurance that the rationality which has up to now succeeded in avoiding nuclear war will never suffer a breakdown in the future. That is one reason why at least some nuclear weapons states have cautiously entered into international arms negotiations.

But when we analyze the problems of disarmament and arms control, we should not lightly dismiss the significance of the paradoxical contribution which nuclear weapons have made to the international system. On the one hand, the miiltary atom presents a frightful specter to people everywhere; even when rejected by the mind as a psychological defensive reaction, it leaves a growing anxiety in man. Yet the same military atom has, on the other hand, made governments more cautious than ever in those relationships that might give rise to a military encounter. Back in 1957, John H. Herz argued that the advent of nuclear weapons had put an end to the "hard shell" defense of the state which had enabled it historically to claim impenetrability and, therefore, to extend security to its population. Twelve years later, however, Herz admitted that his earlier diagnosis concerning the demise of the territorial state had probably been premature. The same nuclear developments which in theory had rendered modern industrial states so vulnerable to the threat of physical annihilation had also, in practice, made all military force, including conventional force, "unavailable" in relations between the major nuclear powers and their alliance blocs.[13] In other words, the condition of nuclear

[13] John H. Herz, "The Rise and Demise of the Territorial State," *World Politics*, vol. 9 (April 1957); and "The Territorial State Revisited: Reflections on the Future of the Nation-State," in James N. Rosenau, ed., *International Politics and Foreign Policy*, revised edition (New York: Free Press, 1964), pp. 76-89.

deterrence is gradually being extended to provide security against attack for larger numbers of states, including many that possess no nuclear weapons.

In the absence of a world peacekeeper, the atom, like a Hobbesian sovereign, holds governments in awe of its power. Those who plan to disarm the nations should be extremely careful in setting out to defuse a mechanism which has produced at least a precarious peace by compelling governments to conduct themselves with unprecedented restraint and uncommon rationality, even amidst an intense ideological-political conflict over the basis on which human society is to be organized in the future—perhaps for centuries to come.

The reader will note that in the following chapters primary emphasis is placed upon the problems of controlling nuclear weapons and other weapons of mass destruction (including biological and chemical weapons). Virtually no attention is paid to the problem of controlling conventional armaments and international transfers in such arms. Despite the fact that conventional forces and armaments account for the greater part of worldwide military expenditures and are capable of feeding regional arms races, increasing the risk of local conflict, and creating the danger of great power embroilment, very little progress—indeed, very little effort—has been made toward negotiating international agreements for arms control in this dimension.[14] As Colin S. Gray has pointed out, the arms traffic flourishes because force is an ever-present reality in international politics. It is not merely a question of regulating arms at the source of supply. Effective regulation also requires control of the demand, and this is something that lies beyond the capability of an international system in which states must keep an apprehensive eye on their own security.[15]

[14] *12th Annual Report to the Congress*, US Arms Control and Disarmament Agency (Washington: US Government Printing Office, 1973), p. 25.
[15] Colin S. Gray, "Traffic Control for the Arms Trade?" *Foreign Policy*, no. 6 (Spring 1972), pp 153-169.

# 3

# Types of Disarmament and Arms Control

The art of definition has been cursed countless times since Aristotle refined it, and many today would insist that it contributes nothing to the sum total of human knowledge. Yet without definitions, we cannot begin to think or analyze with any scientific exactness, much less add anything of value to our knowledge of reality. Weapons are things, and things have names, and from time immemorial men have been inclined to group into vague, general categories things that cannot really be lumped together. Disarmament and arms control are favorite topics of politicians and propagandists, and thus they are usually surrounded by an especially thick fog of linguistic imprecision, which we must try to penetrate if we are to think with clarity.

## Disarmament

When people speak of "disarmament," they usually have in mind some sort of quantitative reduction in the total stocks of existing weapons at the disposal of national governments, or perhaps even their virtual elimination under plans for "general and complete disarmament," except for forces which may be deemed necessary for national and international police or peacekeeping purposes.[1] We must

[1] A variety of safeguards, verification methods, and sanctions is described in Chapter 8.

make clear what we are discussing. Are we talking about complete or partial disarmament? Are we talking about weapons reduction only, or about a form of disarmament which is organically related to the development of an effective international peacekeeping organization capable of guaranteeing the security of all participating nations? Some people would extend the term to encompass the mere freezing of weapons stocks at present levels, on the ground that if nations are capable of expanding the quantity of their armaments but consciously decide not to do so, then they are engaging in some kind of disarmament (or arms control).

Going beyond the *quantitative* dimension, disarmament may also be *qualitative*. If country A and country B both possess the scientific, technological, and economic capability of producing a certain type of complex and costly weapon system, and if both agree under proper safeguard conditions to refrain from producing and deploying such a weapon system, this arrangement would properly fall under the heading of arms control. But under the same circumstances, if country A produces and deploys the weapon while Country B does not, the latter could be said to be following or at least acquiescing in a policy of unilateral qualitative disarmament. (Segments of opinion within country B might contend, of course, that the weapon being deployed by country A is of marginal military-strategic significance, while other segments of opinion in country B might argue with equal vigor that it is of crucial significance.)

Next, it is important to distinguish between various forms of disarmament. Following wars and peace conferences, some nations might voluntarily demobilize and reduce their military expenditures without any disarmament agreement being concluded, simply because they are tired of war and wish to divert their resources to other pursuits. Certain defeated powers may have peace dictated to them and disarmament imposed by *force majeure* (as happened to Germany after both world wars). Occasionally, the powers have agreed to the demilitarization of relatively small, critical areas, and this might be regarded as a sort of selective geographic disarmament. (In recent times, proposals have been made for regional nuclear-free zones. They are potentially of considerable importance, and will be dealt with subsequently.) *But usually in this century, disarmament has implied a general international condition of reduced arms levels to be arrived at through a process of formal diplomatic negotiation, culminating in intergovernmental agreement.*

We must also keep several other clarifying questions in mind:

1. Are we talking about *bilateral* disarmament (negotiated between two adversary powers) or *multilateral* disarmament (among several states, from a few to all or nearly all)? Which nations participate in and which ones abstain from an agreement could have the greatest significance for its success and longevity. Often, when small and middle powers make international pronouncements on disarmament, they are really preaching sermons to the major powers. The homilies do not necessarily reflect a readiness on the part of the homilists to disarm themselves.

2. Are we talking about disarmament in specific weapons sectors only (such as nuclear weapons, biological-chemical weapons, or strategic offensive and/or defensive missiles), or about comprehensive disarmament extending to all weapons systems, including conventional? Naturally, if one side considers itself leading in one area and lagging in another, it will prefer to concentrate on disarmament in the latter dimension. Thus in the early 1950s, when the United States enjoyed an unquestioned superiority in nuclear weaponry, the Soviets called for a ban on atomic bombs; whereas the United States, after the outbreak of the Korean War, was not enthusiastic about negotiating limitations on nuclear arms alone when the Communist powers were assumed to hold the strategic edge in conventional manpower resources both in Europe and Asia.

3. Are we talking about a purely declaratory (or fiduciary) agreement—one that depends on the pledged word and good faith of the parties—or an agreement accompanied by effective controls, including inspection or other means of verifying compliance, as well as a system of sanctions and remedies to be applied, in case of violation, before the security of complying parties could be jeopardized? The majority of American proponents of disarmament insist responsibly that disarmament must be mutual, reciprocal, effectively controlled, and so structured that it will not place any party at an unfair dis-

advantage. But there are some who regard the dangers of nuclear weapons as so grave that in their view the process of destroying arms is much more important than the safeguards accompanying such a process. The latter often recognize that some verification is necessary not only to ensure observance, but also to make the disarmament agreement politically acceptable in a democratic country. But they would accept relatively loose inspection systems, and would rely heavily upon such factors as mutual national interest in keeping the agreement, the deterrent effect of "world public opinion," the technical difficulties of circumventing an agreement on a large scale, and the fear of detection combined with an unwillingness to return to the dangers of an arms race.

Some contemporary writers are so appalled by the risks of nuclear war and so convinced of the futility of military power in the modern world, that they are moved to urge upon the United States government a policy of unilateral action. A few unilateral disarmers, influenced by social-psychological theories of reciprocation in the rise and fall of internation hostility, believe that if the United States would only take a dramatic lead in shifting from a Cold War defense posture toward cooperation and detente by dismantling some weapons, reducing military budgets, withdrawing from forward military bases, and doing other "nice" things, the Soviet Union and other powers might be induced to follow suit.[2] Other unilateral disarmers go further and demand that the United States totally abandon its nuclear defense policy, regardless of the prospects of emulation by other countries, because they think that this will reduce the world's available megatonnage by a sizable percentage (perhaps about half), or that this will reduce the chances of general nuclear war, or that a nuclear defense policy is intrinsically immoral and cannot be supported by any people that calls itself humanitarian or subscribes to a religious ethic.[3] It should be made clear that in this study we are *not* talking about either unilateral disarmament or unverified international dis-

[2] See Arthur I. Waskow, *The Limits of Defense* (Garden City: Doubleday, 1962); and Charles E. Osgood, *An Alternative to War or Surrender* (Urbana: University of Illinois Press, 1962).

[3] See Mulford Q. Sibley, *Unilateral Initiatives and Disarmament* (Philadelphia: American Friends Service Committee, 1962); and Erich Fromm, "The Case for Unilateral Disarmament," in Donald G. Brennan, ed., *Arms Control, Disarmament and National Security* (New York: Braziller, 1961).

armament. Rather we assume, as the United States government has assumed throughout the nuclear era, that whatever disarmament is achieved through diplomatic negotiation must be reciprocal and equitable in its security effects among the nations of the world, and that it must also be safeguarded by a system of controls which prudent, responsible, intelligent political leaders, mindful of historical experience and modern technology, consider necessary.

4. Do we assume that a diplomatically negotiated disarmament agreement would put an end to revolutionary developments in modern weapons technology—nuclear bombs, missiles, laser beams, radars, and so forth? Or would any verbal agreement (such as a treaty) always be in danger of being circumvented or rendered obsolete by new, unforeseen developments in "peace technology" which would have potential military applications?

5. The effort to control technology by the written devices of diplomacy raises another question which comes up frequently in arms limitation negotiations. Is it possible to develop a typology of weapons on the basis of such distinguishing characteristics as "offensive" or "defensive"? "provocative" or "non-provocative"? "strategic" or "tactical"? These are essentially political-military terms. Depending upon the precision with which they are used, they can be useful in the discussion of the arms problem within a given context, and they may conform more or less appropriately to differences in the technological characteristics of weapons. A hardened (that is, well-protected) missile, for example, is generally regarded as less "provocative" than an exposed, forwardly placed missile that would be useful only for a first strike. But it is conceivable that a weapon which side A regards as invulnerable, nonprovocative, and purely defensive and deterrent ("for second strike only") could be used for a first strike. At least, it is conceivable to B if not to A. Therefore, B cannot be expected to agree to A's definitions out of sheer logical necessity, although it is possible that A and B, after intensive communication, formal or informal, might reach agreement as to which types of military postures and weapons systems seem less menacing than others. (While no power can be forced to accept another's logic, two or more powers can negotiate to accept what may impress a disinterested observer as an illogical position.)

The distinction between "strategic" and "tactical" weapons has equal difficulties. (For centuries, military experts have argued in vain over a precise dividing line between strategy and tactics.) American strategic analysts have often been prone to define as "strategic weapons" those of long or intercontinental range, with which one superpower could strike the homeland of another. But the criterion of intercontinental range is unsatisfactory. Both superpowers are bound to look upon intermediate range weapons systems as "strategic" if they jeopardize the homeland (for example, Soviet missiles in Cuba in 1962; US Thors and Jupiters in Turkey and Italy in the early 1960s; medium-range submarine-based missiles which were or still are alternately strategic and nonstrategic while wending their way through the world's oceans; and US "tactical bombers" stationed in NATO Europe). Soviet intermediate range missiles in western Russia, targeted upon Western Europe, are certainly "strategic" in the eyes of the European allies of the United States, even though they do not threaten American cities; and if the United States regards the Atlantic Alliance as of strategic importance to itself, as it does, then it is bound to look upon those Soviet missiles as invested with strategic implications for its allies and thus for itself. The point is that weapons cannot be defined by quantitative or technological characteristics alone. Geographical, strategic, and political factors must also enter into the definition.

6. Is the disarmament under discussion approached exclusively in military terms, as if the destruction of national armed establishments is sufficient to solve the security problems of nations? Or is the plan linked to the creation of an effective international peacekeeping organization? This leads to the further question as to whether the objective of the disarmament plan is to abolish all existing nuclear weapons from the face of the earth—to "put the nuclear genie back in the bottle", as it were—or to reorganize existing national arsenals by "internationalizing" them, that is, placing them at the disposal of an international government which would then be vested with an insuperable monopoly of miliary power adequate to the task of preventing national rearmament and aggression.

At this point, the reader might wonder to himself whether it is not going rather far afield to raise the issue of international organization and, indeed, the radical transformation of the international system. Would it not be better to concentrate upon getting rid of the weapons of destruction which threaten mankind, without complicating the task infinitely by linking it to the political reorganization of the world? The objection can be made that the governments of the world's major powers are not able to overcome their attachment to the sovereign prerogatives of national independence, and to sublimate those deep-rooted political, cultural, and ideological differences now prevailing on the international scene sufficiently to accept a supranational decisionmaking authority endowed with an insuperable global monopoly of legitimate military force. Certainly the creation of such a world organization would require a much greater degree of international homogeneity of political values than presently exists. Even granted that the United States and the Soviet Union both harbor an abiding dread of the consequences of nuclear war, they may still be very far from agreement concerning the basis on which international society is to be organized. The dread of nuclear war does no more than motivate the superpowers to avoid nuclear war. It does not impel them to abandon their familiar political-ideological values and to embrace a new synthetic system of "convergence values" that would enable them to be fused in a genuine community. Thus several writers have suggested that if disarmament is to be achieved, it may be necessary to separate it from a radical rearranging of power and authority relations in the political world.

It might be possible for the major powers, acting out of mutual interest, to bring about a moderate reduction in armaments levels without agreeing to the creation of supranational machinery to ensure disarmament, to guarantee the security of all nations, and to enforce the peaceful settlement of international disputes. But it does not seem possible that general disarmament could ever be attained without drastic political surgery on the international system. It is of the very essence of the nation-state that it seeks its own security within some kind of military power structure—either by maintaining its own military forces, or by allying with a superior power for protection, or by accepting a satellite status, or the status of a neutral buffer, or by looking toward a regional balance, or collective security guarantees, or some such arrangement. It is highly unrealistic to expect that the nations of the world are about to renounce their military capabilities and the concept of a military power structure in the world, and then to let the problem of security "take care of itself." As Hans J. Morgenthau has pointed out, even partial disarmament presupposes an ability on the part of nations to agree concerning the distribution of power between and among themselves.[4] General disarmament goes much further: it presupposes a willingness on the part of nations to relinquish their primary prerogative of providing for their own defense. Thus general disarmament itself, if carried out, would mark such a profound alteration in the nature of the international system as to warrant the conclusion that the nation-state, as known historically for more than three centuries, would have ceased to exist. The executives and foreign offices of every major power in the world realize this simple fact quite fully. Whether general disarmament could be more easily attained with or without the construction of a new worldwide political organization to which all the powers are willing to entrust their security can be debated. But the political question of world order is very germane to the military-technical question of disarmament. That they can be neatly separated in analysis, planning, or negotiation is a dubious proposition, for if nations are unprepared to incorporate themselves into a new international political system for the nonviolent resolution of their differences, then they are not at all likely to subscribe to general disarmament.

## The Scope of "Arms Control"

The term "arms control," in contrast to "disarmament" (which entails the elimination or reduction of armaments), refers to a broad range of policies which presuppose the continued existence of national military establishments and other political-military organizations (such as revolutionary guerrilla movements).[5] Arms control policies usually aim at some kind of restraint or regulation in the qualitative design, quantitative production, deployment, protection, control, transfer, and planned, threatened, or actual use of arms for

---

[4] Morgenthau, *op. cit.*, pp. 380-383.

[5] The ensuing discussion of arms control is adapted from three other works by the author: "The Status of the Arms Negotiations," *Orbis*, vol. 9 (Spring 1965); *Arms Control and Disarmament: The Critical Issues* (Washington: Georgetown Center for Strategic Studies, 1966); and the "Introduction" in the book which he coedited with J. F. Lehman, Jr., *Arms Control for the Late Sixties* (Princeton: Van Nostrand, 1967).

political-strategic purposes. Advocates of arms control assume that general and complete disarmament (GCD), for a number of complex reasons to be examined later in this study, lies beyond the world's reach, at least under present conditions. Some would contend that GCD is not only unattainable; it is not even desirable within the proximate future.

The arms control school is disposed to look upon the contemporary arms problem as a function of the existing system, deeply rooted in the essential characteristics of modern science and technology, the worldwide struggle of competing ideologies and political groupings, and an international structure in which nation-states have little choice but to seek their security through some form of power manipulation. Nevertheless, the arms controllers for the most part do not despair of the present situation. They do not see nuclear holocaust as the inescapable alternative of a failure to achieve GCD within the near future. In fact, they look upon such a line of reasoning as self-defeating because it leads to the dismal conclusion that since GCD is currently impossible, men must passively await the final nuclear cataclysm.

In the view of the arms controllers, it is possible to postpone Armageddon indefinitely *provided* that governments can be persuaded to pursue policies which are based on a realistic understanding of the actual political-military environment. So long as nation-states and dynamic political movements such as communism depend upon armaments either for their security or for the accomplishment of their international objectives, governments must strive to manage power wisely, and to safeguard the international environment against unintended war by minimizing the risks of technical accident, unauthorized use of nuclear weapons, strategic miscalculations, and other undesirable possibilities. Virtually all arms control proponents are agreed, too, that when military conflicts do occur, as is likely from time to time in an armed world, governments should use intelligence and restraint rather than engaging their military forces in operations which lead to uncontrolled escalation or to uninhibited violence and unlimited collateral damage to civilian populations. Most arms controllers support the quest for policies designed to induce all nation-states gradually to set aside the law of force in favor of the rule of law, and to build an international climate of mutual confidence in which peaceful cooperation will predominate over suspicion, hostility, and conflict—although, as one might expect, there are differences of opinion as to what this might mean in respect to the handling of specific critical problems of foreign policy.

Frequently, but not always, the notion of arms control implies some form of collaboration between adversary states—whether it involve formal agreement (embodied in a treaty or joint official announcement), tacit understanding or informal cooperation, or unilateral decisions taken with the expectation of reciprocal action—in those areas of military policy thought to be of common or coincident interest to the parties concerned. We say "not always" because arms control also embraces those unilateral decisions which are deemed worth taking, even if the adversary does not respond, simply because they enhance controllability, stability of the deterrent, and security against unintended war. Thus the concept of arms control encompasses all those restraints that one or more nations consciously select from a wide range of available alternatives and impose upon themselves in the management of their military forces for purposes which, for a variety of reasons, they regard as worthwhile.

The objectives for which governments, groups, and individuals seek arms control may be manifold: (1) to improve the safety of the international environment against the occurrence of dangerous wars by reducing certain risks inherent in the present military situation; (2) to reduce the likelihood and incidence of violent conflict at all levels; (3) to increase the chances that if military conflicts do occur, as they are likely to from time to time, governments will pursue policies of intelligent restraint rather than engage in operations which lead to uncontrolled escalation, uninhibited violence, and unlimited damage to civilian populations; (4) to effect economic savings by avoiding costly and mutually canceling competition in advanced weapons technology; (5) to foster international political settlements by providing a climate of detente and cooperation; (6) to shift resources into other areas, such as international development or the reduction of environmental pollution; and so forth. Many advocates of arms control would insist upon another important purpose—to support policies that will be conducive eventually to disarmament agreements and the growth of peacekeeping institutions in a world where all nation-states have been persuaded to set aside the rules of force in favor of the rule of law. Whether or not this purpose is "realistic" or "utopian" remains a matter of considerable debate among students of international relations. Recent years have witnessed a growing awareness of the necessity for linking arms control with conflict control, but most political scientists are under no illusions as to the difficulties of building the machinery to control limited conflict and to ensure peaceful change in a revolutionary age.

The term "arms control," looked at theoretically, is an extremely permissive one, and may refer to such diverse measures as the following:

1. Administrative, technical, or political arrangements (for example, "failsafe," "two key" systems, the "permissive action link," and the "rules of nuclear engagement") calculated to minimize the risk of nuclear accident, unauthorized use of nuclear weapons, precipitate response to an ambiguous warning, or strategic miscalculation of the adversary's intentions.

2. A program of weapons research, development, and deployment, as well as a strategic doctrine, which stresses the nonprovocative and defensive aspects of national security postures, especially those associated with an "invulnerable second-strike capability."

3. Regional tension-reducing arrangements, such as disengagement, "thinning out" of forces, or the creation of demilitarized or nuclear-free zones.

4. Decisions to hold quantitative rates of weapons production below those levels which a nation is economically and technically capable of sustaining in an uninhibited "arms race."

5. Tension-reducing declarations such as a "no-first-use" pledge, or a "nonaggression pact."

6. The improvement of facilities for emergency communications (for example, the "hot line").

7. Efforts to separate nuclear forces and strategies from conventional forces and strategies through the utilization of various "firebreaks" (for example, time, geography, and command).

8. The prohibition of certain activities, such as the sale of conventional arms and delivery systems to countries in "tinderbox areas," nuclear weapons testing in proscribed environments, the emplacement of weapons of mass destruction in orbit, or the establishment of spheres of influence in outer space.

9. A formal, verified freeze on the production of specified items, such as fissionable materials for weapons purposes or strategic delivery vehicles.

10. Efforts to prevent or retard the proliferation of nuclear weapons to nations not already in possession of them.

11. The prudent management of crisis diplomacy and limited conflict strategy (including such concepts as "sanctuary," "flexible response," "city-avoidance strategies," and conflict de-escalation or termination strategies).

12. The diplomatic institutionalization of arms control dialogues among governments and groups of experts.

This may be, both from a literary and logical standpoint, an unaesthetic inventory; but without being exhaustive, it serves to illustrate the variety of measures that can be comprehended under the rubric of "arms control" as this term has been employed in the literature. (Several of the foregoing arms control measures are discussed in detail in Chapter 9 below.)

**Disarmament and Arms Control**

Naturally there is some overlapping in what the disarmers and the arms controllers advocate. Most of those in both groups, for example, supported the partial nuclear test ban treaty and the quest for ways to inhibit the uncontrolled proliferation of nuclear weapons technology. Most disarmers are in favor of arms control restraints, freezes, regional limitations, and other arrangements insofar as these lead to a diminution of international tensions and pave the way for more substantial disarmament either concurrently or at a later date. In other words, they see many arms control measures as a necessary prelude to, or as part of, the first stage of GCD. Nevertheless, many disarmers are suspicious of the philosophy underlying the arms control movement, because they think that its adherents, by and large, are not committed seriously to the eventual goal of total disarmament, but are merely engaged in a self-deluding search for conditions that will permit the continued existence of national military establishments.

The pure disarmers (as well as some arms controllers) are unmoved by talk of crisis management, stable deterrence, defense-emphasis postures, and city-avoidance strategies. Not a few disarmers fear that a little success in the field of arms control—with the hot line, the Partial Test Ban, the Outer Space Treaty, the Nonproliferation Treaty, the Seabed Treaty, and the 1972 SALT Agreements—might be a dangerous thing, for it could lead to a relaxation of the sense of urgency over the arms problem and to a false sense of security.

Some of the skeptical arms controllers, on the other hand, might be more eager to seek limited, verified arms agreements if they were sure that such agreements would not generate a misleading atmosphere of detente and build up international political pressures for efforts to "preserve momentum" in the "peace race" by devising ill-considered "next steps" toward GCD—steps which could conceivably disturb the existing strategic equilibrium, jeopardize the security of the United States and its allies, and finally bring on a nuclear war which might never have occurred if what they regard as the imprudent philosophy of total disarmament had been clearly rejected. These arms controllers wish to take certain steps to make the defense policies of the United States as rational as possible from the military and political perspectives, but they do not wish to undermine these defense policies by embarking upon what they consider the utopian road to GCD—a road which in their estimate could lead to disaster, not necessarily because a GCD treaty would be signed and later violated, but because GCD is seen as such a patent impossibility in the contemporary world that any government which attempts seriously to move toward it as an immediate policy goal is so mistaken in its approach to the arms problem that it is in danger of making crucial errors in the formulation of its national security policy.

Some arms control analysts hope that a prolonged application of a full spectrum of arms control policies might gradually produce a pattern of international political, social-economic, technological, and armaments competition and a substantial reduction of armaments levels, as well as threats of surprise attack, infiltration, subversion, guerrilla warfare, and other sources of instability and insecurity. This change of pattern presupposes, of course, profound changes in the international state system, and the arms controllers who nourish such hopes are seldom sure that the hoped-for conditions can be brought about within any prescribed time span (for example, by the year 1980 or 2000); some are more optimistic, others less, still others not at all.

Even the most optimistic arms controllers are usually reluctant to embrace the vision of a totally disarmed world which characterizes the radical disarmers. Whereas the latter are inclined to point to the dangers of keeping arms, the former often focus upon the dangers of trying to get rid of them, including on the one hand the instability associated with a rising tide of irregular conflict, and on the other the possible tyranny of a unitary world government.

One's preference for drastic disarmament or for arms control as the goal of national policy almost invariably arises from his philosophy of human nature and society, politics and international relations, especially his interpretation of the East-West conflict, and his preference for a particular military strategy. The more fully a person subcribes to an idealistic concept of man, and the more he is oriented toward a futuristic vision of the transformations that science can produce in the attitudes, emotions, and thoughts of men, the more likely he is to desire the early and complete elimination of national armaments, and the readier he is to believe that the fundamental changes in the state system necessary to usher in GCD can be made through social engineering.

Members of the arms control school tend, on the whole, to be somewhat more conservative in their philosophical outlook. The more one is inclined, on the basis of the historical evidence available, to accept the realistic interpretation of international relations and to shun the utopian approach to politics, the more likely he is to doubt that modern military technology can be banished by legal fiat, or that nation-states can, should, or will relinquish all of their own military power in favor of the United Nations, an international disarmament organization, or any other instrumentality of world government. Such an individual very probably believes that the chances of moving from an armed to a disarmed world under an adequate system of safeguards are extremely remote, and hence he will be interested in various modes of arms control as the best means of minimizing the risks of nuclear catacylsm and, at the same time, of enhancing the security of the United States and those allied countries that depend upon it for their continued independence.

# 4

# The Historical Record of Disarmament Negotiations

One cannot really think about the arms problem if he ignores the historical dimension. What can be learned from human experience with disarmament efforts? Prior to the twentieth century, the record of international disarmament is quite sketchy. Following the major peace conferences concluding Europe's great wars, there had been a natural tendency for governments to reduce arms levels and military expenditures. But this occurred more as a result of unilateral decisions than of negotiated agreement. There were several instances in which treaty provisions called for the destruction of specified fortifications or the demilitarization of particular geographic areas (for example, the Turkish Straits). Sometimes they proved successful, sometimes not. But invariably they applied to one or two nations only. Probably the most famous case of demilitarization negotiated between two modern nations in the nineteenth century was the Rush-Bagot Agreement of 1817, whereby England and the United States made the US-Canadian boundary the longest undefended border in the world.

The idea of an international diplomatic conference to negotiate disarmament among several countries is a relatively recent one. In 1816 the Czar, and in the mid-nineteenth century Napoleon III called for such a gathering, but it never took place. From time to time, various European governments adopted an enlightened posture by declaring that arms expenditures, besides being wasteful, led to a sense of insecurity instead of security. The Swedish parliament in the early 1880s flirted with the idea of permanent neutralization and disarmament. (For a country in Sweden's geographical position, a policy of neutrality can make sense, but present-day Sweden prefers an armed to a disarmed neutrality.) Although the nineteenth century saw very little progress toward disarmament on the diplomatic front, by the end of the century there was a widespread conviction among the Western intelligentsia that Ivan Bloch was correct in his judgment, expressed in *The Future of War*, that war had "become impossible, except at the price of suicide."[1]

The time was ripe for a summons to a disarmament conference. The call came from an unanticipated quarter in 1898, when Czar Nicholas II issued an invitation for an international peace conference at The Hague. The motives of the Czarist regime were far from altruistic. General Kuropatkin, the Russian Minister of War, was anxious to prevent the Austrians from modernizing their artillery. The Russian Finance Minister, Sergius Witte, hoped to reallocate economic resources from armaments to industrial-commercial expansion. Nevertheless, the Czar's appeal fell upon appreciative ears, and was hailed in the Western press as the sound of "beautiful music over the whole earth," the dawn of "a new epoch in civilization," a "most momentous and beneficent movement in modern history," launched by "the new Evangelist on the banks of the Neva." Seasoned politicians and diplomats, however, were much more skeptical in their attitudes towards the gathering, and more suspicious of one another's real intentions; but they found themselves unable to resist public opinion.[2]

Delegates from 26 countries convened at The Hague in May 1899, amidst a good deal of confusion as to whether their mission was to

---

[1] Ivan (Jean de) Bloch *The Future of War* (New York: 1899), p. xxxi. Quoted in Frank M. Russell, *Theories of International Relations* (New York: Appleton-Century-Crofts, 1936), p. 306.

[2] An excellent and highly readable account of the two Hague Conferences may be found in Barbara W. Tuchman, *The Proud Tower* (New York: Macmillan, 1966), ch. 5, on which the following account is largely based.

promote the practice of international arbitration, achieve reductions in the levels of national armaments, prevent the deployment of new weapons, or make more humane the laws regulating the conduct of warfare. The delegates undertook their work in an atmosphere of pessimism, expecting little in the way of results. Proposals for weapons reduction and prevention bogged down over the issue of inspection and control which, in the eyes of practically all delegates, would violate the fundamental principle of national sovereignty. The Conference did vote to outlaw dumdum bullets, the use of asphyxiating gas, and (for a period of five years) the launching of projectiles from balloons. The representatives of several countries were convinced that other nations were concocting proposals solely for the purpose of gaining a unilateral strategic advantage for themselves. The Kaiser, for example, was sure that the other powers, in advancing plans for an international arbitration tribunal, were shrewdly and cynically trying to find a way, in the event of a future dispute with Germany, to temporize and keep the conflict under control until Germany's superior ability with respect to rapid military mobilization had been neutralized. But in the end, an arbitration convention was signed. The limitation of arms was made a subject of further study.

By the time the Second Hague Conference met in 1907, there was considerable reluctance even to put disarmament on the agenda; and when the topic finally came up for lip service, it was dealt with briefly and with embarrassment. The principal effort was devoted to improving arbitration procedures by establishing a Permanent Court, and to refining the Laws of Warfare on Land and Sea. The British warned that if the horrors of war should be attenuated too much, the public detestation of war, which exercised a certain deterrent effect, might be weakened. (Decades later, analogous arguments were advanced against proposals that the United States shift from a "countercity" to a "counterforce" strategy.) The Conference produced agreements on the inviolability of neutral territory, the necessity of a formal declaration of war prior to the outbreak of hostilities, the regulation of the use of underwater mines, and other topics. But no genuine solution to the arms problem was found. The era of the two Hague Conferences began shortly after the Spanish-American War, and was punctuated by the Boer War, the Boxer Rebellion, the Russo-Japanese War, Anglo-German naval rivalry, and the Algeciras crisis. In the wake of the Hague Conferences came the Balkan Wars, which were a prelude to World War I. The spirit of The Hague proved to be a poignant yet futile protest against the titanic forces of destruction that were about to be unleashed in Europe.

Following the holocaust of the First World War, the debate over international disarmament was resumed with more ardor than ever, and with temporary success in respect to naval armaments. One of President Wilson's Fourteen Points of January 1918 referred to "adequate guarantees . . . that national armaments will be reduced to the lowest point consistent with domestic safety." The peace treaties imposed disarmament upon Germany, Austria, Bulgaria, and Hungary. The provisions pertaining to Germany were most important. The General Staff was abolished. The Army was limited to a hundred thousand men, including four thousand officers. No more than five percent of total effectives could be discharged and replaced in any one year. Strict limits were placed on the manufacture, importation, and storage of armaments and munitions. No military aircraft or submarines were permitted, and only a small number of naval vessels of various types was allowed. In addition to these restrictions, the Rhineland was to be demilitarized for fifteen years. "The Germans," wrote E. H. Carr, "made every effort to evade a strict application of these measures . . . But it may on the whole be said that, by 1924, Germany had been subjected to a measure of disarmament more rigorous and complete than any recorded in modern history."[3]

According to the Versailles Treaty, the disarmament of Germany was justified on the ground that it would "render possible the initiation of a general limitation of the armaments of all nations." Article Eight of the Covenant of the League of Nations declared that "the maintenance of peace requires the reduction of national armaments to the lowest point consistent with national safety and the enforcement by common action of international actions."

Several efforts were made throughout the interwar period to achieve disarmament and to outlaw war as an international crime. The

[3] E. H. Carr, *International Relations Between the Two World Wars, 1919-1939* (London: Macmillan, 1965), p. 49.

1924 Geneva Protocol for the Pacific Settlement of International Disputes embodied the idealism of the period, but never came into force. The Locarno Pact of 1925 guaranteed existing Rhine frontiers and strengthened Europe's mood of peace for a few years. The utopianism of the 1920s reached its climax in the Kellogg-Briand Pact of 1927, in which the signatories solemnly renounced war as "an instrument of national policy." But the major powers were never able to reach agreement on what constituted "aggression," and what kind of policies collective security required. The League of Nations became divided between powers committed to the preservation of the status quo and others determined to overthrow it. Except for a ten-year agreement limiting capital ships, the principal governments of the world were not prepared to negotiate arms reduction agreements. One of the major obstacles to progress in the disarmament conference sponsored by the League of Nations was a basic incompatibility in the national objectives of two European countries—the quest of France for security against a future German invasion, and the demand of Germany for a formal recognition of the principle of arms equality (that is, either the victorious powers must disarm or Germany must be accorded the right to rearm).

Before examining the technical problems of disarmament as they were perceived in the League discussions, we should refresh our memories concerning what was probably the most remarkable case of arms limitation in modern history—the Washington Naval Agreement of 1922. The years immediately following World War I found the governments of Britain and the United States interested in avoiding a costly naval arms race, if this were possible without adverse effects upon their security. The Washington Treaty on Naval Arms Limitation was attainable only in the context of a political settlement by which Britain, the United States, Japan, and France exchanged formal assurances in respect to their island possessions in the Pacific, and agreed to consult in the event of controversy over these rights or of the threat of aggression. The Treaty declared a ten-year "naval holiday" during which no new capital ships were to be constructed. (A "capital ship" was defined as one which displaced more than ten thousand tons and carried guns larger than eight-inch caliber.) Within twenty years, there was to be established for total battleship tonnage a ratio of 5:5:3:1.67:1.67 for the United States,

Britain, Japan, France, and Italy, respectively. Battleships were to be limited to a maximum of 35 thousand tons and their guns to sixteen-inch caliber. Aircraft carriers, with a few exceptions, were limited to 27 thousand tons and six-inch guns. In order to comply with the ceilings imposed by the treaty, the leading powers had to scrap a total of 68 ships already built or being built (28 by the United States, 24 by Britain, and 16 by Japan).[4]

Japan at first discerned advantages for itself in the Washington Treaty. Interested only in the Pacific region, Tokyo did not deem it intolerable to be limited to sixty percent of parity with powers of more global interests, although the termination of the Anglo-Japanese Alliance made it fairly clear that henceforth the two largest naval powers would probably be partners in the Pacific. The Washington Treaty set no limits on cruisers, destroyers, and submarines. After 1922, competition among the powers increased in the cruiser category; and a conference was convened at Geneva in 1927 for the purpose of limiting them. But the British were unwilling to accept mathematical parity with the United States, on the ground that the worldwide lines of imperial trade and communications required an unrestricted right to build smaller cruisers; and the Conference ended in failure.[5] At the London Naval Conference of 1930, Anglo-American differences were resolved on the basis of near parity, but this time France, concerned over Mussolini's designs on the Mediterranean, rejected Italy's demand for equality of cruisers. (One much-debated difference of opinion at the London Conference was whether each nation should be assigned a total naval tonnage, and then be free to decide for itself what types of ships it would build, or whether there should be tonnage totals for each category.) By 1934 Japan, now growing dissatisfied with existing limitations, demanded parity with Britain and the United States. When this was denied, Japan gave the required two years' notice of withdrawal from the naval agreements. Henry W. Forbes, evaluating the significance of the Washington Naval Treaty, writes: "The naval disarmament program, which had started with a systematic scrapping

[4] Henry W. Forbes, *The Strategy of Disarmament* (Washington: Public Affairs Press, 1952), pp. 28-29.
[5] *Ibid.*, p. 30.

of battleships and the promise not to fortify the Pacific island bases, had saved funds and reduced friction temporarily, but it also had contributed to the weakness of the United States and Great Britain in the Pacific, a weakness that led to the early and nearly catastrophic defeats in World War II. Whether an extended arms race would have ended in less unhappy results, no one can, of course, say with certainty."[6]

The ten-year period following the Washington Naval Conference witnessed several unsuccessful efforts on the part of the League of Nations to find a solution to the problem of disarmament. One of the first, named after Lord Esher, involved a simple ratio approach. The Esher Plan called for the organization of national armies into units of thirty thousand men each, with a quota of permissible units being assigned to each nation—for example, France, six; Italy, four; Great Britain, three; Spain, three; Czechoslovakia, three; and so forth. This scheme was roundly rejected by nearly all European military experts on the ground that such simple numerical ratios might make some sense in the naval tonnage sector but were meaningless as applied to ground armies, since the power of thirty thousand-man units could vary almost infinitely, depending upon the quality of military-technological equipment available. Lord Esher's scheme was eventually withdrawn at his own suggestion.[7]

A brief note is in order here concerning the interwar attempt to outlaw biological and chemical (B/C) weapons. As we have seen, the Hague Conference of 1899 had produced a convention prohibiting the use of asphyxiating gases. This convention had been signed and ratified by 25 countries. (The United States, doubting the feasibility of such a prohibition, did not sign.) One of the Washington treaties of 1922, noting that the use of poison gas had been "justly condemned by the general opinion of the civilized world," declared such use prohibited among the signatories. (The US Senate ratified the treaty, but the provision cited did not come into effect because its effectiveness was contingent upon ratification by all parties, and

[6] *Ibid.*, p. 31.
[7] F. P. Walters, *A History of the League of Nations* (New York: Oxford University Press, 1952), p. 221.

France failed to ratify.) The Geneva Protocol of 1925, signed by 46 countries, contained this provision:[8]

> Whereas the use in war of asphyxiating, poisonous or other gases, and of all analogous liquids, materials or devices, has been justly condemned by the general opinion of the civilized world; and
>
> Whereas the prohibition of such use has been declared in Treaties to which the majority of Powers of the world are Parties; and
>
> To the end that this prohibition shall be universally accepted as a part of International Law, binding alike the conscience and the practice of nations;
>
> Declare: That the High Contracting Parties, so far as they are not already Parties to Treaties prohibiting such use, accept this prohibition, agree to extend this prohibition to the use of bacteriological methods of warfare and agree to be bound as between themselves according to the terms of this declaration.

Six of the signatories, including the United States and Japan, failed to ratify the treaty. Since the Geneva Protocol did not require unanimous adherence, it came into effect in 1928. By the beginning of World War II, 42 nations had deposited ratifications, but sixteen of these specified that they would consider the terms of the Protocol binding only in respect to States adhering to it, and these sixteen plus three others reserved the right to employ biological and chemical weapons in retaliation against a foe who resorted to them first.[9] Thus, what the Geneva Protocol really proscribed was the first use of B/C weapons. The major governments which did ratify (including Great Britain, France, and the Soviet Union) never interpreted it to mean that they were legally prohibited from developing, producing, and

[8] U. S. Department of State, *Papers Relating to the Foreign Relations of the United States, 1925* (Washington: Department of State, 1940), vol. 1, pp. 89-90.

[9] See Major Joseph Burns Kelly, "Gas Warfare in International Law," *Military Law Review* (July 1960), pp. 1-69; A. N. Sack, "ABC—Atomic, Biological and Chemical Warfare in International Law," *Lawyers' Guild Review*, vol. 10 (Winter 1950), pp. 161-180; and William V. O'Brien, "Biological/Chemical Warfare and the International Law of War," *Georgetown Law Journal*, vol. 51 (Fall 1962), pp. 1-63.

stockpiling B/C weapons in peacetime for defensive use in war, that is, either for deterrence or retaliation. (The status of B/C weapons in post-World War II disarmament discussions and arms control policy will be treated below in Chapter 9.)

In 1925, the Council of the League of Nations appointed a Preparatory Commission for the Disarmament Conference. It included all Council members, six other League members, and three nonmembers —Germany, the United States, and the Soviet Union. The Preparatory Commission worked and studied and argued for five years about the problems of establishing a Draft Convention to be submitted to a World Disarmament Conference, including budgetary limitations on military expenditures; time limits on active military service; limiting the numbers of military effectives in land, sea, and air forces; setting ratios for various categories of naval weapons; the prohibition of chemical and bacteriological warfare; and the creation of a Permanent Disarmament Commission. Although the preparatory body agreed on the need for limiting the number of military effectives, there was serious disagreement over how to determine this number. The French and others who depended upon conscription wanted to exclude trained reserves, while delegates from countries with volunteer armies argued that a man who had just completed several years of military service could be a more effective soldier than a young recruit on active duty.

The proceedings at Geneva were enlivened in 1927 by the appearance of the Soviet delegate, Maxim Litvinov, who startled everyone by demanding the total abolition of all armed forces and weapons, the elimination of all military budgets and military service systems, and the abolition of all military schools, training centers, war departments, and general staffs—all within a period of one year! Total disarmament, he said later, was the only way of putting an end to war, and could be "distinguished from all other plans by its simplicity and by the ease with which it could be carried out."[10] Western diplomats (except for the Germans and the Turks) looked upon Litvinov's proposal not as a serious policy overture but as a piece of propaganda and political warfare—a clever, cynical attack

[10] *League of Nations: Conference for the Reduction and Limitations of Armaments*, Verbatim Records of Plenary Meetings (Geneva: 1932), vol. 1, p. 82.

upon the whole process of Western disarmament diplomacy. It was all the more effective in so far as it appealed beyond governments to a certain simplistic idealism which infuses public opinion in liberal, democratic countries.

The World Conference on the Reduction and Limitation of Armaments was convened at Geneva in February 1932, with representatives from sixty nations in attendance. The crucial technical problem to be resolved was to establish quantitative ratios of military strength satisfactory to the powers. Despite the fact that some progress was made in demonstrating and analyzing the complexities of the problem, solution proved impossible. Factors which had to be taken into account included the size of a nation's population, the nature of its military-industrial potential, its geographic location *vis-à-vis* friendly and hostile powers, the length and vulnerability of its frontiers, patterns of communication and transportation, and so on. At one point, President Hoover proposed a one-third reduction of all national forces larger than that which the Versailles Treaty permitted Germany to retain. Some wanted the reductions based upon the ratios existing in 1900, or 1913, or 1927. Still others contended that, since an industrial state could mobilize quickly for war production, nonindustrial states should be allowed to keep larger standing forces for defense.[11]

It would be going too far, however, to conclude that the failure of the World Disarmament Conference was due primarily to technical obstacles. The kinds of technical security problems which confronted governments in the 1930s might conceivably have been overcome had the major powers possessed the political determination to reach a reasonable agreement. (This is not certain, but it is at least conceivable. Other limited agreements had been reached during the interwar period, including the naval limitation treaties of Washington and London; the 1925 prohibition of chemical and bacteriological methods of warfare; the 1925 Locarno treaties of arbitration and mutual border guarantees; the 1925 International Arms Traffic Convention, which did not enter into force because of insufficient ratifications; the 1931 agreement between the Soviet Union and Turkey

[11] Forbes, *op. cit.*, pp. 15-33.

to prevent competition in naval armaments; the 1935 Anglo-German Naval Agreement, which set a bilateral ratio on naval armaments; and the 1936 Montreux Convention permitting the remilitarization of the Turkish Straits.) But the political climate in the early and middle 1930s was not conducive to a general international disarmament agreement. It was the era of Japanese aggression in Manchuria and China; of Italian aggression in Ethiopia; of Germany's reoccupation of the Rhineland in violation of the Versailles and Locarno treaties; of Japan's notice of withdrawal from the naval limitation treaties; of civil war and intervention in Spain; and of the withdrawal of Germany, Japan, and Italy from the League. Disarmament proved impossible primarily because of the depth of the political disagreement between those countries concerned about security and determined to preserve the status quo, and those countries bent on aggression to alter the status quo. The efforts to achieve disarmament failed to prevent World War II. In fact, a case can be made that the Western democracies' continued quest for disarmament in the 1930s, while the Axis powers pursued a steady policy of arming, helped to create an unstable international climate and to bring on World War II, which Churchill called "the unnecessary war."

The period since World War II has witnessed renewed efforts toward solutions to the greatly increased security problems of the nuclear age, in which the quantum leap in firepower represented by the A-bomb was soon multiplied by a factor of a thousand in the H-bomb, and subsequently matched by the quantum leap in delivery speed made possible by the ICBM. The earliest American disarmament proposal after World War II was in the form of the Baruch Plan, calling for the creation of an International Atomic Development Authority (IADA) within the framework of the United Nations. According to the Baruch Plan, which was based on the Acheson-Lilienthal Report, IADA would conduct all "intrinsically dangerous activities" in the nuclear weapons field; own and control all sources of critical materials and related installations; carrry on continuous research in nuclear weapons and all phases of atomic energy, so that no state could ever surpass it in technical knowledge; license all national and private nuclear activities (such as peaceful atomic projects); approve the structure, design, and capacity of all atomic installations; and reserve the right of inspection in any nation at any time without advance warning. IADA was to be politically responsible to the Security Council and General Assembly of the United Nations, without being subject to any nation's veto power. It was to exercise exclusive control over all stockpiles of atomic weapons, which were to be distributed in such a way that a preponderant amount would never be available within the borders of a single nation. New projects for atomic development would also be located according to the same principle. If an aggressor seized the installations within his country, his move would supply a "signal" to the inspection system, and the facilities of IADA would be placed at the disposal of the UN in sufficient time to enforce its compliance with international obligations under the threat of disaster.[12]

The Baruch Plan was a bold and generous one for the United States to put forward at a time when the US possessed the only A-bombs in the world. Some observers doubted that this country would actually follow through on the proposal if the Soviets should agree to it. Many were puzzled by the adamant Soviet refusal to accept the US offer. Today, however, Western analysts are more inclined to think that it may have been unrealistic for the United States to expect Soviet acceptance of the Baruch Plan. In the Soviet view, IADA would have been established largely on American terms for the simple reason that the United States, by virtue of its great lead over the USSR in nuclear technology, would be able to dominate the international control system to prevent its rival from obtaining independent ownership of nuclear weapons. During the course of the discussions, the Soviets accused the Western powers of trying to infringe the sovereign rights of the USSR, to establish international capitalist control over segments of its industry, to conduct espionage, and to perpetuate the Western nuclear monopoly—thus setting a pattern of argument that was to become all too familiar through future disarmament and arms control negotiations.

Throughout the 1950s and early 1960s, Soviet and US negotiators met thousands of times, at different levels and places and in different bodies, to discuss various types of proposals with greater or lesser

[12] *Documents on Disarmament 1945-1959* (Washington: US Government Printing Office, 1960), vol. 1, pp. 7-16. In 1960, *Documents on Disarmament* became an annual publication. Since 1961, it has been published under the auspices of the US Arms Control and Disarmament Agency.

degrees of seriousness. At one time or another, they called for the following agreements: (a) a "ban on all nuclear weapons;" (b) conventional disarmament; (c) the creation of international police or peacekeeping forces; (d) a "cut-off" in the production of fissionable materials for weapons purposes; (e) a nuclear test ban, either partial or complete; (f) an "open skies" system of aerial inspection to prevent surprise attack; (g) the disengagement or reduction of forces in prescribed geographic zones, especially Central Europe; (h) the creation of "atom-free zones" in Europe and other regions of the world; (i) the liquidation of military bases on "foreign" territory; (j) the reduction of military budgets; (k) the demilitarization of outer space; and other kinds of formal armaments measures. Toward the end of the 1950s, interest began to shift from partial measures to comprehensive or total disarmament plans, as the Soviets presented their proposal for general and complete disarmament (GCD) in September 1959, and the United States submitted its blueprint for GCD "in a peaceful world" to the UN General Assembly two years later.

For many years, the debates were monotonously similar. The Soviets accused the Western powers of desiring control and inspection without disarmament. The Western powers reciprocated by accusing the Soviets of seeking a purely "declaratory disarmament" without adequate verification of compliance. The Soviets charged the West with trying to legalize espionage in the USSR under the guise of inspection. The Western allies in turn suspected that the Soviets were interested in disarmament negotiations primarily for the purpose of bringing about the dismantling of NATO and the severance of the military link between the United States and Western Europe. Nevertheless, international armaments negotiations became what Hedley Bull has called a "persistent theme" in the foreign policies of the leading powers.[13]

## The Lessons of History

Before we turn to an analysis of governmental attitudes toward disarmament and arms control in the nuclear age, it may be instructive

[13] Hedley Bull, *The Control of the Arms Race* (New York: Praeger, 1961), p. 34.

to draw some summary conclusions from the history of arms negotiations up to the late 1950s.

1. The effort to bring modern armaments under political control has become increasingly important in the twentieth century to governments which are interested in placating domestic public opinion or appealing to international public opinion. (Analyzing the interaction of these two levels of public opinion and their implications for foreign policymaking in democratic and totalitarian countries can be an interesting exercise by itself.)

2. The fact that governments periodically express an interest, a desire, or an intent with respect to negotiating international arms agreements constitutes in itself no credible evidence of a genuine commitment toward such a goal. Continued political emphasis upon the importance of such negotiations, however, may generate both domestic and international expectations of real or at least apparent progress in this area. Such expectations, in turn, may create political-diplomatic constraints which operate with differing effects upon various types of political systems.

3. Governments are among the most conservative and cautious of all institutions known to social scientists. Regardless of the liberal or revolutionary ideologies which are supposed to infuse some governments, and regardless of the perennial controversary which goes on within most governments over defense versus nondefense expenditures, when issues of national security are at stake, all governmental bureaucracies tend to act slowly and warily. No government is anxious for sudden, sweeping changes in the environment in which it operates. Every government likes to slice up its problems into digestible proportions. Thus, governmental policymakers take a great deal of time examining any proposal which has serious implications for national security before offering it or accepting it. Not infrequently, an arms proposal which at first glance seems popular and attractive will, upon closer scrutiny, arouse grave suspicions as to its long-range merits. For every government official who is willing to risk gambling on a new arms policy proposal affecting national security, there will very likely be more than one who can be expected to advise caution. (The reader might ask himself whether the "typical" Soviet policy-

maker is more or less likely than the "typical" American policy-maker to take national security risks for the sake of getting a disarmament agreement.)

4. If governments sometimes take years of internal study and debate to evaluate partial arms measures of a limited-liability/risk character, they are likely to shun those farreaching proposals which, if accepted, would be bound to usher in a radical transformation of the international political-strategic environment. Governments usually, in the words of Shakespeare, deem it "better to bear those ills we have, than fly to others that we know not of." This may ultimately prove to be shortsighted and unwise. But it is a bedrock fact of international politics often totally ignored by idealists and others who think that human affairs are entirely governable by their own naive brand of logic.

5. National governments can normally be expected to show interest in international disarmament or arms control negotiations to the degree that they are concerned about the possibility of military-technological developments in rival countries that could have adverse implications for their own national security.

6. Governments may be motivated to negotiate an international arms agreement either if they lag behind in military technology, and fear they may fall even further behind in the absence of an agreement, or if they enjoy a technological lead, and look upon an agreement as a means of preserving an advantageous status quo. Thus, it is at least theoretically possible that a leading and a lagging power can arrive at a temporary mutual agreement, but this is extremely difficult.

7. In an international environment which assigns a high public priority to disarmament as a goal, it is more difficult for open, democratic societies than for closed, totalitarian societies to sustain political support for military defense expenditures, mutual defense alliances, and other national security policies. This is so because of the wide discrepancy between the two systems in their ability to control the content of political communications. In contemporary democratic societies, the dominant tendency of the press is to question and criticize the security policies of the government, whereas in

totalitarian societies the exclusive function of the press is to support and justify the security policies of the government.

8. Nations which enter arms negotiations often seek contrary objectives. Some wish to buttress their security by freezing and preserving the political, military, and strategic status quo; others wish to improve their relative position by altering that status quo.

9. Although the distinction between "offensive" and "defensive" weapons has some validity, it provides no useful basis for negotiating an agreement unless governments are politically willing to arrive at common and more specific definitions concerning the characteristics of weapons to be permitted, regulated, limited, or prohibited.

10. Negotiating nations often interject "jokers" or "riders" into the arms proposals which they advance, for the express purpose of making an otherwise reasonable proposal unacceptable to another power.

11. Over a period of time, governments often reverse their bargaining positions in international arms negotiations. What one government proposes and another rejects at a specific time, the former may find unacceptable a few years later if the latter presses for its adoption.

12. Even when two rival governments are willing to compose their negotiating differences in respect to a particular type of arms limitation, they may find themselves unable to reach or to ratify a final agreement because of the unwillingness of third parties to participate in an arms limitation agreement at a given time.

# 5

# The Attitudes of the Powers: The United States

There is no such thing as a fixed, immutable national attitude toward any policy issue, including disarmament and arms control. Governments, like the men who run them, are subject to the influence of historical change. Concepts of what constitutes "national interest" may undergo alteration—gradually, to be sure, rather than suddenly, over a period of decades if not years. It is important to add that the pace at which attitudes change may differ markedly among nations. All governments move slowly and deliberately; but throughout history, men have recognized that certain types of political systems (the open, democratic variety) have been readier to modify their thinking and their policies on fundamental issues than other types (especially the closed, authoritarian or totalitarian variety).

In the nuclear age, it would be most unusual for any government to state publicly that it was opposed in principle to disarmament. Virtually all governments pay lip service to the concept; but most of them are extremely wary of the concept as it might apply to themselves. Indeed, most of the spokesmen of the smaller states who vote dutifully every year for United Nations resolutions calling for general disarmament really aim at applying rhetorical-political pressure only upon the governments of the leading powers, never on themselves. The bulk of the disarmament discussion of the last 25 years has referred primarily to the United States and secondarily to the Soviet Union. Several governments that are anxious to bring the two superpowers down a peg are not especially interested in disarming China, and some probably perceive a positive value in the growth of China's power on the world scene—particularly those that are immediate neighbors of the two giants, but not of China. (China's neighbors are likely to look at the situation differently.)

So long as nation-states exist, policymakers will be concerned about such things as national security and independence, and international power and prestige. The specific types of policies required for the pursuit of these objectives depend upon concrete circumstances. Moreover, these objectives are often in dynamic tension with the requirements of domestic peace and social well-being, at least in some nations. It is not surprising that governments will sometimes pursue what appear to be—and what actually may be—contradictory policies in a complicated world. This is especially the case in the areas of security, and disarmament and arms control policies and negotiations. National attitudes in this field are usually a function of several different factors: relative military capabilities, geostrategic security requirements, military doctrine, trends in weapons technology, governmental reactions to world and domestic opinion, alliance diplomacy, national ideology, and foreign policy style, and even those scientifically elusive yet politically real phenomena known as "national character" and "leadership personalities."

Thus a government not in possession of nuclear weapons will take a different approach to nuclear disarmament from one that does possess such weapons. A state that possesses nuclear weapon but lacks sophisticated delivery capabilities will probably wish to focus on the need to assign a disarmament priority to the latter over the former category. A state that places exclusive reliance on land-based missiles can be expected to adopt a different negotiating position from one that divides its deterrent between land and sea. A state that seeks "strategic superiority" will not pursue the same policies as one that is content with "strategic parity." In all cases, governments—regardless of their more idealistic statements—can be counted upon in international arms negotiations to promote their national interest, whether conceived narrowly or broadly.

In this and the two succeeding chapters, we shall examine the attitudes of principal powers—the United States, the Soviet Union, and China—toward disarmament and arms control, and also make some brief summary remarks about the positions of other important nations—Britain, France, Germany, India, and Japan.

**The United States**

Generally speaking, the United States has sought throughout the nuclear age to steer a middle course between the extremes of unlimited-power realism, on the one hand, and politically naive idealism on the other.* Since the end of World War II, the United States, of all the world's principal powers, has been the most consistently internationalist in outlook and the most determined to bring advanced weapons technology under effective international control. Even before the war ended, scientists involved in the atom project were deeply concerned with the postwar implications of nuclear weapons for international relations. The Franck Report of June 1945 stressed the dangers of surprise attack in the nuclear age, and concluded that, of "all the arguments calling for an efficient international organization for peace, the existence of nuclear weapons is the most compelling one."[1]

The United States government at an early date adopted a tough, no-nonense, yet radical attitude toward the international control of atomic energy. (The Baruch Plan was described in the previous chapter.) That plan was more farreaching in its implications for the politi-

* The United States was not always among the foremost exponents of arms negotiations. Captain Alfred Thayer Mahan, the US delegate to the first Hague Conference in 1899, was an opponent of arms limitation in almost any form. Later, however, President Wilson was a staunch advocate of disarmament as a pillar of peace, even though this principle was not entirely compatible with his concept of "collective security." During the Harding Administration, Secretary of State Charles Evans Hughes was remarkably successful in his initiatives toward international naval arms limitation, as we saw earlier. In 1927, the idealism of American intellectuals was reflected in the Pact of Paris, which purported to outlaw war as an instrument of national policy. In 1933, President Franklin D. Roosevelt sent a message to the Geneva Disarmament Conference urging all nations to refrain from increasing their armaments and to enter a solemn nonaggression pact. From 1935 to 1939, the United States, in an isolationist mood, tried to insulate itself from international conflict by relying upon a series of neutrality and embargo acts which prohibited or regulated the export of armaments to belligerents, but this policy was abandoned when totalitarian Germany threatened the survival of British democracy.

[1] *The Franck Report,* June 11, 1945. Text reprinted as Appendix B in Alice Kimball Smith, *A Peril and a Hope* (Chicago: University of Chciago Press, 1965), p. 561.

cal reorganization of the world than most American policymakers probably realized at the time. They were not forced to think it all the way through to its conclusion for the simple reason that the Soviets rejected it out of hand. Once it became apparent that the hope of Great Power unanimity in the United Nations Security Council had been a chimera, and that the Soviets had no intention of entering any kind of arms limitation agreement while they were in a distinctly inferior technological position, US policymakers realized increasingly that national security would have to be achieved not through the Baruch Plan but through the maintenance of an effective strategic deterrent.

Throughout the 1950s and early 1960s, the United States remained poised between a readiness to enter into balanced, reciprocal, and effectively controlled arms agreements and a determination to keep a credible strategic nuclear deterrent capable of inhibiting an attack upon the United States and its major allies (especially in the NATO area) in the absence of an arms agreement. The eminent British advocate of disarmament, Philip Noel-Baker, has contended that the United States missed a significant opportunity in May 1955 by reserving all its previous positions and retreating from disarmament as a policy goal just when the Soviets seemed ready to accept a measure of international inspection and control under the new post-Stalin leadership.[2] But the situation was more complex and more confusing than Noel-Baker's analysis would lead us to believe. West Germany had just joined NATO, and the Soviet plan called for the immediate withdrawal of all foreign forces from German territory. Moreover, the Soviet proposal—in a passage of rare honesty—admitted that the production of fissionable materials had reached such a volume as to render impossible a foolproof system of international control against the danger of clandestine accumulation of nuclear weapons stockpiles in violation of a disarmament treaty.[3] (This point will be dealt with more fully later on.) During the two years prior to May 1955,

[2] Philip Noel-Baker, *The Arms Race: A Programme for World Disarmament* (New York: Oceana Publications, 1960), p. 9. See also the Statement by Deputy US Representative Stassen to the Disarmament Subcommittee, September 6, 1955. *Documents on Disarmament 1945-1959*, vol. 1, p. 513.

[3] Soviet Proposal Introduced in the Disarmament Subcommittee May 10, 1955, *ibid.*, vol. 1, p. 465; see also John W. Spanier and Joseph L. Nogee, *The Politics of Disarmament: A Study in Soviet-American Gamesmanship* (New York: Praeger, 1962), p. 88-89.

the problem of hidden stocks had been magnified by a factor of a thousand as a result of the "second quantum leap" from kiloton to megaton weapons. The United States, conditioned since the days of the Baruch Plan to the oft-repeated Soviet *nyet,* had failed to do its homework on the constantly growing problem of devising an effective control system until surprised by the Soviet *da.* The United States was simply caught unprepared by a Soviet initiative which, Moscow planners had reason to believe, Washington could not and would not accept.[4]

The United States, recognizing the decreasing technical feasibility of general disarmament in the mid-1950s, began to develop a "first step" philosophy and to favor partial arms control measures before the Soviets did. Growing fears of the possible genetic effects of radioactive fallout led many scientists to call for a nuclear test ban, which hopefully would also help to inhibit the proliferation of nuclear weapons.[5] At first, the US government linked a nuclear test ban to other partial measures (safeguards against surprise attack, a cut-off in the production of fissionable materials, a start in transferring fissionable materials from weapons stocks to peaceful uses, and so forth); but later agreed to study the problem of a nuclear test ban as a separate item at the Geneva Conference of Experts, July-August 1958, and then to negotiate a test ban at the Geneva Conference on the Discontinuance of Nuclear Weapons Tests, which began in October 1958.[6] At the start of negotiations, there was a widespread assumption in this country that the US enjoyed such a lead in nuclear weapons technology that a test ban would not be detrimental to national security. But the Soviet Union launched a vigorous series of tests of weapons in the fifty megaton range in the late summer of 1961. By the time the Treaty Banning Nuclear Weapon Tests in the Atmosphere, in Outer Space, and Under Water was signed on August 5, 1963, the question as to whether it posed a risk to US national security had become more controversial. Most of the technical experts, including

[4] See Bernhard G. Bechhoefer, *Postwar Negotiations for Arms Control* (Washington: Brookings, 1961), pp. 314-315; and Fred Charles Iklé, *How Nations Negotiate* (New York: Harper and Row, 1964), p. 102.

[5] Robert Gilpin, *American Scientists and Nuclear Weapons Policy* (Princeton: Princeton University Press, 1962), ch. 5.

[6] *Geneva Conference on the Discontinuance of Nuclear Weapon Tests: History and Analysis of Negotiations,* Part I, Department of State Publication 7258 (Washington: US Government Printing Office, 1961).

critics of the treaty, did not attach much military value to the large yield-to-weight ratios enjoyed by the Soviets in the weapons range of ten megatons and above. There was somewhat greater disagreement, however, in respect to the impact of the treaty on US ABM development efforts and knowledge of the effects of induced phenomena on nuclear weapons (including high-altitude blackout).[7] Nevertheless, after weighing the misgivings and the risks, the Senate approved the treaty by an overwhelming vote of 80-19 on September 24, 1963—less than two months after the date of signature.[8]

Between the start of the test ban negotiations and the signing of the treaty, Premier Khrushchev had given a speech before the UN General Assembly that for a period shifted world attention away from partial measures and back to the goal of total disarmament, which was to be accomplished within the short space of four years. John W. Spanier and Joseph L. Nogee have appraised Khrushchev's gambit, and the US reaction to it, as follows:[9]

> Khrushchev's proposal had immediate appeal to a world tired of war and tension and hungry for peace. For it avoided all the complexities of technical questions, stressing in simple terms that "the way to disarm is to disarm," a truism implying the obvious message that since the Soviet Union had proposed disarmament, the continuing arms race was the sole responsibility of the United States. "Complete and general" disarmament was therefore a pure propaganda slogan and nothing else . . . The United States, as usual, was caught without an adequate response . . . Apparently, what was lacking in the US approach was an appreciation of disarmament as an instrument of psychological warfare. Consequently, the United States failed to counter Khrushchev's gambit with any serious effort.

Not until March 1960 did the Western powers reply with their own plan for general and complete disarmament, in a serious yet undramatic proposal at Geneva in which the emphasis was on the

---

[7] See *The Nuclear Test Ban Treaty*, Report of the Committee on Foreign Relations, US Senate, 88th Congress, September 3, 1963.
[8] *New York Times*, September 25, 1963.
[9] Spanier and Nogee, *op. cit.*, pp. 163-164.

creation of an adequate control mechanism and the establishment of an international organization capable of keeping the peace. These same two conditions were essential characteristics of the US Program for General and Complete Disarmament in a Peaceful World, unveiled on September 25, 1961, the same day as President Kennedy's address to the General Assembly on disarmament, and one day before President Kennedy signed the Act of Congress creating the United States Arms Control and Disarmament Agency.[10]

In the early 1960s, the Soviet Union was clearly ahead of the United States on the propaganda front as far as general and complete disarmament was concerned. Since that time, the US government has done more to advance man's understanding of the profound dilemmas implicit in the arms problem by: (1) insisting that general and complete disarmament, if it is ever achieved, would involve a radical change in the political structure of the world; (2) linking the reduction of national armaments to the building up of international peacekeeping machinery; (3) demanding the effective verification of all disarmament measures from beginning to end, so that each state can be confident that every other state is fulfilling its commitments; (4) calling for all disarmament measures to be balanced, so that at no point could one state gain a military advantage over another;[11] and (5) promoting the serious scientific study, both inside and outside the government, of the requirements and implications of total disarmament, partial arms control measures, and the relation of the latter to the former. In the last decade, the United Sates—including the government and private institutions—has probably devoted more resources to the scientific analysis of disarmament and arms control than all the other major powers of the world taken together.

Since the mid-1950s, and prior to the 1972 Moscow Agreements, the United States had agreed jointly with the Soviet Union on the following arms control measures: (1) the Antarctica Treaty of December 1, 1959, demilitarizing that region and preventing weapons tests therein; (2) the establishment of a direct communications link (the "hot line") between Washington and Moscow, June 20, 1963, and

[10] *Documents on Disarmament 1961*, pp. 475-496.
[11] See US draft statements submitted during bilateral talks with the Soviet Union from June to September 1961. *Ibid.*, pp. 196, 246-247, 360-361, and 431-438.

technologically updated September 30, 1971; (3) the Partial Test Ban Treaty of 1963, mentioned above; (4) the Outer Space Treaty of January 27, 1967, prohibiting the emplacement of weapons of mass destruction in orbit, on the moon, or on other celestial bodies; (5) the Nonproliferation Treaty of July 1, 1968, whereby the nuclear countries agree not to transfer such weapons to states not already possessing them; (6) the Seabed Treaty of February 11, 1971, which prohibits the emplacement of nuclear weapons and other weapons of mass destruction on the ocean bed or subsoil; (7) the Agreement on Measures to Reduce the Risk of the Outbreak of Nuclear War, September 30, 1971, by which the superpowers undertake to improve arrangements to guard against the accidental or unauthorized use of nuclear weapons, and to notify each other immediately concerning events which could create a risk of war. In the latter part of 1971, the United States and the Soviet Union also began to discuss ways of reducing the risks of mutual surveillance at sea, submitted a joint draft to ban biological weapons to the UN General Assembly, and showed some interest, however fluctuating, in undertaking negotiations toward mutual balanced force reduction (MBFR) in Europe. (All of these measures will be treated in subsequent chapters.)

Generally speaking, the United States has been opposed to arms control and disarmament proposals which aim: (1) to place an absolute ban on the use of weapons prior to the creation of an effective control system (except for biological weapons, the use of which by the United States, even in retaliation, was renounced by President Nixon on November 25, 1969[12]); (2) to weaken the North Atlantic Treaty Organization *vis-à-vis* the Warsaw Pact; (3) to liquidate entirely the sea-based deterrent (Polaris submarines) in an early stage of disarmament; or (4) to create an impression that progress is being made toward disarmament where such progress cannot be verified. Thus, the United States has steadily resisted proposals for a declaratory pledge of "no first use" of nuclear weapons. It has opposed the establishment of a nuclear-free zone in Central Europe which would denuclearize Germany but not apply to Soviet territory. For many years, it was distinctly cool to proposals for a nonaggression pact

[12] See *9th Annual Report to the Congress,* US Arms Control and Disarmament Agency (Washington: US Government Printing Office, 1970), pp. 45-46.

between NATO and the Warsaw Pact countries, and insisted that such an agreement must be accompanied by guarantees for West Berlin.[13] (During 1971, the ratification of the Bonn-Moscow and Bonn-Warsaw treaties, which contained "nonaggression" pledges, was clearly linked to the final working out of an accord on Berlin. The United States, the Soviet Union, Britain, and France signed such an accord on September 3, 1971, which left the details on guaranteed access and communications to East and West Germany. An agreement to facilitate traffic between West Germany and West Berlin was initialed in December 1971, and came into force along with the Quadripartite Berlin Accord in June 1972.[14])

A word should be said about the political sensitivity of the United States to the attitudes of its NATO allies toward superpower arms negotiations. At times in the past, some European allies—especially the Federal Republic of Germany—have become nervous or chagrined at US-Soviet diplomatic maneuvering. Both the Test Ban Treaty and the Nonproliferation Treaty filled many West Europeans with mixed emotions. On the one hand, they welcomed the willingness of the superpowers to tone down the hostility of their confrontation and to enter an era of "detente." But on the other hand, there was fear that the two nuclear giants, in their quest for mutual interest agreements, might strike bargains over the heads and at the expense of the Europeans in between. In recent years, the United States has taken steps to allay European apprehensions and to assure its allies that further US-Soviet negotiations on arms control and related European security matters would be preceded by consultations within NATO. The US had taken care not to allow the German Democratic Republic (East Germany) to exploit either the arms control negotiations or the signing of arms control treaties to upgrade its diplomatic status in the eyes of the Western powers.[15] (This was especially important prior to November 1972, when East and West Germany finally concluded their own negotiations on a treaty which normalized

[13] President Kennedy, shortly after the signing of the Test Ban Treaty, noted that a major US interest in a nonaggression pledge would be to obtain greater security and access guarantees in respect to Berlin. *New York Times,* August 2, 1963.

[14] *Ibid.*, June 4, 1972.

[15] *Nuclear Test Ban Treaty*, Report of the Committee on Foreign Relations, US Senate, *op. cit.*, pp. 6-7; and the Verbatim Proceedings of the Eighteen-Nation Disarmament Committee, ENDC/PV. 238, February 8, 1966, pp. 21-25; and ENDC/PV. 291, March 7, 1967, pp. 11-13.

their relations and opened the way for the admission of both states to the United Nations.) The creation of a Nuclear Planning Group in NATO, by which the allies have been admitted to a greater share in formulating alliance defense strategy, has helped to make US opposition to the spread of nuclear weapons to other nations more palatable. Since 1969, a new disarmament and arms control section has been operating within the NATO Secretariat to intensify the consultative process.[16] Finally, the United States takes the position that negotiated mutual balanced force reductions in Europe, East and West, should be sought to create a more stable military situation at lower levels and lower costs.[17] The Nixon Administration looks upon such negotiated withdrawals as vastly preferable to the kind of unilateral US withdrawal envisaged in the Mansfield Senate Resolution. Diplomatic probings toward negotiating mutual force withdrawals actually got under way early in 1973 and will be discussed in the final chapter.

Potentially the most important of all the US-Soviet negotiations, of course, have been the Strategic Arms Limitation Talks (SALT), carried on in Helsinki and Vienna since late 1969, and which have already led to the 1972 Moscow Agreements. SALT was largely a product of US initiative. It resulted from several years of American insistence, dating from January 1964, that the arms race could not be reversed until after it had been brought to a halt through a verified freeze on offensive and defensive strategic delivery vehicles.[18] One of the principal US objectives in SALT has been to determine whether the Soviet Union will be content with the rough strategic parity that was generally assumed to prevail at the beginning of this decade, or whether the USSR intends to push ahead in the deployment of land-based and sea-based missiles in an effort to achieve a kind of missile superiority which could be politically significant even if not militarily decisive.

What has motivated American policymakers to seek SALT agreements? There has been a variety of factors, national and international,

[16] A. G. Kuhn, "Active Disarmament Consultations in NATO," *NATO Letter,* vol. 18 (March 1970), pp. 20-23.
[17] *U. S. Foreign Policy for the 1970's,* A Report to the Congress by Richard Nixon, President of the United States, February 25, 1971, p. 195.
[18] *Documents on Disarmament 1964,* pp. 17-21.

several of them interrelated. As a nation, the United States had become frustrated by the Vietnam War and the effort to establish an equilibrium in Asia (despite a certain degree of success). We have experienced internal social disorders arising from urban crises, racial and generational conflicts, and campus unrest, as well as a pervading inflation which has contributed to general discontent with the existing institutional structure. A substantial portion of the intelligentsia and youth has become alienated from the nation's political, economic, and technical culture—seeking but not finding a viable "counterculture." American elites, it would seem, are growing weary of America's role as "policeman of the world." In a word, they are losing the sense of "manifest destiny," of "imperial will," and of what Peter Wiles calls "international self-confidence."[19] A particular antiwar sentiment is being generalized into a growing indifference among elites, or even growing hostility, toward national military defense policies and expenditures. Politicians discern a rising demand for a reordering of national priorities from defense and outer space to the environment and the inner city.

These trends should be neither underestimated nor exaggerated. They do not necessarily mean that the United States is about to become a second-class power all of a sudden. But they probably mean that the United States will in the coming decade reduce its relative emphasis on defense technology and become somewhat less active on the world scene—compared to the last 25 years. This, at least in part, is what the Nixon Doctrine means. This, in part, is what SALT means. It is a mode of adjustment to a more complex world—to a multipolar rather than a bipolar world, to the emergence of Europe, China, and Japan as potential new power centers, and to the dangers of additional proliferation of nuclear weapons to a larger number of states if the superpowers fail to make any progress toward limiting their own vast military power. (More will be said about the SALT in the concluding chapter.)

[19] Peter Wiles, "Declining Self-Confidence," *International Affairs* (London), 1971.

# 6

# The Attitudes of the Powers: USSR and Communist China

## The Soviet Union

The analysis of Soviet policy attitudes toward disarmament and arms control brings us face to face with a militant revolutionary ideology, the traditional modes of behavior of an old nation-state interested in both the status quo and expansion, an historic defense-mindedness strengthened by the destructive experience of World War II, and various emotional complexes almost too numerous to mention—xenophobia, suspicion, universal messianism, a desire to project enlightenment to the world, a fear of internal upheavals, and a determination to impose rational political controls upon science and technology as tools of social development. For decades, scholars have argued inconclusively as to whether Soviet imperialism is essentially Czarist or Communist, and whether the growth of the Soviet economic-technological power base would make Russia a more "bourgeois," satisfied power, or whet its appetite for global prestige, influence, and power, or produce both effects, as happened in the case of other modern imperialisms, British, French, German, and American, to mention only the leading examples. No definite, reassuring answers to this dilemma can be given.

Let us begin with Lenin, who never thought that the newly established Soviet Union could persuade the capitalist powers of the West to conclude a genuine disarmament agreement. For many years, Lenin condemned disarmament and pacifism as sentimental bourgeois dreams. He was convinced that significant social change resulted only from violent revolution, and that genuine, lasting peace could be achieved only after the establishment of a classless society. Thus, Lenin held explicitly that the objective of communism should not be international disarmament, but rather the arming of the proletariat for the purpose of disarming and defeating the bourgeoise.[1] Four decades later, when Premier Khrushchev was anxious to pose as the great champion of disarmament agreements, Soviet propagandists often invoked the mantle of Lenin for his policies, especially against Chinese Communist critics. A distinguished group of scholars of Soviet affairs commented on these efforts as follows:[2]

> Moscow's current attempts at establishing the Leninist orthodoxy of its disarmament policy are highly debatable. Lenin and his associates had, after all, been candid enough in their days to deny the possibility of any firm and binding compacts among inherently hostile states in an inevitably fluid world. As has since been suggested, the Leninist outlook affirmed, in essence, that in a system of capitalist powers, negotiated disarmament was impossible; in a Communist system, negotiated disarmament was unnecessary.

The Leninist skepticism about disarmament did not inhibit Soviet diplomats from advocating it at international conferences as early as Genoa in 1922. Then in 1928, Maxim Litvinov, the Soviet delegate to the Preparatory Commission of the League of Nations Disarmament Conference, startled virtually everyone by proposing total disarmament within a period of one year. The Sixth Congress of the Communist International, meeting that same year in Moscow, declared:[3]

---

[1] V. I. Lenin, *Sochineniia*, second edition, 30 vols. (Moscow, 1926-1932), vol. 8, pp. 395-397; Lincoln P. Bloomfield and others, *Khrushchev and the Arms Race* (Cambridge: MIT Press, 1966), pp. 5-10; Walter C. Clemens, Jr., "Ideology in Soviet Disarmament Policy," *The Journal of Conflict Resolution*, vol. 7 (March 1964), pp. 9-10.

[2] Alexander Dallin and others, *The Soviet Union, Arms Control and Disarmament: A Study of Soviet Attitudes* (New York: School of International Affairs, Columbia University, 1964), pp. 117-118. See also Richard J. Barnet, *Who Wants Disarmament?* (Boston: Beacon Press, 1960), p. 61; and Lincoln P. Bloomfield and others, *op. cit.*, pp. 118-120.

[3] Quoted in Alexander Dallin, *The Soviet Union at the United Nations* (New York: Praeger, 1962), p. 72.

> The aim of the Soviet proposals was not to spread pacifist illusions but to destroy them . . . Disarmament and the abolition of war are possible only with the fall of capitalism . . . It goes without saying that not a single Communist thought for a moment that the imperialist world would accept the Communist proposals.

During the greater part of the interwar period, the Soviets kept up their calls for universal disarmament. Besides showing contempt for buorgeois diplomatic conferences and advertising their own radically new approaches to the world's problems, the disarmament theme may have served as a defense mechanism, designed to create a pacifist climate of opinion, first against the danger of renewed anti-Bolshevik intervention by the capitalist powers, and later against the growing menace of German fascism. But on two counts Soviet interwar policy proved counterproductive. In the early 1920s, the Soviet Union was actively helping Germany to evade the disarmament provisions of the Versailles Treaty. Moreover, international Communist propaganda for peace and disarmament produced a greater effect in the democratic countries than in the fascist countries, and may have helped to delay timely defense responses by the former to the aggressive behavior of the latter.

Following World War II, the Soviet Union would have liked to resume its role as leader in the world struggle for peace and disarmament, but now the situation was different. The Red Army had brought Soviet power into Eastern Europe, and Stalin was more interested in consolidating his position there than disarming. Besides, the United States was actually pressing for effective international control of atomic energy in the United Nations. The Soviets insisted that these problems must be subject to the veto, and they rejected the Baruch Plan as an attempted infringement of their sovereignty. "Within the governing elite of the Soviet Union," Nogee writes, "the harmful expectations that would result from placing its atomic energy resources under international control exceeded the threat inherent in an atomic arms race and the possibility of a war involving atomic weapons."[4] During those years of Soviet military-technological in-

[4] Joseph L. Nogee, *Soviet Policy Toward International Control of Atomic Energy* (Notre Dame: University of Notre Dame Press, 1961), p. 233.

feriority, when the United States held a monopoly of atomic power, Stalin's policy was to deemphasize the importance of atomic weapons in war[5] and to focus propaganda efforts on a campaign for a purely declaratory "banning of the bomb," without what the Western governments would have regarded as adequate controls.

From 1955 to the early 1960s, the USSR managed to pose as the leading advocate of general and complete disarmament. During those years, the West often accused the Soviets of seeking "disarmament without controls." The Soviets countered with the charge that the West wanted "controls without disarmament" and sought to legalize espionage in the USSR under the guise of "international inspection." Some Western observers were inclined to think that the Soviet Union really wanted total disarmament; but, being a xenophobic dictatorship, Moscow was unwilling to pay the inspection price. Nothing more than irrational complex stood in the way of GCD, and this might be circumvented by devising "nonintrusive" inspection systems. Certainly the Russians' historic suspicion of Western intervention and prying, coupled with the controlled state's instinctive aversion to inspection by the "open society," cannot be lightly dismissed. These attitudes undoubtedly figured in the Soviets' rejection of President Eisenhower's "open skies" proposal put forth at the Geneva Summit Conference in July 1955, and also in their rather neurotic reaction to the U-2 incident in May 1960. There probably lurks among the Soviet military a real fear—not entirely without foundation—that effective international inspection can shade off into espionage.

But aside from the issue of inspection, on which the Soviets have been adamant, it is very difficult to make out a plausible case that the USSR really wants disarmament. On the contrary, there is reason to believe that the Soviet leaders are quite content with the condition of mutual deterrence. Russian elites have historically labored under a sense of technological and military inferiority *vis-à-vis* the Western powers. But since *sputnik* and the advent of the ICBM, they have felt an abiding self-confidence for the first time in centuries, believing that so far as the power of weaponry is concerned they now stand, for all practical purposes, on a par with the West. They know that no country

[5] H. S. Dinerstein, *War and the Soviet Union* (New York: Praeger, 1959), pp. 5-9.

can attack the Soviet Union with impunity, and this knowledge gives them an unprecedented sense of security. Not only can the USSR defend the Socialist states of Eastern Europe; it is in a position to extend its protective umbrella and its aid to client states in Southern Asia, the Middle East, and even the Caribbean. As its naval capabilities grow, Soviet communism accumulates the respect that accompanies global mobility. This, too, provides a pleasant sensation to a traditionally landlocked power—a satisfaction not readily to be forfeited. It is likely that the Soviets abhor the prospect of nuclear war just as much as Americans do—perhaps more, in view of the fact that their national experience in World War II was much worse than ours. But the Soviets have never thought that any statistical correlation could be drawn between the total size of nuclear stockpiles in being and the probability of a deliberate choice for nuclear war. If there is any correlation at all in their view, it is an inverse one: the growth of stockplies on both sides serves to deter war rather than to cause it.

Moreover, there is no convincing evidence that the Soviet leaders have carefully thought through, much less accepted, the long-range political implications and consequences of total disarmament. Richard J. Barnet once pointed out that the Soviet Union "has never appeared to accept the proposition that radical disarmament, which it espouses, will necessitate many profound changes in the world, including a drastic reorientation of the techniques of Soviet rule affecting both domestic and foreign policy."[6] Soviet theoreticians have long viewed the United Nations as a product of Western bourgeois liberal idealism; and Soviet diplomats have always been extremely reluctant to consider the strengthening of peace enforcement machinery within the framework of the UN.[7] Arthur I. Waskow writes:[8]

[6] Richard J. Barnet, "The Soviet Attitude on Disarmament,"*Problems of Communism*, vol. 10 (May-June 1961), p. 37.

[7] This attitude was particularly evident in the refusal of the Soviets to pay their assessments in support of UN peacekeeping operations in the Congo and the Middle East. For the background of the Soviets' theoretical atittude, see J. I. Coffey, "The Soviet View of a Disarmed World," *Journal of Conflict Resolution*, vol. 8 (March 1964).

[8] Arthur I. Waskow, "Alternative Models of a Disarmed World," *Disarmament and Arms Control*, vol. 2 (Winter 1963/64), p. 63. In contrast to US plans for an international peace force that would be, in effect, a "world army," Waskow notes that the Soviets propose no force except militia units controlled by national governments and placed at the disposal of the Security Council, always subject, of course, to the veto.

> The Soviet image of the disarmed world is quite different from that of the United States. The Soviet proposals seem to be based on the belief that in a world where resort to armed force has once been ruled out as a means of pursuing national interests, intense conflicts can be pursued without either using military force or resorting to agreed international institutions for achieving settlements of disputes.

The United Nations is seldom mentioned very favorably in Communist statements which look to the future organization of the international system. Even if the Communist states of the world should some day come to command a majority of the votes in the General Assembly, it is highly doubtful that Moscow would pay any more attenion to majoritarian position-taking in the United Nations than it has done in the past.[9] At the present time, there is no reason to expect that the Soviet Union will agree to the negotiated creation of a universally effective international peacekeeping force in lieu of national military establishments (even though it is at least conceivable that Moscow might, under certain circumstances, agree to such a force in a particular locality, such as the Middle East, to damp down a specific crisis that would otherwise involve unacceptable risks of war).

If the Soviets do not really want disarmament, what do they stand to gain by advocating total disarmament so insistently? Disarmament negotiations, to quote one group of scholars commenting on Czarist and Bolshevik diplomacy, serve "as a device to manipulate the atmosphere of world politics."[10] Lenin himself, after once condemning disarmament negotiations as a "snare and an illusion," later perceived them as a useful means of strengthening the influence of the pacifist bourgeoisie within the Western states and of dividing the bourgeois governments among themselves.[11] Undoubtedly, Soviet leaders from the time of Khrushchev onward have been compelled by the nature of modern weapons technology to adopt a more serious attitude toward international arms negotiations than Lenin did. But

---

[9] In July 1961, Khrushchev declared: "Even if all the countries of the world adopted a decision which did not accord with the interests of the Soviet Union, the Soviet Union would not recognize such a decision and would uphold its rights, relying on force." *New York Times*, July 12, 1961.

[10] Lincoln P. Bloomfield and others, *op. cit.*, p. 5.

[11] *Ibid.*, p. 8.

despite the fact that the Soviet leaders cannot entirely discount the danger of accidental or other unintended nuclear war, their behavior suggests that they do not regard such a danger as so intolerable as to make disarmament an imperative object of policy.[12]

By continuing to call for total disarmament, the Soviets no doubt hope to achieve some beneficial results. The Soviet proposals help to create a "world public opinion" which can be expected to have a greater effect upon the decisionmaking processes in Western democratic countries than in Communist countries. By maintaining the propaganda initiative in the struggle for peace and disarmament, the Soviets are able to appear more dynamic in the eyes of the emerging nations, which often equate superpower disarmament with substantial increases in international development aid. By hammering away at the notion that the Western powers resist general disarmament because they fear its economic consequences, Communist propagandists have helped to implant in many Western intellectuals an abiding suspicion of capitalist institutions, particularly the "military-industrial complex." The Soviet campaign for total disarmament has contributed toward the rise of an organized peace movement within the Western countries (but not in Communist countries, of course). Growing numbers of citizens become skeptical of the wisdom and cost of defense policies. Scientists gradually feel more ill at ease about working on weapons programs. The psychosocial gap widens between the "peaceful" pursuits of universities and the "militaristic" policies of Western governments. Western governmental institutions are set to working at the cross purposes of maintaining an adequate defense establishment while simuitaneously seeking avenues that lead to disarmament. Western statesmen become increasingly reluctant to pursue foreign policy objectives which would jeopardize disarmament negotiations, while the negotiations themselves contribute their share toward the political crisis of confidence that arises within the Atlantic Alliance whenever the two superpowers appear to be seeking agreement over the heads of the European allies.[13]

---

[12] Malcolm Mackintosh and Harry Willets, "Arms Control and the Soviet National Interest," in Louis Henkin, ed., *Arms Control: Issues for the Public* (Englewood Cliffs, N. J.: Prentice-Hall, 1961), pp. 159-160.

[13] Soviet diplomats for many years were incapable of speaking about disarmament without assigning a high priority to the elimination of "foreign bases"—a term which usually referred to US bases in NATO Europe.

All of the abovementioned results cannot but represent tangible benefits in the eyes of the Soviets. This is not to suggest that there is anything particularly sinister in the Soviet espousal of total disarmament. Given their understanding of how the social dialectic operates, and their appreciation of the asymmetries which exist between the Communist states of Eastern Europe and the Western democracies, it makes a great deal of sense for the Soviets to place heavy stress on the disarmament theme in their foreign policy, since this helps to create a political climate which enables them to exert some influence upon the strategic responses of the economically and technologically superior West. A pacifist, pro-disarmament atmosphere, however partial it may be, makes for an international environment safer for the conduct of Soviet foreign policy operations than probably would be the case without that atmosphere.[14]

To say that the Soviets neither seek nor expect a disarmed world at the present time is not to say, however, that they are uninterested in reaching any arms limitation agreements. From the end of World War II until the early 1960s, the Soviets were inclined to dismiss the concept of "arms control" as little more than a capitalist deception designed to justify the retention and growth of Western military establishments. During that period, the Soviets spoke frequently of "disarmament," but practically never of "arms control."[15] Some change was noticeable after the Cuban missile crisis, when the Soviets became more willing to admit that partial measures might be valuable if they served to advance the cause of general disarmament.[16] During the past decade, there have been signs that the Soviets have begun to take more seriously the Western idea of "arms control." probably as a result of intensified exchanges at governmental and nongovernmental levels. Soviet intellectuals and policymakers have become

[14] For a fuller account of Soviet attitudes, see James E. Dougherty, "Soviet Disarmament Policy: Illusion and Reality," in Eleanor Lansing Dulles and Robert Dickson Crane, eds., *Détente: Cold War Strategies in Transition* (New York: Praeger, 1965), pp. 138-178.

[15] Bechhoefer, *op. cit.*, p. 7. Three RAND specialists noted in the early 1960s that the technical aspects of arms control which fascinated so many Western analysts seemed to hold virtually no interest for Soviet military planners. Herbert S. Dinerstein, Leon Gouré, and Thomas W. Wolfe, "Introduction" to the English translation of *Soviet Military Strategy*, edited by Marshal of the Soviet Union V. D. Sokolovskiy (Englewood Cliffs, N. J.: Prentice-Hall, 1963), p. 77. Yuri Sheimin, a Soviet academician, expressed strong reservations over the American concept of arms control in the article, "A Soviet Scientist Looks at Disarmament," *Bulletin of the Atomic Scientists*, vol. 20 (January 1964).

[16] Victor Karpov, then First Secretary of the Soviet Embassy in Washington, made this point in "Soviet Stand on Disarmament," in J. David Singer, ed., *Weapons Management in World Politics*, Proceedings of the International Arms Control Symposium, Ann Arbor, Michigan, December 17-20, 1962, Joint Issue of *Journal of Arms Control* (October 1963) and *Journal of Conflict Resolution* (September 1963).

more familiar with Western strategic and arms control literature. Soviet and US scientists have intermingled at Pugwash Conferences and other gatherings. Communist, Western, and "neutral country" diplomats have been engaging in an arms limitation dialogue in Geneva, New York, Helsinki, Vienna, and other capitals. The Soviets have gradually perceived various motivations for participating in negotiations which lead to limited-cost, limited-risk agreements with the "capitalist" powers.

Some Soviet policymakers are probably interested in using arms negotiations to gain or perpetuate military advantages in specific weapons sectors or geographic regions; some to reduce the risks of unintended nuclear war; some to modulate the rate of US arms development and deployment; some to promote detente with the West while the Sino-Soviet dispute is in progress; some to discourage the spread of nuclear weapons to other countries, and thus make the dangers of the international environment less unmanageable in the future; some to keep Germany under control while sowing the seeds of discord among the NATO allies; some to facilitate the promotion of pacifism and occasional agitation against Western defense establishments and weapons policies in what is obviously a nondisarming world; some to control the costs of defense; and some for other purposes.

As early as November 1956, the Soviet Union proposed several specific, partial measures for force reductions, disengagement, and safeguards against surprise attack in Europe, but linked them to total disarmament. Those proposals served, among other purposes, to deflect unfavorable international opinion from the Soviet suppression of the Hungarian uprising two weeks earlier. The Soviets permitted Polish Foreign Minister Adam Rapacki to press for the establishment of a nuclear-free zone covering Germany, Poland, and Czechoslovakia; and later allowed Polish Prime Minister Wladyslaw Gomulka to advocate a nuclear freeze in the same region. (Both of these proposals were regarded by the West as directed at NATO defense strategy; acceptance of either at the time would have caused a crisis of confidence over the alliance in West Germany.)[17] The

[17] See James E. Dougherty, "Zonal Arms Limitation in Europe," *Orbis*, vol. 7 (Fall 1963).

Soviets also adhered to the Antarctica Treaty in 1959, providing for the demilitarization of a region quite remote from the vital interests of the USSR.

Following the "narrow escape" of Cuba, the Soviet Union entered a "hot-line" agreement with the United States to facilitate emergency communications between Washington and Moscow. Shortly thereafter, it entered a partial nuclear test ban treaty which involved no onsite inspection on Soviet territory—and thus no espionage or infringement of Soviet sovereignty. Still later, the Soviet Union collaborated with the United States in producing the Nonproliferation Treaty. (After having pulled back in the late 1950s from extending nuclear weapons aid to China, Moscow wanted a commensurate pledge from the United States that it would not allow nuclear weapons to pass to the national control of West Germany, and the Soviet leaders obtained the scrapping of the projected NATO multilateral force—MLF—as the price for their support of the Nonproliferation Treaty.) From the mid-1960s onwards, the Soviets became a party to the Outer Space Treaty, the Seabed Treaty, the agreement on reducing the risks of war by nuclear accident, and the Strategic Arms Limitation Talks.

Have the Soviets really become committed to arms control in recent years? By cooperating as they have with the United States, they have exposed themselves to the charge—made by the Chinese Communists—of "collusion" with the leaders of capitalist imperialism and reaction. (In view of the turnabout in United States-Chinese relations in 1971, such a charge may diminish in intensity and significance.) It makes sense that Moscow would wish to reduce as much as possible the uncertainty about Washington's future weapons deployment plans, and to avoid the economic futility of a mutually canceling, yet costly, arms competition with the United States, while watching China carefully—somewhat as Britain and the United States were interested in attenuating their naval rivalry after World War I, while keeping a nervous eye on Japan. The Soviet leaders are certainly aware that the rigid assumptions of Cold War bipolarity have been undergoing change for several years. The world is becoming more complicated as Western Europe, China, and Japan continue to move toward potential superpower status.

The Soviets problably now feel the pull of contradictory forces and desires. On the one hand, whether their fears are really justified or not, they do appear to have serious apprehensions when they contemplate their future relations with China, with which they share a 4,500-mile border. Western analysts have long assumed that the Soviet leaders are anxious to promote detente with the West for the purpose of "safeguarding their western rear" while involved with the Maoist regime in a dispute over national interests, interpretations of Marxist ideology, and the leadership as well as the strategies of the world revolutionary movement. Such an assumption is quite compatible with the classic Russian-Soviet strategy of avoiding conflict on opposite fronts simultaneously. It might be no less logical to argue that the USSR has adopted a militant posture toward a nuclear-weak China to "safeguard its eastern rear" so that it could pursue a more dynamic policy in Europe.[18] But regardless of which interpretation is currently correct, the possible strategic threat which China may pose in the future probably sets definite limits to what kinds of arms agreements the Soviets are willing to negotiate with the United States, irrespective of Moscow's interest in promoting detente.[19]

The European scene itself is also fraught with ambiguities for the Soviets. For many years, the Soviets demanded the liquidation of US bases overseas, the dissolution of NATO, disengagement from Central Europe, reduction of the US military presence in Europe, and an East-West nonaggression pact—long one of Moscow's favorite arms control measures. Today, the Soviets seem to be on the verge of achieving some of their long-cherished objectives. As a result of the Vietnam War and other factors, the American mood has been moving slowly but inexorably in recent years toward a reduction of international commitments in favor of domestic concerns. Since the West Germans signed the Nonproliferation Treaty, the Bonn-Moscow and Bonn-Warsaw treaties have been concluded, renouncing the forceful alteration of Central Europe's postwar boundaries. These

[18] This has been suggested by Michel Tatu, *The Great Power Triangle: Washington-Moscow-Peking* (Paris: Atlantic Institute, Atlantic Papers No. 3, 1970).

[19] The "triangular relationship" in its implications for arms control negotiations is analogous to the insoluble "three body" problem in Newtonian physics. For a treatment of some of the complexities of this relationship, see Pierre Maillard, "The Effect of China on Soviet-American Relations," in *Soviet-American Relations and World Order: The Two and the Many* (London: Institute for Strategic Studies, Adelphi Papers No. 66, March 1970).

constitute, in effect, the nonaggression pacts which Premier Khrushchev's diplomacy sought so eagerly in the late 1950s and early 1960s. In the meantime, the European Economic Community has been politically strengthened by the entrance of Britain; and Moscow is not likely to look with favor upon future West European efforts to develop a unified foreign or defense policy, particularly if the latter would involve a joint nuclear force.

This may partially explain why the Soviets, after showing no interest for several years in negotiating an equitable scaling down of the Atlantic and Warsaw Pact alliances, finally in mid-1971 indicated a cautious, by no means enthusiastic, willingness to undertake talks looking toward mutual balanced force reduction (MBFR) in Europe. The Soviets are well aware of mounting political and economic pressures within the United States for a unilateral cut in US forces in Europe, as reflected in the Mansfield Resolution in the Senate. Perhaps the Soviets have concluded that a unilateral US withdrawal would be more likely to result in stepped-up efforts for West European political unity and common defense, whereas negotiated mutual force reductions would be more conducive to Soviet objectives in the European Security Conference. Whether it will prove possible to work out a mutual force reduction which will not upset the existing political-military equilibrium in Europe is at present a highly debatable subject. In the NATO view, as Chalmers Roberts writes, "a one-man for one-man cut would give an unfair adavntage to the East, since US troops would travel thousands of miles to come home whereas Russian troops would move back only a few hundred miles into the Soviet Union."[20]

Within recent years, the Soviets have been steadily improving the armor and mobility of Warsaw Pact forces. It is generally conceded that any mutual withdrawal will leave the Soviets with a definite advantage in respect to reinforcement capability, since US reinforcements would have to be carried out over long distances, across an ocean barrier which would either necessitate a slow redeployment by surface carrier or a costly airlift which would limit the movement

[20] *Washington Post*, May 19, 1971.

of heavy equipment.[21] There is good reason, therefore, to wonder whether really equitable force reductions—perhaps based on such tradeoffs as quick-reaction aircraft for tanks—can be negotiated, given the differences in force structures and in the political-military geography of the situation. (MBFR will be treated in Chapter 10.)

The assumption concerning strategic parity has been an important factor in the background of US-Soviet arms negotiations, because this has been the first time in the history of the nuclear era that such a condition has been thought to exist. In a sense, American decision-makers seemed to be "marking time" all through the latter half of the decade of the 1960s in refraining from the deployment of additional strategic launcher capabilities, as if waiting for the Soviets to "catch up" to the point where serious negotiations on the size of missile forces could get under way. But the Soviets have been "coming abreast" at a disturbingly rapid rate on land and sea during the last few years. They have surpassed the United States in the number of landbased launchers by more than fifty percent, and they have deployed at least half the number of US submarine-launched missiles.[22] In these circumstances, the United States sought to reinsure its own security position by scheduling the deployment of the Safeguard sysem (around two or four missile sites), and by arming half its land-based Minuteman missiles and three quarters of its submarine missiles with multiple-warhead weapons.[23]

The crucial question has been, How long could prudent strategic planners in the United States assume that "crude parity" existed, given recent Soviet deployment rates? The third edition of *Jane's Weapons Systems,* published in late 1971, carried this conclusion: "Russia now has the initiative in weapons technology. Whereas for a long time it was assumed—with considerable justification—that the NATO countries had a clear lead in the development of sophisticated

[21] See Admiral Sir Nigel Henderson, "NATO Facing the Warsaw Peace Forces," General A. J. Goodpaster, "The Military Situation in Europe," and Major F. H. C. Koch, "Problems of Comparing Force Levels," all in *NATO Letter,* vol. 19 (March/April 1971); Timothy W. Stanley, "Mutual Force Reductions," *Survival,* vol. 12 (May 1970); and also Roger J. Hill, "Mutual and Balanced Force Reductions: The State of a Key Alliance Policy," *NATO Letter,* vol. 19 (September/October 1971).

[22] See *SIPRI Yearbook of World Armaments and Disarmament 1969/70,* Stockholm International Peace Research Institute (Stockholm: Almqvist and Wiksell, 1970), pp. 36-58; *The Military Balance 1971-1972* (London: Institute for Strategic Studies, September 1971), pp. 1-2.

[23] *New York Times,* February 27, 1971, and October 3, 1971.

weapons, it is now clear that the USSR has extinguished that lead and is now outstripping the West."[24] For some years, US defense and arms control planners have wondered whether the Soviets would be content to level off at crude parity, or whether they might try to sustain and increase their recent momentum in an effort to achieve the kind of strategic superiority which the United States has for all practical purposes renounced.

Was there any reason to believe that the Soviets were willing to level off at "crude parity?" What does the concept of "parity" mean to the Soviets, if anything? Certainly the idea does not loom in Soviet strategic literature. US security analysts feared that the Soviets, having been Number Two for so long, and now perceiving it to be within their grasp to become the world's Number One military power, would find the temptation irresistible.

What was there to inhibit them? First of all, they did not relish the prospect that an operational ABM might be deployed in the United States if the SALT Talks failed. They still have a healthy respect for the productive capabilities of the American economic-technological system. They realized that if SALT were to issue in no agreement, there would be a danger of increased competition in military research, development, and deployment. Furthermore, Soviet leaders undoubtedly feel economic pressures to limit spending for strategic arms—pressures for increased investment in agriculture and consumer industries, increasing imports, narrowing the "technological gap" with the West in nondefense sectors, and for a reallocation of defense resources to the Army and Navy. The Soviets may experience differences of opinion, too, among orthodox militants and revisionist modernizers, among party leaders, diplomats, the military, and the R & D scientists.[25] Yet the Soviets are not under as much domestic political pressure to reallocate national budgetary resources to nondefense purposes as US political leaders are. They might already have

---

[24] *New York Times,* November 21, 1971. Just a few weeks earlier, US satellite reconnaissance produced evidence that the Soviets were continuing to build new classes of silos, or emplacements, for large missiles, and were doubling the production facilities for missile submarines. *Ibid.,* October 11 and 20, 1971.

[25] For analyses of the conflicting economic, strategic, and political pressures upon Soviet decisionmakers, see Thomas W. Wolfe "Soviet Approaches to SALT," *Problems of Communism* (September/October 1970). See also Lawrence T. Caldwell, *Soviet Attitudes to SALT* (London: Institute for Strategic Studies, Adelphi Papers No. 75, February 1971).

reached the conclusion that the United States, having lost its "imperial will" and now preoccupied with domestic demands for a shift in national priorities, would not really be able to step up its efforts in the realm of defense technology as the USSR gradually acquiries a numerically impressive missile superiority—not necessarily one that would so upset the military balance as to reintroduce the actual threat of a deliberate surprise attack, but one that would enable the USSR to project a politically effective image, especially in Europe, of the world's most powerful nation, against which a US guarantee no longer holds.[26]

Since President Nixon's trip to Moscow and the signing of the SALT Agreements in May 1972 (as well as agreements to cooperate in space, the environmental field, scientific research, and the avoidance of incidents at sea), the Soviet Union and the United States have shown signs of being interested in cultivating more cordial relations with each other. The general trend toward friendlier Washington-Moscow ties has been strengthened by several other subsequent developments—the withdrawal of Soviet military personnel from Egypt following President Sadat's demand of July 1972; the benign diplomatic posture adopted by the Soviets in their effort (reflected in the Prague Declaration of January 1972 and their role in negotiating the network of German treaties) to lay the groundwork for a European Security Conference; the apparent willingness of Moscow to wield its influence behind the scenes for the purpose of facilitating the cease-fire agreement reached by the United States and North Vietnam in January 1973; and the conclusion of an agreement concerning the USSR's World War II debt and the extension of US credits for Soviet trade, especially in agricultural products. It can be said that since mid-1972, the climate of US-Soviet relations has definitely undergone a change. It is much too early, however, to predict what kind of effect this change will have upon the defense and arms control or disarmament policies of the two countries, and upon their ability to avoid future conflict situations which might heighten international tensions.

[26] Walter Slocombe has noted that one of the principal advantages to be derived from a SALT agreement is that it would reduce the danger that "parity is merely a prelude to substantial American inferiority"—an inferiority with "great potential for creating continued and politically disturbing anxiety." *The Political Implications of Strategic Parity* (London: Institute for Strategic Studies, Adelphi Papers No. 77, May 1971), p. 18.

**The People's Republic of China**

China's outlook upon the world is conditioned by traditional cultural elements (such as Confucianism), the effects of historical isolation and ethnocentrism, nationalism, and the Marxist-Leninist ideology of Socialist development as interpreted by Mao. In the nineteenth century, the Chinese empire was overrun by foreign nations seeking spheres of influence. Since the empire gave way to a republic in 1912, much of China's history has been marked by the violence of civil war, foreign invasion, and revolutionary upheaval in various forms. Anxious to wipe out the humiliations of the past, China has frequently asserted a determination to regain territories lost to other powers in the nineteenth century (Russia, Great Britain, France, and Japan), even though some of these "lost territories" are now separate states or belong to such independent states as India, Afghanistan, the Philippines, and the succession states of Indochina. Communist China has refused to renounce force as a means of settling boundary disputes and other territorial questions, as Tibet, India, Russia, South Korea, and the offshore islands in the Taiwan Strait have learned by experience since 1950.[27] The new trend in Chinese foreign policy symbolized by the "normalization" of relations between Peking and Washington announced in February 1973 might perhaps lead to a growing presumption that the problem of Taiwan will be allowed to evolve toward a nonviolent solution. It is doubtful, however, that all of China's neighbors can feel assured that the "Middle Kingdom" has turned permanently peaceable.

Although the experts are often divided as to whether Chinese policy is predominantly nationalist or Communist, there is little doubt that in its formulation it is essentially elitist. The role of public opinion in setting directions can for all practical purposes be ignored. The most commonly accepted interpretation of Communist China's foreign policy during the past decade has been that China has been attempting to replace the Soviet Union as the leader of the forces of

[27] See Robert A. Scalapino, "The Foreign Policy of the People's Republic of China," in Joseph E. Black and Kenneth W. Thompson, eds., *Foreign Policies in a World of Change* (New York: Harper and Row, 1963), pp. 549-588; Allen S. Whiting, "Foreign Policy of Communist China," in Roy C. Macridis, ed., *Foreign Policy in World Politics*, third edition (Englewood Cliffs, N.J.: Prentice-Hall, 1967); Robert C. North, *The Foreign Relations of China* (Belmont, Calif.: Dickinson, 1969).

world revolution, especially in the eyes of the Third World peoples of Asia, Africa, and Latin America, while accusing Soviet leaders of revisionism, "bourgeoisification," and betraying the revolution by entering into agreements with imperialist governments. The appearance of China as a Great Power rival for leadership of the world revolution has done much to alter the image of communism from a "monolithic" to a polycentric movement. Whether this has strengthened or weakened communism in relation to the West is a matter of debate. In the meantime, the Western nations have had to confront two different emphases in Communist strategies with respect to the arms problem.

China has played no direct part in international disarmament and arms control negotiations throughout the nuclear era. Prior to achieving a successful nuclear explosion, and for a considerable time thereafter, China followed the Stalinist line of depreciating the importance of nuclear weapons. Mao himself, of course, has long maintained that weapons technology is less important in war than the power of man and the strength of the masses. When Khrushchev in 1956 replaced Stalin's naively confident assertion that a third world war would destroy capitalism and assure the victory of socialism with the more realistic assessment that a general nuclear war would mean mutual suicide for both systems, the Chinese demurred and accused Khrushchev of being afraid to support the world struggle against imperialism with sufficient vigor. The Chinese took the position that general nuclear war was not likely to result from stepping up the pace of revolution; but that even if it did, capitalism would perish and communism would emerge triumphant on a world scale. We cannot be sure that the Chinese themselves believed this. But the net effect of their position in the late 1950s was to make Khrushchev look by comparison like "the prudent man" of the English common law tradition, especially when the Soviet Premier decided in 1962 to withdraw Soviet assistance from Peking's nuclear weapons program.[28] (As we have noted previously, the Chinese Com-

[28] "The Disarmament Issue in the Sino-Soviet Dispute: A Chronological Documentation," Appendix in Dallin and others, *op. cit.*, pp. 238-239. For representative Chinese statements on the Chinese-Soviet dispute over nuclear weapons policies in the early 1960s, see *ibid.*, pp. 239-276; see also Walter C. Clemens, Jr., *The Arms Race and Sino-Soviet Relations* (Stanford: Hoover Institute on War, Revolution and Peace, 1968), pp. 13-68.

munists themselves may have reached a point in the late 1950s where they deemed it preferable to develop nuclear weapons on their own rather than remain dependent upon and controlled by a foreign source of aid.)

Several years before acquiring nuclear weapons, the PRC had expressed unqualified support for the goal of universal disarmament, but insisted that no agreement to which the PRC was not a direct party would have any binding force on it.[29] Moreover, said Premier Chou, it was inconceivable that the PRC would attend a Great Power disarmament conference before being granted recognition.[30] While suppressing the Tibetan revolt in 1959 (an action which greatly alienated Indian sentiment) and refusing to renounce the use of force in the Taiwan Strait, the PRC proposed that "all countries of the Asian and Pacific area conclude a peace pact of mutual non-aggression and make this area a nuclear weapon-free zone."[31] Throughout the early 1960s, Chinese Communist spokesmen saw the nuclear weapons of the United States "imperialists" as the only significant threat to world peace. On the subject of proliferation and testing, Vice Premier Ch'en made this comment to Japanese reporters on November 9, 1962:[32]

> It is unfair for the nuclear powers to try to prevent the expansion of nuclear weapons. China will not abandon its right to possess nuclear weapons, even though it might take over a hundred years for China to possess them. It is important to ban all nuclear weapons, then nuclear testing would be suspended. The more nuclear powers there are, the better will be the conditions to eliminate nuclear weapons ultimately. We demand that all nuclear weapons be abandoned and nuclear testing be banned.

When the Nuclear Test Ban Treaty was signed in August 1963, the Chinese Communists were extremely critical of the Soviet leaders,

[29] Resolution of the National People's Congress of Communist China, January 21, 1960. *Documents on Disarmament 1960*, p. 26.
[30] News Conference by the Chinese Communist Premier, May 8, 1960. *Ibid.*, p. 87.
[31] Message from Premier Chou to the Sixth World Conference Against Atomic and Hydrogen Bombs, July 30, 1960. *Ibid.*, p. 181.
[32] *Documents on Disarmament 1962*, p. 1038.

calling them "betrayers" and "deceivers" for adhering to a treaty advantageous to the forces of war headed by US imperialism. The Chinese expressed fear that, since the United States was more experienced in underground tests (which are permitted by the treaty), the agreement would only retard Soviet progress and enhance US superiority. China, their statement said, did not depend completely upon Soviet nuclear weapons for protection against aggression. "The Chinese government has always fully appreciated the importance of the Soviet Union's possession of nuclear weapons. However, such possession must in no way be made a justification for preventing other Socialist countries from increasing their own defense capabilities."[33]

Aware that the Test Ban Treaty might be a prelude to US-Soviet cooperation to prevent nuclear proliferation, the Chinese declared:[34]

> Whether or not nuclear weapons help peace depends on who possesses them. It is detrimental to peace if they are in the hands of imperialist countries, it helps peace if they are in the hands of Socialist countries. It must not be said indiscriminately that the danger of nuclear war increases along with an increase in the number of nuclear powers . . . As long as the imperialists refuse to ban nuclear weapons, the greater the number of Socialist countries possessing them, the better the guarantee of world peace.

The Chinese admitted that the Soviet acquisition of nuclear weapons had strengthened the chances of peace. But now Khrushchev, by entering into an agreement with Kennedy, was committing a fraud against the peoples of the world by leading them to believe that US imperialists were "peace fighters." The Soviets were warned that if they allied themselves with US imperialism against the revolutionary struggle of the fraternal Socialist countries, "eventually it will not be possible for the Soviet Union itself to be preserved."[35] The Chinese accused the Soviets of terminating nuclear weapons assistance to China in order to please Eisenhower. Later, the Soviets "brazenly ganged up with the imperialist bandits in exerting pressure

---

[33] Chinese Communist Statement on the Soviet Union and the Test Ban Treaty, August 15, 1963. *Documents on Disarmament 1963*, p. 359.
[34] *Ibid.*, pp. 359-360.
[35] *Ibid.*, p. 363.

on China" to abstain from acquiring nuclear weapons. Not surprisingly, the Chinese announced that they were ending their reliance on the Soviets and would develop their own nuclear strength to resist the US.[36] If it served no other purpose, the Chinese statement helped to convince the West that there was a serious breach between Moscow and Peking over the Soviet Union's approach to "peaceful coexistence" through arms control agreements with the United States.

Whenever the Chinese professed their support for the disarmament proposals put forward by the USSR, they usually added that it was inconceivable that the imperialist countries could ever accept such proposals. "The purpose of putting forward such proposals is to arouse the people throughout the world to unite and oppose the imperialist scheme for arms drive and war preparations, to unmask the aggressive and bellicose nature of imperialism before the peoples of the world in order to isolate the imperialist bloc headed by the United States."[37] It is illusory to expect peace through disarmament, the Chinese leaders steadfastly held in Leninist fashion, while imperialism still exists. Not until the whole world is Socialist will it be free from war and free to disarm. At one point, the Soviets felt compelled to justify their position to other Communist parties by having Boris Ponamarev circulate a lengthy letter which Edward Crankshaw partially paraphrased as follows:[38]

> As for disarmament, the Chinese objection to the call for disarmament, namely, that it encouraged "illusions" among the masses, was based on a failure to appreciate the real meaning of the Soviet proposals. This was that, by concentrating on disarmament, the creation of broad popular fronts and mass movements in favor of peace would be facilitated, thus embarrassing "bellicose circles" in their efforts to intensify the arms race.

But the Chinese continued to brand as "sheer illusion" the expectation of general and complete disarmament while the system of

[36] *Ibid.*, pp. 364-365. The Chinese elsewhere criticized the Test Ban Treaty as an instrument aimed at preventing China from acquiring nuclear weapons, perpetuating the superpowers' nuclear monopoly, and paving the way for US-Soviet cooperation to dominate the world. See Dallin, *op. cit.*, p. 268.

[37] Speech of Lin Chang-sheng, June 7, 1960. In Dallin, *op cit.*, pp. 247-248.

[38] *Ibid.*, p. 249.

imperialism still existed. "An elementary knowledge of Marxism-Leninism tells us that the armed forces are the principal part of the state machine and that a socalled world without weapons and without armed forces can only be a world without states." (This passage was in the letter of the Chinese Communist Party Central Committee, June 14, 1963, in reply to a letter from the Soviet Communist Party Central Committee, March 30, 1963.)[39] The Chinese letter then quoted that famous passage from Lenin on disarmament cited previously, which Soviet Communists apparently would prefer that the West forget.

On the occasion of detonating their first nuclear weapon in October 1964, the Chinese reiterated the famous saying of Chairman Mao that "the atom bomb is a paper tiger." They also declared that China "will never at any time and under any circumstances be the first to use nuclear weapons." They called for a summit conference of all the countries of the world to discuss the complete prohibition and destruction of all nuclear weapons. As a first step toward such a goal, they proposed an agreement among nuclear powers and soon-to-be-nuclear powers not to use nuclear weapons against anyone.[40] All of these positions made a good deal of sense for a brand new nuclear power with no weapons stockpiles or delivery systems.

Before Communist China was ever invited to take part in the eighteen-nation Geneva disarmament talks, spokesmen for Peking made clear that China would not participate. Two reasons were given. First, those talks were being conducted within the framework of the United Nations, where the PRC was deprived of its rights as the "sole legal government" of the Chinese people. Second, the UN had proved itself "completely incapable of handling the disarmament question." The PRC was also opposed to any suggestion of five-power nuclear talks, because there were at least a hundred other sovereign states that should have a say on the disarmament question.[41] (At that time, the Soviet Union endorsed the Chinese

[39] *Ibid.*, p. 264.
[40] Chinese Statement on Nuclear Weapons, October 16, 1964. *Documents on Disarmament 1964*, pp. 448-451. Communist China, as soon as it was admitted to the United Nations, reiterated its demand for a no-first-use pledge by all nuclear powers. *New York Times*, November 16, 1971.
[41] Peking *People's Daily* Editorial on Nuclear Disarmament, November 22, 1964. *Documents on Disarmament* 1964, pp. 485-487.
[42] Address by Foreign Minister Gromyko to the General Assembly, December 7, 1964. *Documents on Disarmament 1964*, p. 503.

Communist proposal for a world conference of heads of state to agree upon a pledge renouncing the use of nuclear weapons by anyone against anyone.)[42] Up to the present time (1973), China has steadfastly refused to adhere to the Nuclear Test Ban Treaty or the Nonproliferation Treaty. On the question of continued testing in the atmosphere, the Chinese have justified their policy on grounds of its "peaceful" and "defensive" character against "the threats of the imperialists," while blithely ignoring Indian criticisms that Chinese testing policy stands condemned by the language of General Assembly resolutions, the Bandung Declaration, the Nuclear Test Ban Treaty, and the Cairo Declaration of Nonaligned States, which was issued just a few days before the first Chinese test.[43] (Actually, only a few nonaligned states later made specific statements that could be regarded as critical of the Chinese testing program.)

As for proliferation, China began its career as a nuclear power by sounding a distinctively revolutionary note, yet one that contained some built-in reservations for the future. In September 1965, Vice Premier Ch'en said:[44]

> In my opinion, the most important task for the Afro-Asian countries today is to shake off imperialist control politically, economically, and culturally, and develop their own independent economy . . . Any country with a fair basis in industry and agriculture and in science and technology will be able to manufacture atom bombs, with or without China's assistance. China hopes that Afro-Asian countries will be able to make atom bombs themselves, and it would be better for a greater number of countries to come into possession of atom bombs.

Despite Mao's famous dictum that "political power grows out of the barrel of a gun," China has not yet stopped professing its traditional conviction that man rather than weapons technology consti-

[43] Statement by Indian Ambassador V. C. Trivedi on the Second Chinese Communist Nuclear Test, May 14, 1965. *Documents on Disarmament 1965*, pp. 169-170.

[44] News Conference by Vice Premier Chen, September 29, 1965, *Documents on Disarmament 1965*, p. 463. For a discussion of Chinese Communist attitudes, see Morton H. Halperin, *China and Nuclear Proliferation* (Chicago: University of Chicago Center for Policy Study, 1966). See also *Communist China and Arms Control: A Contingency Study 1967-1976* (Stanford: Hoover Institution on War, Revolution and Peace, 1968).

tutes the decisive strategic factor. While praising the achievements of the scientists at Lop Nor as "a great victory of Maoist thought," and while enjoying a new global prestige as a nuclear power, especially in the eyes of the Third World, China frequently reasserts that it will never place blind faith in nuclear weapons and warns nonnuclear states against placing too much emphasis upon the role of atom bombs in world politics. Peking has displayed no eagerness in practice to encourage the diffusion of nuclear weapons to states not yet possessing them.

The strategic position of the PRC *vis-à-vis* the superpowers has remained one of relative inferiority. A. Doak Barnett has given the following estimate of the situation:[45]

> One of China's basic aims . . . has been and still is to acquire at least a minimal nuclear deterrent to improve its ability to deal with the United States and the Soviet Union . . . . While its technological progress has been impressive in many respects, its actual capabilities are very limited and will remain so for a long time to come because of the relative weakness of China's resource base. By the middle or latter 1970s, China will at best have accumulated 15 to 40 operational intercontinental ballistic missiles (ICBMs), plus one to two hundred medium-range ballistic missiles (MRBMs) and a limited number of other bombs deliverable by aircraft.

Barnett concludes that within the foreseeable future, China cannot possibly hope to achieve strategic parity with the superpowers, nor approach anything resembling a first strike capability. US Secretary of Defense Melvin R. Laird also pointed out in March 1971 that China "probably could not have significant numbers of ICBMs deployed until late in the decade.[46]

---

[45] A. Doak Barnett, "A Nuclear China and U. S. Arms Policy," *Foreign Affairs*, vol. 43 (April 1970), pp. 427-428. Some Western observers have argued in the past that the Chinese, recognizing the symbolic significance of nuclear weapons, would be content with merely a token nuclear force. For a persuasive presentation of the view that Peking is interested in much more than a token force, see Yuan-li Wu, *Communist China and the World Balance of Power* (Washington: American Enterprise Institute for Public Policy Research, 1971).

[46] *Toward a National Security of Realistic Deterrence*, Statement by the Secretary of Defense on the FY 1972-76 Defense Program and the 1972 Defense Budget, before the Senate Armed Services Committee, March 15, 1971, p. 48. See also *The Military Balance 1971-1972* (London: Institute for Strategic Studies, 1971), pp. 40-41.

During its periods of nuclear infancy and childhood, China appears to have recognized its great strategic vulnerability. Confronting an American military presence in Southeast Asia while simultaneously involved in a tense border situation with the Soviets along the Amur-Ussuri Rivers, the Chinese have carefully refrained from provoking either superpower into a preventive strike against Lop Nor. The Chinese do not appear to be too worried about the danger of accidental nuclear war—less so than the Soviets, who in turn have been less concerned than American arms controllers. The Chinese, writes Morton H. Halperin, "attack the Soviet view . . . that a small war of national liberation can grow very rapidly into a nuclear war," and accuse the Russians of advancing such an argument "mainly as an excuse for not supporting wars of national liberation."[47] On the whole, the Chinese leaders do not get excited about the dangers of uncontrollable war, probably because they themselves are masters in the art of applying controlled strategy. They are nurtured in a tradition which bids them to avoid strategic adventurism. They are intelligent enough to realize that, so long as they act with caution, each passing year brings them closer to the time—however far off it may be—when no sensible policymaker in Washington or Moscow will be able to deny that China has entered the charmed circle of mutual deterrence. From a strictly military standpoint, China will not achieve such a posture until it has deployed an operational force of IRBMs (on which the Chinese are now concentrating) and ICBMs (which they are pursuing on a high priority basis) sufficient to overcome the self-immunizing effects, *vis-à-vis* China, of the relatively "thin" antimissile capabilities which will be available to the USSR and the United States after the SALT Agreements. China's present nuclear force was limited to, at most, about 300 weapons at the end of 1971, deliverable by a small but growing force of jet bombers and perhaps 25 medium-range missiles. Thus, concludes one expert: "First use of nuclear weapons will not be a realistic alternative for Chinese decisionmakers for many years to come."[48] But, he adds, the mere existence of even a small number of Chinese ICBMs—expected to appear after 1975—may be quite sufficient, from the

[47] Halperin, *op. cit.*, p. 18. For official Chinese statements on the SALT negotiations, see *Documents on Disarmament 1969*, p. 529; and *Documents on Disarmament 1970*, pp. 695-696.

[48] Charles H. Murphy, "Mainland China's Evolving Nuclear Deterrent," *Bulletin of the Atomic Scientists*, vol. 28 (January 1972), p. 34.

standpoint of practical realism, to deter the United States from assuming a posture of risk in a future confrontation with China.

Undoubtedly, President Nixon's new diplomatic stance toward the PRC, and the seating of the PRC in the United Nations, will have some effect upon China's future attitude toward questions of disarmament and arms control. When the first SALT talks were just getting started, the Chinese Communists branded it a "big plot"—a mixture of Soviet-US competition, each trying to achieve superiority over the other, and of collusion to develop their alliance in order to maintain their nuclear monopoly and to step up their joint opposition to China. They referred to "the criminal designs of US imperialism and social imperialism in conducting the nuclear talks." Western and Soviet analysts have been saying for many years that there can be no serious international arms negotiations so long as China does not participate. Whether China is now ready to enter the "arms control club," no one can predict with certitude—except perhaps a few Chinese leaders. The longer China remains outside, while the US and USSR continue to accumuate agreements, the more difficult it may be to arrange entry. In view of the position that Chinese leaders have taken in the past concerning the proliferation of nuclear weapons, it would now be difficult—but not impossible—for them to sign the Nonproliferation Treaty. It might be easier to adhere to the Nuclear Test Ban Treaty. Within recent years, China has been the power primarily responsible for the nuclear pollution of the atmosphere. But Peking has also been developing its underground testing capabilities. China might be willing to demonstrate its reasonableness and "peaceableness" by renouncing further atmospheric testing, even if not yet ready to enter into "collusion" with the superpower "imperialists" by adhering to their Test Ban Treaty. Incidentally, those who advocate a comprehensive test ban treaty seldom consider the possibility that China might regard such a pact between Washington and Moscow as directed against Peking—assuming that the two former capitals would be willing to subscribe to a total test ban which did not include China.

China, like the two superpowers, can be expected to exploit the "triangular relationship" for whatever it is worth on the international political-strategic scene. Peking can be expected to behave with the discretion appropriate to an inferior nuclear power. At present, China seems to be using the Sino-American relationship to deter the Soviet Union. It is not inconceivable—stranger things have happened—that at some future time, the Communist regime in Peking might move toward a rapprochement with the Communist regime in Moscow to present a united front against the United States.

China's position within the international diplomatic system has undergone a dramatic change since mid-1971. Within a year of President Nixon's trip to Peking in February 1972, China and Japan agreed to end the state of war between them and to normalize relations; Peking and Bonn established diplomatic relations; and China and the United States announced that they would set up "liaison offices" in each other's capitals.[49] The ending of the US involvement in Vietnam has undoubtedly proved to be an important factor enabling the People's Republic and the United States to view each other as natural counterweights to the Soviet Union in the emerging multipolar balance.

It is not easy to say what effect these developments will have on Peking's policies with respect to weapons programs and international arms control discussions. No one has suggested that the Chinese, in the new climate of international relations, will slow down the rate at which they are building their strategic nuclear capabilities. It seems quite likely that Mao and his advisers will continue to look upon US-Soviet arms control negotiations as a potential forum for superpower collusion against China's nuclear weapons program.

A few years ago, opposing a Soviet-sponsored proposal for a disarmament conference made up of the five nuclear powers, China countered with a call for a world disarmament conference made up of the heads of *all* governments (including the "mini-states")—but only after the superpowers follow China's lead in renouncing the first use of nuclear weapons, especially against nonnuclear countries and nuclear-free zones. But when the Soviet Union in 1971 proposed a world conference of 136 countries, the Chinese delegate to the UN General Assembly, after reiterating the demands previously men-

[49] *New York Times,* September 30 and October 1, 1972; February 23, 1973.

tioned, warned that the world disarmament conference should not be convened under the threat of the superpowers.[50] There was reason to believe that the PRC, aware that it was still far behind the two superpowers in the development of advanced nuclear weapons technology, was not yet ready to enter into serious international armaments discussions, particularly in bodies hitherto dominated by the US and the USSR.

Perhaps China perceives an advantage in remaining aloof from the "imperialist" superpowers at this juncture, and in identifying as closely as possible with the countries of the Third World. China's Vice Minister for Foreign Affairs, Chiao Kuan-hua, lent credibility to such an interpretation in his militant address before the UN General Assembly in October 1972. He scored the United States for supporting Zionist aggression in the Middle East, and criticized the Soviet Union not only for failing to give greater support and assistance to the Arab people but also for spreading the "nonsense" that "no counterattack should be made against Israel's armed aggression for that would spark a world war."[51] In that same address, Chiao Kuan-hua reiterated a classic Marxist-Leninist-Khrushchevist doctrine which implies a somewhat different philosophy of arms control and disarmament from that to which the West has become accustomed in the nuclear age:

> People condemn war and consider it a barbarous way of settling disputes among mankind, but . . . there are two categories of war, just and unjust. We support just wars and oppose unjust wars. If a Socialist still wants to be a Socialist, he should not oppose wars indiscriminately.[52]

---

[50] *World Armaments and Disarmament: SIPRI Yearbook 1972*, Stockholm International Peace Research Institute (Stockholm: Almqvist and Wiksell, 1972), pp. 494-499.
[51] *New York Times*, October 4, 1972.
[52] *Ibid.*, October 8, 1972.

# 7

## The Attitudes of Other Countries

It is not possible in a short work to survey in detail the attitudes of a large number of contries toward disarmament and arms control. Several countries have not articulated a clearly defiined position. But most of the world's states have taken at least a general position within the United Nations General Assembly or Disarmament Commission —where they more often criticize the arms policies of the Great Powers than advocate a form of universal disarmament applicable to themselves. During the last decade, a dozen or so countries have become identified with specific positions, either by propounding them in the Eighteen-Nation Disarmament Committee (ENDC) (or the Conference of the Committee on Disarmament),* or by opposing particular arms control measures. Sweden, for example, has long pressed for a comprehensive test ban which would prohibit underground tests as well as those in the atmosphere, in outer space, or under the oceans. India has refused to sign the Nonproliferation Treaty for reasons discussed below. West Germany and Italy delayed approving that treaty until they had received certain assurances concerning the implications of international inspection for the peaceful reactor industry and the role of Euratom in European integration. Brazil held out against the same treaty because of resentment over

* The Disarmament Committee, which existed from 1962 to 1969, consisted of Brazil, Bulgaria, Burma, Canada, Czechoslovakia, Ethiopia, France, India, Italy, Mexico, Nigeria, Poland, Rumania, Sweden, UAR, UK, US, and USSR. In 1969, it was replaced by the Conference of the Comittee on Disarmament (CCD) and its membership was expanded to 26 by adding Argentina, Hungary, Japan, Mongolia, Morocco, the Netherlands, Pakistan, and Yugoslavia, France has never participated.

dependence on the nuclear powers for the conduct of future peaceful explosions on Brazilian soil.[1]

**Britain and France**

There is no need to describe the policy attitudes of the British government toward disarmament and arms control, since for all practical purposes they have been, for more than two decades, virtually indistinguishable from those of the United States. There have been minor differences of emphasis from time to time; but on the whole, close cooperation in international arms negotiations has been a part of the "special" Anglo-American relationship that has prevailed throughout the period since World War II. The British government often cosponsored disarmament proposals with the United States and signed the major arms control treaties as soon as they were opened for signature. Now that Britain has entered the Common Market, we can expect some diminution of the "special relationship" with the US government in nearly all areas. London will probably have to accommodate itself to the fact that Paris frequently differs, while Bonn and Rome sometimes differ, from Washington and Moscow in the approach taken to international arms control.

Since early in the Gaullist era, France has refused to participate in the Geneva arms negotiations. Although a place was reserved for France in the Eighteen-Nation Disarmament Committee, Paris never occupied it, nor did it sign the Nuclear Test Ban Treaty and subsequent agreements worked out by the United States, the Soviet Union, and the UK. De Gaulle resented the special Anglo-American relationship, especially the fact that the United States, after helping the British to acquire nuclear weapons, first tried to exclude the French from entering the "nuclear club" through dissuasion and the withholding of assistance, and later manifested disdain for the value of the *force de frappe*. Lacking an underground testing capability (particularly in view of the loss of Algeria), the Gaullist government felt compelled to continue atmospheric testing or else renounce the

[1] See James E. Dougherty, "The Treaty and the Nonnuclear States," *Orbis*, vol. 11 (Summer 1967); and Elizabeth Young, *The Control of Proliferation: The 1968 Treaty in Hindsight and Forecast* (London: Institute for Strategic Studies, Adelphi Papers No. 56, April 1969).

development of the nation's nuclear deterrent. Although France has not adhered to the Nonproliferation Treaty, Paris has manifested no desire to encourage the diffusion of nuclear weapons to additional nations, and has given public assurances of an intention to "behave in this area exactly as do those states that decide to adhere" to the Nonproliferation Treaty.[2] Now that the de Gaulle era has come to an end, it might be possible for France to return to the international conference table during the 1970s, but France seems to be in no hurry to reverse Gaullist policies in this respect. The government in Paris might very well make overtures to London for a demonstration of Britain's European-mindedness through the establishment of an Anglo-French *entente nucleaire* as the foundation of a joint European Community deterrent. Thus, Britain may find itself under some political pressure to move away from the United States and closer to France in order to create the basis of a common European foreign policy more independent of superpower dominance. Such a course has been frequently discussed since the early 1960s, but thus far it has not come to pass.[3] We shall return to this subject in the final chapter.

**West Germany**

For many years, Germany has figured prominently in the thinking of the World War II victors about arms control, and will continue to do so for many years to come. After the Second World War, as after the first, Germany was subject to a greater degree of arms control than any other power. A protocol to the Treaty of the Western European Union, to which the Federal Republic adhered in 1954, prohibits West Germany from producing atomic, biological, and chemical weapons, as well as guided missiles (except for air defense), heavy warships, submarines, and strategic bombers, unless permitted by the WEU Council; and also placed West Germany under the inspection supervision of an Armaments Control Agency.[4]

[2] *Documents on Disarmament 1969*, p. 579.

[3] See James E. Dougherty, "European Deterrence and Atlantic Unity," *Orbis*, vol. 6 (Fall 1962); Alastair Buchan and Philip Windsor, *Arms and Stability in Europe* (New York: Praeger, 1963), pp. 201-212; Karl W. Deutsch, *Arms Control and the Atlantic Alliance* (New York: Wiley, 1967), pp. 34, 99, 136; Ivor Richards, "A European Defence Policy," *Survival*, vol. 12 (March 1970); Robert Ellsworth, "Europe and America," *ibid.*, vol. 13 (April 1971).

[4] The text of the protocol can be found in A. H. Robertson, *European Institutions* (New York: Praeger, 1958), pp. 294-297; see also Raymond Fletcher, "Existing Arrangements for International Control of Warlike Material—Western European Union," *Disarmament and Arms Control*, vol. 1 (Autumn 1963), p. 149.

Ever since West Germany joined NATO in 1955, most of the debates about arms control strategy within the alliance, as well as arms negotiations with the Soviet bloc over Central Europe, have centered on Germany, and have made either the West Germans or their neighbors nervous. This has been the case in respect to debates over the following subjects: whether the Bundeswehr should be armed with nuclear weapons; the credibility of the Western deterrent *vis-à-vis* Berlin; nuclear *versus* conventional strategies, such as "massive retaliation," "flexible response," "conventional pause," and so forth; the various plans for disengagement, denuclearization, nuclear free zones, and nonaggression pacts, as well as proposed pledges for "no-first-use-of-nuclears"; and whether NATO should create a multilateral force (MLF) in which West Germany could share in the control of the alliance's nuclear capabilities.[5] The MLF idea was finally scrapped in 1967, partly because it had become a bone of contention among the allies, and partly to attenuate the professed Soviet fears of German "revanchism," thereby paving the way for a US-Soviet agreement on the Nonproliferation Treaty.

At the time both the Test Ban Treaty and the Nonproliferation Treaty were being negotiated, the United Sates had to give the Federal Republic special reassurances that East Germany's diplomatic status would not be enhanced as a result of being allowed to adhere to those instruments.[6] After the shelving of the MLF, the United States shifted emphasis within NATO to the Nuclear Planning Committee, whereby the European allies, including West Germany, were to have a greater share in formulating alliance defense strategy. This move helped to render more palatable the US policy of opposing the spread of nuclear weapons to nations not already possessing them.[7] Later, the Bonn government contended that the Non-

[5] In addition to items referred to in ch. 6, fn. 16, and ch. 7, fn. 3 above, see Robert E. Osgood, *NATO: The Entangling Alliance* (Chicago: University of Chicago Press, 1962), ch. 6; Michael Brower, "Nuclear Strategy of the Kennedy Administration," *Bulletin of the Atomic Scientists*, vol. 18 (October 1962); Morton H. Halperin, "A Proposal for a Ban on the First Use of Nuclear Weapons," *Journal of Arms Control*, vol. 1 (April 1963); Alvin J. Cottrell and James E. Dougherty, *The Politics of the Atlantic Alliance* (New York: Praeger, 1964), ch. 3; Kai-Uwe von Hassel, "Detente Through Firmness," *Foreign Affairs*, vol. 42 (January 1964), and "Organizing Western Defense," *ibid.*, vol. 43 (January 1965); James L. Richardson, *Germany and the Atlantic Alliance* (Cambridge: Harvard University Press, 1966); and George R. Bluhm, *Detente and Military Relaxation in Europe: A German View* (London: Institute for Strategic Studies, Adelphi Papers No. 40, September 1967).

[6] See ch. 5, fn. 15, above.

[7] Walter Schutze, "European Defense Cooperation and NATO," *NATO Letter* (January 1970), p. 22; and W. F. van Eckelen, "Development of NATO's Nuclear Consultation," *ibid.* (July/August 1970), pp. 2-6.

proliferation Treaty failed to protect the Federal Republic's interest in peaceful nuclear reactors. West Germany has invested heavily in fast-breeder reactors, and it feared that the provisions of the treaty might someday be cited by commercial rivals in other countries to prevent the Germans from exporting plutonium.[8] The West Germans were also apprehensive that if East European Communist inspectors from the International Atomic Energy Agency (IAEA) were allowed to visit West German plants, they might carry out industrial espionage and transmit to the Soviet Union secret design characeristics of German reactors. Finally, the Germans and their partners in the European Community did not want to see the European Atomic Energy Commission (Euratom) pass under the IAEA control system. They feared that this could have adverse repercussions upon the European unity movement, since it might well close out the "European option"—that is, the possibility of developing a joint European nuclear deterrent in the future.[9] (See the discussion under "The Nonproliferation Treaty in Chapter 9.)

One by one, the Federal Republic's misgivings over the Nonproliferation Treaty were removed or reduced to the point where the Bonn government signed the treaty on November 28, 1969, while pledging to continue efforts to obtain clarification, before the treay was ratified, of some political and technological aspects. Obviously, West Germany was anxious to make certain that the treaty would not hinder the peaceful uses of nuclear energy, jeopardize the prerogatives of Euratom, or endanger military security and cooperation in NATO.[10] Since the Brandt government signed the Nonproliferation Treaty, the climate of West Germany's relations with its Eastern neighbors has noticeably improved. The Bonn-Moscow and Bonn-Warsaw treaties—which are tantamount to "little nonaggression

[8] "Commercial Nuclear Development is Big Business," *Die Welt*, February 24, 1967. English translation in *German Tribune*, March 4, 1967.

[9] See James E. Dougherty, "Introduction" to Dougherty and Lehman, eds., *Arms Control for the Late Sixties*, pp. xxxviii-xxxix. When the Nonproliferation Treaty was completed, it provided for the members of the European Atomic Energy Commission (Euratom) to negotiate in concert with IAEA on safeguards. Negotiations between IAEA and Euratom began in late 1971. They had been held up because of an intra-Euratom problem—the demand by West Germany that France (exempt under the Nonproliferation Treaty from IAEA controls) allow its nonmilitary production facilities to be inspected by Euratom. *New York Times*, November 19, 1971. The negotiations were completed in 1972.

[10] *Bulletin*, Press and Information Office of the Government of the Federal Republic of Germany, November 18 and December 2, 1969.

pacts," insofar as they recognize the unchangeability of existing boundaries by force—have been signed. An accord has been reached on Berlin. All of these Eastern treaties came into effect in mid-1972, and the electoral victory scored in late 1972 by Chancellor Willy Brandt's Social Democratic Party testified to the popularity of the *Ostpolitik,* despite the misgivings of some Western observers that the new Eastern orientation of the Federal Republic's foreign policy might lead to the unraveling of Bonn's earlier *Westpolitik.*

The final ratification of all these agreements has been a delicately interdependent process, and all of them were interrelated with the prospects for SALT, MBFR, and a European Security Conference. In any event, the West Germans have emphasized that the network of force-renunciation pacts does not render superfluous the balance in Europe, for which NATO and the political-military presence of the United States are essential.[11] We cannot lose sight of the possibility that if the United States, unable to arrive at a satisfactory agreement with the Soviets on mutual, balanced force reduction, should unilaterally reduce its military presence in Europe, neither NATO nor the intricate network of agreements negotiated in recent years, including West German adherence to the Nonproliferation Treaty, will survive. The evolution of German political attitudes after the entry of the German states into the United Nations will be of crucial significance for the future of international arms control, especially if the "national question" continues to move toward the center of the German political consciousness.

## India

For many years, India has been beset by gnawing doubts and dilemmas with respect to the acquisition of nuclear weapons. Indian officials for whom the Gandhian tradition is still important want India to refrain from becoming the world's sixth nuclear power. They look upon India as the *n*th-power "firebreak." For if the mem-

[11] Statement by FRG Defense Minister Helmut Schmidt at Georgetown University, Washington, February 9, 1971. *Bulletin,* February 16, 1971. See also Chancellor Brandt's statement to the 18th North Atlantic Assembly, Bonn, November 22, 1972. *Bulletin,* November 28, 1972.

bership of the "nuclear club" expands to six, it could very easily expand to ten or more within a relatively short time, through the processes of reaction and emulation. The Indians have no assurance, of course, that their abstention will induce other potential nuclear powers to abstain. Nevertheless, having been for many years critical of nuclear weapons development, nuclear tests, and nuclear strategies, they are still reluctant to see their country embark on the nuclear weapons path, despite the fact that events during the 1960s —including the India-Pakistan War and China's actions in Tibet and along the northern borders—have made many Indian intellectuals less moralistic and pacifist than they seemed to be in the 1950s.

Other voices in India have called for a decision by the government to build nuclear weapons. Certain politicians, civil servants, journalists, scientists, and military planners have contended that nuclear weapons provide massive firepower available in no other form. China, whose intentions worry India more than those of Pakistan, possesses nuclear weapons; and it is argued that, in such circumstances, India can assure its national security only if it obtains such weapons, too. If deterrence works in the West, why should it not work in the East? India does not have to be concerned about achieving a credible deterrent against the Soviet Union or the United States, but only against China, which ought to be a much easier undertaking. In this respect, India's task is less formidable than that facing France, which must acquire some semblance of credibility against the USSR. As a defensive state, India may not need expensive, long-range delivery systems, at least not in the beginning, when it may be sufficient to wield a tactical nuclear capability denying China the mountain approaches through the Himalayas.

Economically, the advocates of "going nuclear" point out that such weapons are no longer prohibitive in cost, especially for a country such as India which has been moving steadily toward the creation of a substantial civil nuclear energy program. India is one of the very few nonnuclear-weapon states that has already built a plutonium separation plant; consequently, it has come a long way toward paying for a weapons program. In fact, each passing year brings India closer to a position in which a governmental decision to manufacture weapons on a relatively large scale could be implemented within a short time. A full-scale weapons program would, of course, siphon off scarce scientific and engineering talent from national development projects. But this is a lesser problem for India than it would be for a country starting to build a nuclear industry from scratch. Moreover, some Indian scientists and economists argue that a weapons program, even though it entails certain sacrifices, also contributes to the growth of a sophisticated technology that could produce economic benefits in the future.

The political arguments for acquisition, it is safe to say, are the strongest of all, just as they were with Britain, France, and China. In today's world, nuclear weapons alone seem to provide the ultimate guarantee of a country's independence and territorial integrity in the absence of effective international peacekeeping machinery or a reliable alliance bond. Under the pressure of Chinese expansionism, Indian nationalism has begun to stir in recent years. Nehru has been criticized for having neglected India's defense and ignored the realities of international politics.

Nationalists everywhere are inclined to agree with the Gaullist contention that it is intolerable for a nation to rely permanently upon outside powers for its defense. Indian realists fear that if India signs the Nonproliferation Treaty and thus forecloses the nuclear option, New Delhi may be relegating itself to a permanently inferior political-strategic position *vis-à-vis* China within the international system. They argue that an Indian hand on the nuclear lever would serve to preclude the danger of "crisis deals" by the superpowers, which might be tempted to make future concessions to China at India's expense rather than risk a military encounter.[12] More idealistic nationalists in the Gandhi-Nehru tradition have rationalized the case for acquisition by pointing out that it could strengthen the country's position in international disarmament negotiations.[13]

[12] The foregoing summary of the pro-acquisition position in India is adapted from the author's article, "The Treaty and the Nonnuclear States," *loc. cit.*, pp. 361-364. See also G. D. Deshingkar, "China's Earth Satellite: The Case for Indian Bomb," *China Report*, vol. 6 (May-June 1970), 28-33.

[13] For an account of the arguments over this issue, see Sisir Gupta, "The Indian Dilemma," in Alastair Buchan, ed., *A World of Nuclear Powers* (Englewood Cliffs, N.J.: Prentice-Hall, 1966), pp. 57-58.

During the latter 1960s, the Indians made a number of demands that reflected their sense of insecurity. First, they demanded evidence that China's possession of nuclear weapons would not lead to a permanent enhancement of its international political status at India's expense. India had always been sensitive concerning the grant of the veto power to China at the 1945 San Francisco Conference, at which the United Nations Charter was drafted, and has not wanted to see the veto merged with, and reinforced by, the possession of nuclear weapons. Ambassador V. C. Trivedi, who represented India in the Eighteen-Nation Disarmament Committee when the Nonproliferation Treaty was being negotiated, wrote:[14]

> There are some who even think of equating possession of these evil weapons with permanent membership of the Security Council of the United Nations, as if the nuclear bomb were a special symbol of the right to enforce the veto. No wonder, therefore, that the world society in general has come to the conclusion that the possession of nuclear weapons does bestow prestige, and that consequently the road to sanity lies in taking away these dread instruments from the hands of the five powers rather than placing them in the hands of more countries.

Second, India demanded assurances that the Nonproliferation Treaty would not adversely affect the peaceful uses of nuclear technology, which is expected to become increasingly important in the development plans of several nations. (On this score, India acquired significant allies in such countries as West Germany, Sweden, and Brazil.)

Third, India demanded adequate security guarantees in return for signing the treaty. In 1967, Mrs. Gandhi preferred to have the guarantees come from powers "in different camps," so that India's nonalignment posture might be preserved.[15] But a joint US-British-Soviet security guarantee credible to Indian defense planners always seemed

[14] V. C. Trivedi, "Vertical Versus Horizontal Proliferation: An Indian View," in Dougherty and Lehman, eds., *op. cit.*, pp. 199-200.
[15] Statement by the Prime Minister in the Lok Sabha on July 17, 1967, as quoted in *Weekly India News*, July 28, 1967, p. 6.

a rather remote contingency. The superpowers were not willing to promise more than that they would concert action through the United Nations Security Council in the event of a nuclear attack upon a nonnuclear signatory of the treaty. Throughout the 1960s, India was concerned about the threat of conventional aggression, more from China than Pakistan. Indians had no reason to expect that, if their northeast frontier should again come under Chinese attack, they would receive help from the British (who were withdrawing irreversibly from "east of Suez"), from the Americans (who were planning under the Nixon Doctrine to reduce their Asian military commitments in the post-Vietnam era), or from the Russians (who had to worry about their own troop commitments both in Eastern Europe and along the 4,500-mile Chinese border). Moreover, India could not afford to ignore the possibility that in a future crisis, the superpowers might find themselves on opposite sides. (This actually happened, of course, in the India-Pakistan War over Bangladesh in late 1971; but since the Indian forces proved victorious, the Indians experienced no such trauma as they might in a future conflict with China.)

In 1970, an Indian writer characterized his country's position as one of "three negatives—no bomb, no treaty, no guarantees."[16] Indian decisionmakers undoubtedly realize—after all the efforts that have been made in recent years to induce them to sign the Nonproliferation Treaty—that their decisionmaking process is of crucial importance in international arms control efforts. Thus the Indian government is not without political leverage *vis-à-vis* the delicate triangular relationship of the United States, the Soviet Union, and China. Certain developments in Asia during the last few years might serve to convince the Indians that their security position is less tenuous than they had earlier thought. The Soviet Union, which has been gradually extending its naval presence to the Indian Ocean,[17] signed a Treaty of Peace, Friendship, and Cooperation with India

[16] Hans R. Vohra, "India's Nuclear Policy of Three Negatives," *Bulletin of the Atomic Scientists*, vol. 26 (April 1970), 25-27. See also George H. Quester, "India Contemplates the Bomb," *ibid.*, vol. 26 (January 1970), 13-16.

[17] See T. B. Millar, *The Indian and Pacific Oceans: Some Strategic Considerations* (London: Institute for Strategic Studies, Adelphi Papers No. 57, May 1969); *The Indian Ocean: Political and Strategic Future*, Committee on Foreign Affairs, US House of Representatives, 92nd Congress, September 26, 1971.

on August 9, 1971. Despite protestations to the contrary from New Delhi, this treaty has put an end to the Indian policy of nonalignment. Since Pakistan had been supported by the United States and China, India's military victory in support of the Bangladesh secession may serve to offset, at least for a time, Indian misgivings over the country's strategic inferiority—misgivings which were exacerbated by President Nixon's trip to Peking. Whether this Indian triumph in a situation in which China acted with restraint will be sufficient to persuade India to adhere to the Nonproliferation Treaty must await the verdict of history. In any event, now that India has been drawn into the circle of Soviet deterrence, New Delhi will probably wish to see Moscow maintain as wide a margin of strategic superiority as possible over Peking. Thus the Indian government, long an advocate of superpower nuclear disarmament and a reduction in the symbolic importance of nuclear weapons in international politics, is bound to adopt an ambivalent attitude toward strategic arms limitation negotiations between the United States and the Soviet Union.

By 1973, India was well aware that the pattern of Great Power relations in Asia had begun to change profoundly. There has been some fence-mending between India and Pakistan in the Simla Agreement, but relations between India and China remain strained, as Peking continues to oppose the entry of Bangladesh into the United Nations. That India has moved politically closer to the USSR is reflected in the upgrading of New Delhi's diplomatic links with East Germany. Some Indians might wonder whether their country has allowed itself to become too dependent upon Moscow and too far removed from forms of US assistance (including food) which may yet prove necessary. But for the time being, Indians perceive no compelling reasons for embarking upon a new course with respect to nuclear armaments. It is to India's advantage to continue moving toward a technical capability to acquire nuclear weapons quickly if they should be needed for security reasons, but to stop short of an actual, publicly known political decision to "go nuclear." Like Israel, India undoubtedly wants a nuclear capability for use *in extremis,* but it prefers to avoid the political onus and strategic-military complications which would probably accompany the status of a nascent nuclear power. In short, there may be more to be gained from keeping open the nuclear option than from closing it by exercising it.

**Japan**

Since the postwar occupation of Japan ended in 1951, that country has been a defense protectorate of the United States. The Japanese people have recovered an unquestioned status as a first-class economic power. But the nation has not been in a position to achieve autonomy with respect to security. A national consensus on defense and foreign policies has been lacking, and "there is a basic uncertainty about the world status of Japan."[18]

Japan was demilitarized after the war. Article Nine of the new constitution renounces war "as a sovereign right of the nation," and asserts that "war potential" will never be maintained. During the Korean War, however, Japan was allowed to establish Self-Defense Forces, and these have never posed a threat to any other countries. The government has had several classic justifications for relying upon the US-Japan Security Treaty for military protection: (1) the experience of Hiroshima and Nagasaki made the thought of possessing nuclear weapons abhorrent to the Japanese people; (2) the acquisition of nuclear weapons would run counter to the "pacifist" spirit of the 1946 constitution and would alarm Japan's Asian neighbors; and (3) a credible nuclear deterrent force is an expensive proposition, and is unnecessary so long as Japan can depend upon the US guarantee.[19] Critics of the government and of the United States have often protested against the presence of US nuclear weapons on submarines in Japanese ports or on Okinawa; but the government has realized that Japan cannot totally disassociate itself from the deterrent forces on which its security rests. Though the government was long opposed to nuclear weapons on the national territory, it tolerated their presence on Okinawa until the island reverted to Japanese jurisdiction on May 15, 1972. One of the principal advantages of the American umbrella is the fact that, although the US is committed to come to the defense of Japan in case of an attack upon its territory, Tokyo has no corresponding obligation to assist in case of an armed attack upon US territory or bases outside Japan. Given Japan's stra-

[18] I. H. Nish, "Is Japan a Great Power?" *The Year Book of World Affairs 1967* (New York: Praeger, 1967), p. 72.

[19] *Ibid.*, pp. 73-76. See also Robert A. Scalapino, "The Foreign Policy of Modern Japan," in Macridis, ed., *op. cit.*, especially pp. 300-307.

tegic vulnerability to attack in terms of geographical size and concentration of population, it would seem logical for any government in Tokyo to want to rely on an outside deterrent protector as long as possible.

Within recent years, the longstanding assumptions of Japan's official policy have been increasingly questioned, and not only by the political left, as in the past. The shift of opinion began after China started testing nuclear weapons in 1964. As Japanese skills in nuclear reactor technology grew, so did the capability to manufacture nuclear weapons. It does not seem that an economy with a GNP approaching $200 billion should find the cost of developing a nuclear force intolerable. Indeed, if China can do it, Japan certainly can. Strategic analysts in Japan have been asking how credible the extended US deterrent is in the Western Pacific, now that China's nuclear force is growing. Just as it was being asked in Europe ten or twelve years ago whether the United States would risk New York for Berlin, the Japanese are now asking whether the United States would risk San Francisco for Tokyo. Observers have noted a marked decline in the degree of popular emotional and political opposition to the idea of nuclear weapons in Japan, and a greater willingness to discuss openly a subject which used to be avoided with embarrassment. A *Mainichi Shimbun* poll, however, has shown that during the period April 1969–April 1972 those opposed to acquiring nuclear weapons increased from 46 to 58 per cent, and those in favor dropped from 45 to 35.[20] Japan belatedly signed the Nonproliferation Treaty,[21] but has not yet ratified it. According to a Japanese White Paper on Defense published October 20, 1970, the government announced that Japan would not manufacture or possess nuclear weapons, "even if it is constitutionally possible to do so."[22] One nuclear specialist has been quoted as saying: "Japan has become a nuclear power minus two years. That is something of a deterrent in itself.[23] Japan is expected to ratify the Nonproliferation Treaty once

[20] Cited in Kei Wakaizumi, "Japan's Role in a New World Order," *Foreign Affairs*, vol. 51 (January 1973), p. 314. See also Richard Halloran, "Japan Is Losing Aversion to Idea of Nuclear Arms," *New York Times*, December 26, 1971; and Ryukichi Imai, "Japan and the Nuclear Age," *Bulletin of the Atomic Scientists*, vol. 26 (June 1970).
[21] See Ryukichi Imai, "The Non-Proliferation Treaty and Japan," *Bulletin of the Atomic Scientists*, vol. 25 (May 1969); and George H. Quester, "Japan and the Nuclear Non-Proliferation Treaty," *Asian Survey*, vol. 10 (September 1970), 765-778.
[22] "Japanese Defence Policy," *Survival*, vol. 13 (January 1971), p. 5.
[23] Richard Halloran, *op. cit.*

negotiations with the International Atomic Energy Agency on peaceful reactor technology have been concluded.

The People's Republic of China has often denounced the US-Japan Security Treaty and called for its termination. More recently, the Peking regime has expressed fear of Japanese remilitarization. In the 1970 White Paper on Defense, the Japanese government announced that it would more than double its military budget during the period 1972-76. Chinese misgivings about Japanese rearmament have been cited as one factor in China's willingness to explore a new policy course toward the United States. [24] (It is not the only factor, by any means.) But if there is any one development bound to make the Japanese more security-minded, and readier to increase their military capabilities, it is a fear or expectation that the United States will retreat from its strategic responsibilities in the Asia-Pacific region. If this should come to pass (and it does not seem likely), Japan would then be motivated to strike out in a new direction—for example, to seek a mutual defense pact with the USSR or to acquire its own nuclear deterrent. With the improvement in Peking's relations with President Nixon and Prime Minister Tanaka, the PRC has refrained from attacking the US-Japanese Defense Treaty.

In the light of their historical experience from 1931 to 1945, Chinese misgivings are not unintelligible. But neither are Japenese fears of China's growing nuclear arsenal. Japanese observers were perplexed by the reversal of the US position on Vietnam[25] and stunned by the sudden change in US policy toward China. Looking ahead, the Japanese cannot but wonder what the possible annexation of Taiwan to the mainland and the eventual projection of Chinese power onto the oceans might imply for Japan's vital maritime interests and routes in the region. The Japanese are not sure that a Chinese naval force would guarantee freedom of navigation for Japanese vessels as well as the Seventh Fleet has done.[26] Such suspicions, of course, pertain to the future. At present, China is a long

[24] Edwin O. Reischauer, "As China Sees It, the Enemy is Japan," *New York Times*, August 15, 1971.

[25] Kiyoshi Nasu, "Japan and America—A Special Relationship?" *Interplay* (December 1969/ January 1970), pp. 11-12.

[26] This point was made by Turakeshi Muramatsu in a paper delivered at the Fifth International Arms Control Symposium in Philadelphia in October 1971 and published subsequently in William R. Kintner and Robert L. Pfaltzgraff, eds., *SALT: Implications for Arms Control in the 1970s* (Pittsburgh: University of Pittsburgh Press, 1973).

way from becoming a formidable naval power. If a serious naval rivalry were to develop between the two Asian powers, Japan would have a decided edge. Furthermore, if Japan decides to acquire nuclear weapons, its geostrategic situation as an island off the mainland will compel it to move immediately to a sea-based deterrent. The Japanese are not unaware that they hold these cards, and they believe that they have time to make up their minds which way to go, as they watch the unfolding complexities of the quadrilateral relationships of their own country with the United States, China, and the Soviet Union.

## Conclusion

From the foregoing cursory survey of the attitudes of the leading powers and selected other countries toward disarmament and arms control, one can safely infer that the world is not on the verge of complete political agreement on these matters. If we take the Non-proliferation Treaty as a touchstone of a country's current official policy on arms control, it is a sobering thought that the list of states which have not yet signed the treaty includes Argentina, Brazil, China, France, India, Israel, Pakistan, South Africa, and Spain. Those that have signed, but not yet ratified, the treaty are Belgium, the Federal Republic of Germany, Italy, Japan, the Netherlands, and Switzerland.

Several of these nations regard the arms control agreements entered into by the superpowers as efforts to freeze the favorable position of the latter, or even to "disarm the unarmed." The Non-proliferation Treaty has been particularly criticized for failing to provide an acceptable balance of mutual obligations and responsibilities as between the nuclear and nonnuclear states. The Strategic Arms Limitation Talks between the United States and the Soviet Union represent an effort by the superpowers to comply at the diplomatic level with the demands of the nonnuclear states that the nuclear powers make some progress toward disarmament. Whether these medium and smaller powers expect much real progress to be made, whether they really want the progress for which they call, or whether their political rhetoric is merely calculated to prepare their own publics for the arguments which may subsequently be advanced to justify their own decisions to acquire nuclear weapons—this is very difficult to know for certain.

But this much we can say. The international system, made up of more than 135 political entities of varying atomic weights, is shot through with all sorts of political, social, geographical, economic, technological, military, and strategic asymmetries. Scarcely any two states in the world, in calculating their security problems and requirements, find themselves in really comparable situations. Every state will approach arms control negotiations from a perspective distinctly its own, as to the proper timing for trying to derive a favorable net balance after trading off the available options and the unavoidable necessities, the various advantages and disadvantages, of this or that agreement. This is a fact of international political life which will always complicate the armaments problem and render viable solutions not impossible, but extremely difficult to achieve.

# 8

# General Disarmament

In the early 1960s, US and Soviet leaders were competing in the international forum as champions of something called "general and complete disarmament" (GCD). In retrospect, it is difficult to believe that either government could have looked upon the blueprints for GCD as a feasible policy goal to be achieved within the plannable future—four years, according to the Soviet proposal, and perhaps up to twelve years in the US proposal. Total disarmament was a popular policy idea in the early 1960s. Government agencies, research institutes, and private individuals produced a number of studies, books, monographs, and articles on the subject.[1] Indeed, for a time it was almost considered imprudent, impolite, or immoral for any intellectual in the United States to suggest that GCD was not, given the existing international context, a practically achievable

[1] See, for example, Noel-Baker, *op. cit.*; Seymour Melman, ed., *Disarmament: Its Politics and Economics* (Boston: American Academy of Arts and Sciences, 1962); Louis B. Sohn and David H. Frisch, "Arms Reduction in the 1960's," in David H. Frisch, ed., *Arms Reduction: Program and Issues* (New York: Twentieth Century Fund, 1961); Arthur Lawson, *A Warless World* (New York: McGraw-Hill, 1962); Jerome B. Weisner, "Comprehensive Arms Limitation Systems," in Brennan, ed., *op. cit.*; F. A. Long, "Immediate Steps toward General and Complete Disarmament," *Disarmament and Arms Control*, vol. 2 (Winter 1963/64), pp. 1-9; Evan Luard, ed., *First Steps to Disarmament* (New York: Basic Books, 1965); and US Arms Control and Disarmament Agency, *Fourth Report on U. S. Government Research and Studies in the Field of Arms Control and Disarmament Matters*, Submitted to the Director, Bureau of the Budget, September 15, 1964.

goal, and perhaps not a politically desirable goal. It took only a few years of analysis and negotiation, however, to demonstrate that the chasm between the rhetoric of total disarmament and the reality of the international political, strategic, and military-technological situation was wide and deep—a chasm not likely to be bridged within a short time and without profound systemic changes which no national was ready to accept.

### The Economics of Disarmament

As a result of the Leninist theoretical heritage, large numbers of intellectuals, students, and journalists both in the Western and non-Western worlds still entertain the suspicion that economics somehow lie at the bottom of the disarmament impasse. They trace the lack of progress in negotiating disarmament to that sinister grouping known as the "military-industrial complex," with its "vested interest in perpetuating the arms race." Such an attitude represents a modernized and somewhat more sophisticated version of the older "devil theory of war," in which US entry into World War I was blamed on the profit-seeking motives of munitions-makers.[2] This *neodiabolus* theory, which has achieved the status of religious dogma within the ranks of the American New Left, is admittedly more subtle and comprehensive than its predecessor, which has long since been thoroughly discredited by social scientists. But it can never transcend its limitations as a mere corollary of the Leninist theory of imperialism, which is itself a simplistic explanation of the complex phenomena of international relations.

Undoubtedly, general disarmament would cause serious economic dislocations. The cancellation of military contracts following upon a disarmament agreement could be expected to have an adverse multiplier effect upon prices, employment, public spending, and general confidence in the health of the capitalist or mixed enterprise economy. But if nation-states should ever manage, consistently with their

[2] For a criticism of this simplistic explanation of war and imperialism, see Morgenthau, *op. cit.*, pp. 46-50; and Joseph A. Schumpeter, *Capitalism, Socialism and Democracy*, third edition (New York: Harper, 1950), fn., pp. 52-53.

political and strategic objectives, to reach agreement on substantial arms reductions, these would certainly have to be phased over several years, probably at least a decade, thereby providing ample opportunity for national economies to make the transition without unmanageable disturbances. We should not forget that even in a GCD world, governments would still have to allocate resources to support sophisticated monitoring systems and international peacekeeping machinery. Western economists have learned a good deal since the days of Lord Keynes about the use of compensatory, antideflationary policies for the purpose of bolstering aggregate demand when it is in danger of sagging. Such policies as timely tax cuts, changes in interest rates and other investment incentives, and shifts to nonmilitary forms of spending in the public sector can help to ensure a fairly stable period of adjustment. It is precisely in the most advanced economic systems that pent-up demands for the reallocation of resources away from defense expenditures are greatest—for transportation, education, health and medical programs, advanced scientific research, welfare, space exploration, environmental control, weather and ocean technology, and a variety of other purposes. Moreover, even though some Third World economists may have been excessively optimistic a decade ago concerning the possibility of shifting world expenditures from armaments to international development, nevertheless the needs of the disadvantaged nations will continue to pose a major economic, political, and moral challenge to the industrially advanced nations for several decades to come. Emile Benoit writes:[3]

> Even if disarmament remained elusive, one could count . . . on tens of billions of dollars in savings from an arms freeze . . . Moreover, much of the released resources in research and development, systems analysis, and large-scale program administration capability, could usefully be diverted to the basic analytic, innovational, and creative programs required to achieve the needed breakthroughs in the field of economic

[3] See Emile Benoit, "Interdependence on a Small Planet," in the book which he edited, *Disarmament and World Economic Interdependence* (New York: Columbia University Press, 1967), p. 25. It should be noted, however, that the poorer countries of the world often suffer from their own military expenditures, which since the mid-1960s have been growing faster in developing than in developed countries. *World Military Expenditures 1970*, US Arms Control and Disarmament Agency Publication 58 (Washington: US Government Printing Office, December 1970), p. 4.

development. Examples of such breakthroughs are the inexpensive desalination of water, the effective tapping of unconventional energy sources, sharply reduced building costs via prefabricated modules, mass production of cheap protein food additives to remedy nutritional deficiencies, and the speedy achievement of universal literacy and advanced skills through the use of teaching machines and satellite-transmitted TV programs, and so forth.

The main point is that Western man need not burden himself unnecessarily with a complex of guilty self-recrimination on the ground that the lack of progress in disarmament efforts has been due to crass economic causes. In terms of pure economics, the problems of disarmament should prove no more intractable for a capitalist system than for a Socialist one—indeed, the former might very well possess the flexibility which would enable it to adjust more readily to a substantially changed defense environment.[4] The principal obstacles to general disarmament up to the present time, far from being economic, have been technical, strategic, and political in nature. The armaments problem in the age of the nuclear-tipped ICBM is not an aberration imposed upon the contemporary international system by the profiteering of certain industrialists, the aggressiveness of certain military leaders, and the misguided conservatism of certain politicians. Rather it is an intrinsic part of the system. It is integrally related to the essential characteristics of modern science and technology, of the global ideological-political competition, and of a world environment in which nation-states inevitably seek their security by engaging in some form of power balancing. In the final analysis, it is deeply rooted in man's psychological, sociological, and cultural structures. Thus, the arms problem does not readily lend itself to complete

[4] The literature of the 1960s on the economic feasibility of disarmament was ample and never really controverted. See Gerard Piel, "The Economics of Disarmament," *Bulletin of the Atomic Scientists*, April 1960, pp. 117-122 and 126; *Economic Impacts of Disarmament*, US Arms Control and Disarmament Agency Publication No. 2 (Washington: US Government Printing Office, 1962); *Economic and Social Consequences of Disarmament*, Report of a Study by the United Nations Economic and Social Council E/3593/Rev. 1 (New York: United Nations, 1962); Emile Benoit and Kenneth Boulding, eds., *Disarmament and the Economy* (New York: Harper and Row, 1963); Otto Feinstein, "Disarmament: Economic Effects," *Current History* (August 1964), pp. 81-87; *Report of the Committee on the Economic Impact of Defense and Disarmament*, Submitted to President Johnson July 30, 1965 (Washington: US Government Printing Office, 1965); *United States Report to Secretary-General Thant on the Economic and Social Consequences of Disarmament*, March 26, 1968, in *Documents on Disarmament 1968*, US Arms Control and Disarmament Agency Publication 52, September 1969 (Washington: US Government Printing Office, 1969), pp. 196-203.

solution by resort to the rational, verbal devices of traditional diplomacy known as treaties. Those who were the staunchest advocates of GCD in the early 1960s allowed themselves to be carried along by their own optimistic idealism, and they failed to estimate properly the magnitude of the armaments dilemma confronting contemporary governments.

**Political-Strategic Obstacles to GCD**

Ever since the dawn of the atomic era, countless voices have insisted that unless the nations achieve complete nuclear disarmament, they will eventually find themselves propelled inevitably into nuclear war. Yet more than 25 years after Hiroshima and Nagasaki, there is no reason to think that any one of the five existing nuclear powers—not even China, perhaps especially not China—hopes to accomplish any political purpose by initiating nuclear war. Paradoxically, despite the terrors of the thermonuclear age, not a single one of the five—not even Britain—has acted consistently during the last decade as if it looks upon total nuclear disarmament as the only way, or necessarily the best way, of safeguarding its security. Probably in all five countries, we would find varying numbers and proportions of intellectuals, government officials, military leaders, and others who, in moments of philosophical reflection, regard general disarmament as a desirable goal to be striven toward in the diplomatic forum. But it would seem that in all five countries, most of the people in positions of ultimate political responsibility have concluded that the very same advanced weapons technology which makes disarmament a more ethically imperative objective than ever before in man's history also makes it more difficult than ever to attain—in technical, strategic, and political terms.

We need not dwell at length on the political difficulties of moving toward GCD. Several of them have been discussed or alluded to in previous sections. Here it will suffice to summarize briefly as follows:

1. Two nuclear powers—France and China—have not participated in international disarmament and arms control negotiations. Even with respect to the limited agreements that have been reached,

these two countries are at least a decade behind the superpowers; and this fact serves as a brake upon the rate at which the superpowers can proceed.

2. Serious discrepancies persist in the positions adopted by the United States and the Soviet Union toward the building of those international peacekeeping institutions which would be necessary to safeguard the security and political rights of nations in a disarmed world. Generally speaking, the United States has pressed officially for a more radical approach to the creation of an effective world authority backed up by an adequate international military force, while the Soviets have been unwilling to entertain the notion of anything more than national military contingents earmarked for possible UN Security Council use, subject as always to Great Power veto.[5]

3. Even within the Anglo-American cultural context, several scholars have questioned the wisdom of the US government in formally subscribing to the concept of GCD and world government. Lincoln P. Bloomfield has observed that, in putting forward proposals for GCD, American policymakers had not thought through the political and military implications of such a position, partly because "the question of feasibility is so overwhelming in today's world that the matter seems totally academic."[6] Although some US disarmament planners wish to defer indefinitely the question as to whether the international military force should be nuclear-armed (probably because they were opposed to such a concept), Bloomfield insisted that such a force, if it ever came into being, would have to be able to discourage evasion of the disarmament agreement and clandestine production of nuclear weapons by possessing a preponderant nuclear capability.[7] Bloomfield was inclined to think that the ideological-political struggle between communism and the West would continue indefinitely, and that it was unlikely both sides would subordinate themselves to a supranational authority. Even assuming that the two nuclear titans could compose their differences and

[5] See Lincoln P. Bloomfield, "The Politics of Administering Disarmament," ch. 7 in Richard J. Barnet and Richard A. Falk, eds., *Security in Disarmament* (Princeton: Princeton University Press, 1965), pp. 123-138; and Lincoln P. Bloomfield and others, *International Military Forces: The Question of Peacekeeping in an Armed and Disarming World* (Boston: Little, Brown, 1964), ch. 4, "The Soviet View of International Force."

[6] Lincoln P. Bloomfield, "Arms Control and World Government," *World Politics*, vol. 14 (July 1962), 634.

[7] *Ibid.*, 640.

achieve mutual trust, it is not at all clear that they could impose world government on all other nations. "Perhaps," he notes, "the most sobering consideration about world government is the nightmare prospect of world order at the price of world tyranny—a kind of global Holy Alliance to preserve the *status quo*."[8]

4. As we have seen, there are good reasons to conclude that the Soviet Union's leaders, when they contemplate the prestige, security, and foreign policy flexibility that a highly developed nuclear weapons technology has bestowed upon them, and when they consider the possible growth of Chinese power in the future, are more interested in maintaining the implements of deterrence than in reposing their faith in the creation of a radically transformed international system. This probably also holds true for most US policymakers. In a study undertaken for the Arms Control and Disarmament Agency, Arnold Wolfers suggested that a world balance of power, based upon mutual deterrence, constitutes a highly rational goal for the United States, both as the minimum and maximum objective of its military effort. He pointed out that while proportionate arms reductions are attractive in theory, they are extremely difficult to attain in practice, and that complete disarmament can be expected to prove disadvantageous to the side which originally enjoyed military superiority. Finally, he questioned whether an international peacekeeping force of the kind proposed in the US Outline Plan for General and Complete Disarmament could be seriously relied upon by this country in cases where matters of national security and other important interests were concerned, or whether "American vital interests could become exposed to new threats emanating from such a force, instead of being protected by it."[9]

5. Reference has already been made to the fact that superpower negotiations often cause nervousness among allies and threaten alliance cohesiveness if allies think that their vital interests are being bargained away. Such fears can affect Warsaw Pact countries (especially East Germany) as well as NATO countries in Europe; but undoubtedly the dangers of distrust are more serious in alliances

[8] *Ibid.*, 643.

[9] Arnold Wolfers, "Disarmament, Peacekeeping and the National Interest," in *The United States in a Disarmed World* (Baltimore: Johns Hopkins Press, 1966), pp. 12, 25 and 32.

among democratic countries, since centrifugal political pressures are usually stronger in relation to centripetal forces within such coalitions.

6. Other political obstacles to GCD can merely be cited without elaboration. The Soviet phobia with respect to free-access inspection systems and their oft-expressed fear of "espionage" are perhaps deeply rooted in Russian national psychosocial-cultural attitudes, always suspicious and resentful of influences intruding from the West; but they are probably also linked to a political desire by orthodox Communists to maintain internal social control and ideological purity against the temptations, corruptions, and machinations that a prying international inspectorate (including "capitalist agents") might eventually introduce into remote corners of Soviet society. Even the more pluralist, "open" American society might find the kind of inspection system needed to police a totally disarmed world increasingly intolerable, if "institutionalized snooping" should come to impinge upon the rights of private individuals (for example, in their homes), academic freedom, the patent rights of industrial firms, and the desire of citizens to be free of constant surveillance.[10] Finally, those who looked ahead to the time when a general disarmament agreement would be in effect and an inspection system would be operating asked disturbing questions as to the kinds of political and military responses which would probably be made to violations when they became known. Even the legal idealists have recognized the importance of having an adequate system of proportionate responses and sanctions to deter future violations of a disarmament agreement that might lead to its eventual breakdown. Louis B. Sohn pointed out "that in later stages, the desire to prevent an interruption of the disarmament process might be so powerful that it would prove difficult to respond properly to dangerous violations."[11] Sohn conceded that the threat of economic sanctions, which might prove effective against

[10] The author has contrasted Soviet and American attitudes toward the prying aspects of inspection in "The Disarmament Debate: A Review of Current Literature (Part One)," *Orbis,* vol. 5 (Fall 1961), esp. pp. 349-351 and 354-357. Louis Henkin, who studied the legal aspects of inspection, concluded that there are no insuperable legal obstacles in the American constitutional-legal system, but he admits that there could be serious political problems, noting that the US constitution might prove less resistant to controlling the activities of the government than those of the citizen. *Arms Control and Inspection in American Law* (New York: Columbia University Press, 1958), p. 22.

[11] Louis B. Sohn, "A General Survey of Responses to Violations," *Journal of Arms Control,* vol. 1 (April 1963), p. 95.

smaller nations, would not deter Great Powers and their bloc allies. In serious cases, military sanctions, either unilateral by one nation or multilateral by an international peacekeeping force, would be necessary.[12]

Fred Charles Iklé has noted that potential violators would not be deterred by the mere risk of discovery, or by fear of adverse "world opinion" reactions, but only by an expectation that the gains of violation would be outweighed by the losses. He cited Soviet indifference to world opinion and UN resolutions at the time of the Hungarian uprising as an illustration of the impotence of such amorphous political inhibitors in the face of determined national action. Iklé focused on the problems faced by a democratic government in responding to a detected evasion—the arguments about the evidence and the seriousness of the evasion, the interaction of rival political parties, leaders, and government agencies, the reluctance to jeopardize international cooperation by scrapping the entire disarmament agreement, and the difficulty of convincing legislatures and the public that the nation must embark upon retaliatory rearmament.[13] It is clear from Iklé's analysis that the problem of response to violation is in the first instance a political problem, and uncertainty as to what the future might hold in this crucial respect constitutes a definite political obstacle to GCD, or to any substantial program of arms reduction.

Several strategic difficulties inhere in the concept of total disarmament. These are closely related, and they all have implications for national security planning. It is erroneous to think that only US planners need worry about these problems. At least some of them must cause fundamental concern to those responsible for national security in Moscow and other capitals.

The first question is how to make sure that the 1961 McCloy-Zorin principle can be fully observed, so that neither side would at any time be placed at an unfair disadvantage as a result of the disarming process. To begin with, the geostrategic requirements of the

[12] *Ibid.*, 101-104.
[13] Fred Charles Iklé, "After Detection—What?" *Foreign Affairs*, vol. 39 (January 1961), 208-220.

two superpowers are different, because of differences in geographical location, size, borders to be defended, proximity to other powers or to allies, access to the oceans, patterns of population concentration, interests to be protected, and so forth. The weapons systems at the disposal of each nation are unique to that nation. They are a function of the nation's technological capabilities and preferred military-strategic doctrines. Because of these asymmetries, it is always difficult to reach agreement on where the dismantling of arms ought to begin in the first stage. Since general disarmament cannot take place instantaneously, the first stage inevitably has to consist of a large package of "partial" measures. Governments often propose partial steps to others, but they are slow to take up the offers made by other governments. Each nation tends to suspect that the other nation, in proposing a partial measure, is seeking a one-sided military advantage. It is not easy to conceive of specific arms reductions or alterations in military postures which would appear "equal" to both sides and which would actually lead to symmetrical improvements in the security situation of each side. It is possible, of course, that a mutually satisfactory arms agreement can be negotiated after a lengthy period of intensive bargaining. Indeed, a modest number of limited-risk control measures have been negotiated by the United States and the Soviet Union during the last decade. But no arms reduction measures have ever been negotiated in the nuclear age, and the difficulty of reaching even modest agreements of this sort should not be underestimated.

Assuming that it would be possible to get the disarmament process started, additional strategic questions arise. How fast and how far down the scale should the United States (and other powers) be willing to go in reducing their strategic arms levels? In the case of ICBMs, for example, should the United States seek a verified parity with the Soviet Union at lower levels than are presumed to exist at the time the agreement is made—regardless of whether this parity would be expressed in the number of comparable vehicles, or in total "throw weight," or in some other way? By now, other questions must have occurred to the reader. On what intelligence estimates of the existing military situation do policymakers base their formulae for reducing armaments levels, and how reliable are these estimates for the scientific planning of disarmament? (This presupposes accurate information with respect to our own and the adversary's weapons—numbers, types, ranges, yields, location, protection, multiplicity of warheads, state of readiness, reliability, penetration capabilities, accuracy, and other performance characteristics, and the kinds of command, control, and communications systems to which they are subject.) How do we define "strategic weapons"—merely as those which can strike the homeland of the superpowers? Or must we also count those weapons (for example, MRBMs and IRBMs in western Russia) which are targeted upon the cities of the European allies of the United States, on the assumption that the Atlantic Alliance is of "strategic" political-military importance to the United States?

If one side is taken to be strategically superior to the other at the start of the reduction process, there is a question as to whether, in specific stages, the two sides go down to a point of mathematical parity or to agreed fractions of the force levels which existed before the disarmament process began. Let us suppose that side A has 2,000 ICBMs and side B has 1,000, and they are discussing the first stage of a three-stage agreement. If they should decide to cut by 500 ICBMs, A's advantage would increase from 2:1 to 3:1. On the other hand, if they should decide to reduce to 500 ICBMs each, A would be giving up a substantial advantage in order to achieve parity—something that governments are usually not wont to do. If both agreed to cut by half, A would be left with 1,000 ICBMs and B with 500, in which case B might fear that, although the ratio had remained steady, nevertheless at lower numerical levels his capability to deter attack had been reduced.

The foregoing simplified model leads us into the crucial strategic problem of total disarmament. How far can strategic arms be cut before the condition of international military stability known as "mutual deterrence"—and presupposing high levels of armaments, a degree of invulnerability of missile forces sufficient to assure a capability for inflicting a retaliatory blow which would produce an "unacceptable level of damage," and rational decisionmaking by policymakers—be corroded to the point of ineffectiveness? The early 1960s heard a good deal of discussion about the possibility of exchanging "maximum deterrence" for "minimum deterrence," by working toward a strategic situation in which the United States and the Soviet Union would eventually agree to keep not the thousands or several hundreds of ICBMs which they were capable of producing and deploying over time, but a much smaller number—say, 50 or 100—very well protected missiles.[14] Unfortunately, there was no compelling rational basis for the belief that as the level of strategic armaments keeps dropping, the safety of the international environment against the outbreak of war necessarily improves commensurately.

Several leading strategic analysts have warned that there may be a point below which it becomes unwise to reduce nuclear forces, because this might create an imbalance that degrades the existing "mutual deterrent" and give way to renascent incentives for surprise attack, based on an expectation of achieving a decisive advantage. Granted that it is virtually impossible to determine what constitutes "unacceptable damage" to an adversary with a different value system (or even to one's own government), nevertheless we can safely conclude that it is more profitable to try to cheat at lower levels than at higher levels of strategic arms, easier to alter rapidly the ratio of power-in-being and easier to deliver a knockout blow against an adversary's stationary forces.[15]

Prior to early Fall 1962, the Soviets had called for the elimination of all rockets in Stage One of the disarmament process. On September 22 in that year, the USSR submitted to the ENDC at Geneva a revised draft GCD treaty with provision for "an agreed and strictly limited number" of missiles to be retained by the two superpowers "exclusively in their own territory, until the end of the second stage."[16] A year later, Soviet Foreign Minister Andrei Gromyko, in an address to the UN General Assembly, declared that the Soviet Union was willing to extend the concept of the "nuclear unmbrella" as a guarantee against aggression until the end of the third stage.[17]

[14] See, for example, Leo Szilard, "'Minimal Deterrent' Versus Saturation Parity," *Bulletin of the Atomic Scientists*, vol. 20 (March 1964).

[15] See Thomas C. Schelling, "Surprise Attack and Disarmament," ch. 10 in his book, *The Strategy of Conflict* (New York: Oxford University Press, 1963), esp. pp. 235-236; Henry A. Kissinger, "Arms Control, Inspection and Surprise Attack," *Foreign Affairs*, vol. 38 (July 1960), pp. 559-561; Bull, *op. cit., pp.* 168-169; Glenn H. Snyder, *Deterrence and Defense* (Princeton: Princeton University Press, 1961), pp. 97-103.

[16] *Documents on Disarmament 1962,* vol. 2, pp. 916-917.

[17] *Documents on Disarmament 1963,* pp. 515-516.

These Soviet moves were widely interpreted in the West as a concession to Western fears of possible surprise attack incentives in a disarming world. But Western diplomats remained unimpressed for several reasons: (1) The West wanted details of the proposal before accepting it, but the Soviets refused to supply component numbers. (2) Since the Soviet proposal stipulated retention by the superpowers "in their own territories," this meant that the US sea-based deterrent (which provided added invulnerability through dispersal, mobility, and partial sequestration) would have to be dismantled in Stage One. (Now that the Soviets have developed a submarine-launched missile capability, they are less able to seek a unilateral advantage—thereby rendering the proposal unacceptable to the United States—by insisting upon a purely land-based "nuclear umbrella.") (3) The Soviet proposal was politically unrealistic, since it ignored the attitudes of three other nuclear powers. (4) Adoption of the Soviet plan would have required the liquidation of all US forces, weapons, and bases in Europe during the first stage. (5) The retention of the "nuclear umbrella" would not have solved the problem of hidden stockpiles, which would remain as a threat after the legal minimal deterrent force had been destroyed.[18]

Finally, those responsible for security must take that long look into the future, and ask how safe a completely disarmed world would be. Governments would have no choice but to remain on their guard under any kind of disarmament arrangement, for nations would always possess, in the words of Hedley Bull, the technical capacity to "reestablish what has been disestablished, to remember or to reinvent what has been laid aside."[19] In a disarmed world, wrote Thomas Schelling and Morton Halperin, in "the absence of some effective policing force, primitive war is still possible, rearmament is possible, and primitive wars that last long enough may convert themselves by rapid mobilization into very modern warfare."[20] Eugene Rabinowitch, the Editor of the *Bulletin of Atomic Scientists*, once warned that war might break out more easily between disarmed powers than between armed nations, and that such a war, once

[18] See Dougherty, "The Status of the Arms Negotiations," *loc. cit.*, pp. 62-65.
[19] Bull, *op. cit.*, p. 34.
[20] Thomas C. Schelling and Morton H. Halperin, *Strategy and Arms Control* (New York: Twentieth Century Fund, 1961), p. 60.

initiated, would inevitably become nuclear.[21] Apprehensions such as these naturally open onto the analysis of the major technical problem of total disarmament—namely, verifying to the satisfaction of each party to the disarmament agreement that all other nations are complying with their obligations under the agreement.

## The Technical Problems of Verification and Inspection

During the late 1950s and the decade of the 1960s, many useful theoretical studies of inspection and control problems were performed by governmental agencies, the military services, scientific organizations, private research institutes associated with universities and industry, and individual analysts throughout the country.[22] But in spite of all the theoretical analyses that have been undertaken, an observation made in 1961 by the former science advisor to President Kennedy is still valid today:[23]

> (It) is extremely difficult to get agreement on a specific inspection system designed to monitor a specific reduction in the level of a specific force or weapon. This situation will persist until there is adequate understanding of the capability of the various systems and until there have been enough weapons system studies to establish limits on the uncertainty tolerable in inspection system performance.

The complexity of the task of setting up inspection methods and control institutions in an age of fast-moving technological change was amply demonstrated during the Geneva test ban negotiations, when a technical inspection system once accepted by the experts was later

---

[21] Eugene Rabinowitch, "Defenders and Avengers," *Bulletin of the Atomic Scientists,* vol. 16 (November 1960).

[22] Among the many studies that have been published, the following warrant special mention: Bernard T. Feld, Donald G. Brennan, and others, *The Technical Problems of Arms Control,* for the Committee on the Technical Problems of Arms Limitation of the American Academy of Arts and Sciences, n. d.; Seymour Melman, ed., *Inspection for Disarmament* (New York: Columbia University Press, 1958); Bernard T. Feld, "Inspection Techniques for Arms Control," in Brennan, ed., *op. cit.*; Jerome B. Wiesner, "Inspection for Disarmament," in Louis Henkin, ed., *Arms Control: Issues for the Public* (Englewood Cliffs, N. J.: Prentice-Hall, 1961); Report of the Woods Hole Summary Study, 1962, *Verification and Response in Disarmament Agreements* (Washington: Institute for Defense Analyses, 1962); and Lawrence S. Finkelstein, *Arms Inspection,* International Conciliation No. 540 (November 1962). In addition, there have been several articles in *Bulletin of the Atomic Scientists, Journal of Conflict Resolution, Journal of Arms Control,* and other scholarly periodicals.

[23] Wiesner, "Inspection for Disarmament," *loc. cit.*, p. 114.

rendered obsolete by the discovery of scientific evasion techniques even before a start could be made on the construction of the projected control network. Here, too, though the Geneva talks failed to produce a control system, they yielded important insights into the technical and organizational problems of control. The test ban negotiations constituted the most exhaustive dialogue on the issues of international control ever engaged in by the official representatives of governments.

American, British, and Soviet delegates bargained at length over such issues as the following: (1) the total number of control stations needed on land and sea to police a comprehensive ban; (2) the number of stations to be located on the soil of each nuclear power; (3) the number and nationality of the staff needed to man a control station; (4) the possibility of using unmanned technical detection stations; (5) the basic structure and operating principles for a control organization; (6) the types of questions over which the veto should be retained (such as the exact location of control post sites on a state's territory); (7) financing the control organization; (8) the functions and powers of the Control Commission and the Administrator; (9) the staffing of headquarters; (10) the role of the "third third" (that is, the neutral component in the organization); (11) the scientific problem of detecting underground explosions and distinguishing them from earthquakes; (12) the need for "on-site" inspections and the method of determining the annual number of them; (13) the staffing and dispatching of "on-site" inspection teams and air sampling flights; (14) methods whereby "on-site" inspections could be conducted (for example, aerial overflight, ground surveys, drilling operations); (15) localization of the area to be subjected to "on-site" inspection; (16) the schedule of installation of control posts; (17) nuclear explosions for detection research and for peaceful purposes; (18) a moratorium for underground tests falling below the threshold of detectable explosions; (19) methods of detecting outer space tests; and (20) the adequacy of purely national means of detecting tests in all environments.[24]

[24] See *Geneva Conference on the Discontinuance of Nuclear Weapons Tests: History and Analysis of Negotiations*, Department of State Publication 7258 (Washington: US Government Printing Office, 1961); and *International Negotiations on Ending Nuclear Weapons Tests, September 1961-September 1962*, US Arms Control and Disarmament Agency Publication No. 9 (Washington: US Government Printing Office, 1962).

There is no possibility of devising a single technical system for the international control of nuclear weapons. The type of system required varies with the nature of the specific objective; it depends upon what is being controlled and the extent to which it is being controlled. In each case, the projected control system is different. In fact, for each of many different disarmament objectives, it is possible to select among alternative control systems. Some systems may be formally institutionalized to a high degree; others may rely upon informal or tacit communication;[25] still others may combine the two approaches.

It would be dishonest to suggest that foolproof inspection and control systems can be devised for most types of disarmament agreements between states that are hostile to and suspicious of each other. Conversely, it is easy to show that, among states which are essentially friendly to one another, elaborate control systems are not necessary to furnish a sense of security. The need for stringent controls arises when two powers which have long been adversaries and have still not found a way to reconcile their political and ideological objectives nevertheless become interested, for a variety of reasons, in avoiding nuclear war, enhancing the safety of the international military environment, damping the rate of arms competition, or reducing armaments levels by substantial amounts. The question then arises as to how much reliability is needed in the control system.

Certain optimistic observers suggest that when two nations enter into an arms agreement, it is because they perceive an interest in observing its provisions, and that this fact can be relied upon to compensate for deficiencies in the control system. Moreover, the optimistic argue, as the atmosphere of detente spreads with each succeeding agreement, tensions and suspicions will subside, both sides will mutually relax, and the demand for high-reliability systems will diminish.

Most American arms control specialists, however, would insist that, although limited risks and margins of error might be tolerable

[25] Thomas C. Schelling has frequently called attention to the importance of tacit understandings. See his "Bargaining, Communications and Limited War," *Journal of Conflict Resolution*, vol. I (March 1957), pp. 19-36; and "Reciprocal Measures for Arms Stabilization," in Brennan, ed., *op. cit.*, p. 174.

in the earlier stages when total arms levels are high, the overall reliability of the control system should increase as physical disarmament proceeds, and that something is radically wrong if it does not. United States planning for arms control and disarmament has always been predicated upon the assumption that safeguards are necessary precisely because the other side may cheat, and that its efforts to deceive might prove to be highly intelligent, strategically imaginative, and economically costly.

Formal nuclear disarmament, whether partial or complete, would have to be preceded by the exchange of authoritative information pertaining to the precise objects of the agreement—for example, the size of nuclear stockpiles; the numbers and types of nuclear weapons; the location of bases of nuclear weapons delivery systems; nuclear research and development facilities; the number, location, and capacity of production plants; data relating to scientific and engineering personnel; and so on. In order to inspire confidence in the reliability of the information received, each government would certainly require satisfactory verification of the veracity of the other's disclosures.

Verification might be accomplished in the first instance through aerial or satellite reconnaissance employing "high resolution" photographic methods, followed by ground inspection of randomly selected parts of each country's territory, review of governmental fiscal and military records, industrial records, transportation records, and interrogation of key personnel. Naturally, some things are easier to control and inspect than others: delivery systems are generally easier to find than nuclear weapons; strategic bomber bases are more difficult to hide than carefully camouflaged, underground missile sites; surface warships are more readily spotted than submarines.

The two superpowers have long disagreed as to whether inspection should be confined, as the Soviets demand, to "declared facilities" (that is, to the arms and forces which are actually being dismantled in the presence of the disarmament organization), or whether it must be extended, as the United States insists, to make sure that whatever arms and forces remain do not exceed agreed levels. In an effort to bridge the gap between the two positions, analysts have suggested the concept of "progressive verification," under which the amount of inspection during any stage would be proportionate to the amount of disarmament being undertaken and to the degree of risk involved. One variant of this concept envisages a "zonal inspection" scheme, in which each power divides its territory into a prescribed number of zones of relatively equivalent military worth and then invites the other power to select any zone it wishes for complete disarmament and complete inspection.[26]

Another variant, called "graduated access inspection," provides for initial disarmament in categories which can be inspected tolerably well with a minimum of intrusion into sensitive areas of Soviet secrecy. Thus aerial inspection is less intrusive than ground inspection; for certain types of arms reduction plans, the inspection of production facilities, transport centers, and bases may be more significant than the inspection of secret communications centers and command posts, but the inspectors' rights of access to sensitive areas must increase as disarmament proceeds.[27] It must be admitted, however, that at the present time the Soviets still seem extremely reluctant to permit any kind of international inspection on their territory. The SALT Agreements of May 1972, as we shall see presently, provide for purely national verification rather than international inspection.

Theoretically, it is possible to postulate many different forms of physical inspection to check on the disarming process and on the continuing state of disarmament that follows. The supervision of weapons destruction by international teams is itself a form of inspection. Permanent aerial and satellite reconnaissance could detect the construction of new production plants or missile sites. Ground observers stationed at airports, railheads, ports, and highway centers could be on the lookout for suspicious movements of goods or personnel. Resident inspectors could be stationed at those factories

[26] See Louis B. Sohn, "Zonal Disarmament and Inspection: Variations on a Theme," *Bulletin of the Atomic Scientists*, vol. 18 (September 1962).
[27] See Leonard S. Rodberg, "Graduated Access Inspection," *Journal of Arms Control*, vol. 1 (April 1963); and Lincoln P. Bloomfield, "The Politics of Administering Disarmament," *Disarmament and Arms Control*, vol. 1 (Autumn 1963).

that formerly manufactured critical components of nuclear weapons and missile systems, while other plants could be subjected to spot checks against conversion.[28]

Strict accounting of industrial materials and skilled labor could be instituted. Scientists could be placed under a sytsem of registration and random surveillance. Although the monitoring of governmental budgets and expenditures is of highly dubious value in the early stages, it might become more useful as an additional indicator in a disarmed world.[29] The experts readily concede that there are ways of evading every single technique. But they argue that the reliability of a system increases as multiple techniques are crossed with each other to be applied according to scientific sampling methods.

Most disarmament experts in this country would probably agree—albeit with caution—that it is technically feasible to formulate a moderately reliable system of controls against the future clandestine production of fissionable materials and long-range delivery vehicles, and the future deployment of these weapons to secret sites. But a majority of the experts would emphatically deny that a physical inspection scheme can yet be devised which can offer any assurance against the danger of nuclear weapons caches diverted from past production—that is, hidden away out of stockpiles which had been accumulated prior to the disarmament agreement. One of the pioneers in the study of inspection writes:[30]

> One of the gravest hazards for international disarmament lies in the possibility that secret stockpiles of highly destructive weapons could remain undeclared even after agreements for stopping the production of these weapons had been signed. This danger exists whenever critical weapons have been produced in large quantities over a long period.

[28] See the articles by James H. Boyd, John B. Walsh, Eugene A. Avallone, Bruno A. Boley, Henry Burlage, Jr., and Charles J. Marsel in Melman, ed., *op. cit.*; also Wiesner, "Inspection for Disarmament," *loc. cit.*

[29] See Jesse Burkhead, "The Control of Disarmament by Fiscal Inspection," in Melman, ed., *op. cit.*; Morris Bernstein, "Inspection of Economic Records as an Arms Control Technique," in Singer, ed., *op. cit.*

[30] Seymour Melman, "How Can Inspection Be Made to Work?" *Bulletin of the Atomic Scientists*, vol. 14 (September 1958), pp. 271-272.

Another scientific authority has concluded that "there is not at present any mechanical means for detecting clandestine stockpiles, and ground search without special equipment is a practical impossibility."[31] In 1962, a British paper submitted at Geneva contained the assertion that the total past output of plutonium from a reactor can be falsified by as much as fifteen to twenty percent.[32] If the bulk of the hidden nuclear material should be in the form of thermonuclear weapons, it is not difficult to imagine one or two thousand megatons of destructive power sequestered for years in a few remote caches, waiting to be delivered by commercial jet aircraft converted to military use. Such potential margins of error or deception pose enormous risks to the superpowers, and make both of them extremely cautious in disarmament negotiations. In fact, this one technical problem makes it virtually impossible for either side to think seriously of *complete* disarmament as a feasible goal for the foreseeable future.

Perhaps it is the problem of clandestine stockpiles more than anything else that prompted some analysts to suggest novel and radical methods of control. Instead of concentrating on the search for *physical* evidence that a violation has occurred, these scientists would prefer to seek *nonphysical* evidence, mainly in the form of human knowledge—either (a) volunteered knowledge (or "inspection by the people"), which implies that individual citizens are motivated by a system of rewards and punishments to inform against their own government officials or fellow citizens who engage in prohibited activities; or (b) detected knowledge, which involves the use of modern psychological testing techniques upon personnel most likely to know whether a violation has occurred.[33] It seems highly unlikely, however, that nations are at all ready to enter such sweeping disarmament agreements as entail drastic revisions of human political atti-

---

[31] Wiesner, "Inspection for Disarmament," *loc. cit.*, p. 126. See also Finkelstein, *op. cit.*, p. 24: "It is apparent . . . that in today's circumstances, no agreement can be reached to eliminate nuclear stockpiles because no known methods would provide high assurance . . . that the total existing stockpile had been declared at the beginning of the control period."

[32] See *Documents on Disarmament 1962*, US Arms Control and Disarmament Agency Publication No. 19 (Washington: US Government Printing Office, 1963), vol. 2, p. 844.

[33] See Lewis C. Bohn, "Non-Physical Inspection Techniques," in Brennan, ed., *op. cit.*; Jay Orear, "New Approaches to Inspection," *Bulletin of the Atomic Scientists*, vol. 17 (March 1961); Elton B. McNeil, "Psychological Inspection," *Journal of Arms Control*, vol. 1 (April 1963); and Thomas C. O'Sullivan, "Social Inspection," in Singer, ed., *op. cit.*

tudes (for example, citizen loyalty), or require key officials to undergo polygraph tests, depth interviews, or the use of "truth serum" injections.

**Decline of Interest in GCD**

As we look back today upon the efforts of idealistic analysts in the early 1960s to devise a variety of physical and nonphysical verification and control methods to ensure either compliance with a disarmament agreement or timely warning and effective sanctions in case of violation, we cannot but be impressed by the remarkable creativity of some of the ideas which they invented. The whole intellectual exercise, however, despite its admirable imaginativeness, remained rather "academic" in the most impractical connotations of that term. Most of the proposals were vulnerable to one or another criticism: they could be circumvented by parties bent on violation; they were politically obnoxious to the Soviets, and some of them perhaps would be unacceptable even within the more permissive framework of American political culture; they failed to dispel the crucial danger of "hidden stockpiles" which might be sufficiently large to pose a future threat to the national survival of a disarmed power; and in their orientation to radical disarmament, they contributed little if anything toward the solution of more practical and immediate problems associated with the task of achieving those much more modest and limited arms agreements which might be brought within the circle of feasibility. (It should be noted here that there is only one weapons sector in which governments are now undertaking genuine disarmament—biological warfare weapons. See the discussion on The Prohibition of Biological and Chemical Weapons in the next chapter.)

It is a sobering thought that after hundreds of negotiating sessions over the course of a quarter century, not a single weapon—not even a rifle, a carbine, a pistol, or a hand grenade, much less a bomber or missile—has yet been destroyed as the result of an international disarmament agreement in the nuclear age. A perusal of *Arms Control and Disarmament: A Quarterly Bibliography with Abstracts and Annotations* from volume one in 1964 to volume eight in

1972 serves to illustrate a marked decline in the amount of literature published on the subject of General and Complete Disarmament. By the mid-1960s, there was a perceptible increase in the publication of books and articles questioning the necessity, urgency, or likelihood of rapid progress toward GCD, or lamenting the growing difficulties of achieving it.[34] Thomas C. Schelling noted that the conclusion of the Nuclear Test Ban Treaty reversed the momentum toward GCD by removing "a provocative symbol of the arms race."[35] By the end of the decade of the 1960s, although Soviet and American spokesmen still occasionally paid lip service to the goal of GCD, no serious analyst was writing about it as a practicable objective toward which contemporary governments are striving. Several years after the Test Ban Treaty, the two superpowers were still engaged in a protracted discussion as to how they would begin not to dismantle but merely to freeze strategic weapons. Governments have probably always recognized the dangers that J. David Singer described so trenchantly as early as 1962.[36]

> First, even with the establishment of a thorough inspection system, there will always be the gnawing fear that the other side may not only *attempt* to conceal weapons or produce new ones, but may possibly succeed . . . Second, there is the possibility that while the reduction has ceased, the adversary may develop a new device not covered by the agreement . . . In any partial distarmament scheme, the risks of evasion are significant but not tragic; in a complete and total disarmament program, the hazard is almost intolerable . . . (for) there may come a time when a government subscribing to it is virtually incapable of self-defense, and when, if another has successfully concealed significant offensive weapons, it may be faced with the choice between surrender and annihilation.

[34] See, for example, James E. Dougherty and J. F. Lehman, Jr., eds., *The Prospects for Arms Control* (New York: Bartell-Macfadden, 1965); Jeremy J. Stone, "Whither the Arms Race?" *Correspondent*, no. 35 (Autumn 1965), pp. 11-13; James E. Dougherty, *Arms Control and Disarmament: The Critical Issues*; Curt Gasteyger, "The Problems of International Disarmament," *Military Review*, vol. 46 (January 1966), pp. 23-29; and Dougherty and Lehman, eds., *Arms Control for the Late Sixties*.

[35] Thomas C. Schelling, "Perspective on Disarmament," *Disarmament*, no. 9 (March 1966), p. 11.

[36] J. David Singer, *Deterrence, Arms Control and Disarmament* (Columbus: Ohio State University Press, 1962), pp. 190-191.

It may safely be said that it is the awareness of this haunting possibility that will, in the final analysis, deter most national elites from pursuing any total disarmament schedule, no matter how objectively effective the inspection provisions may be. Under the Moscow SALT agreements, some land-based missiles may be actually dismantled (see Chapter 10), but if so they will be replaced by an equivalent number of sea-based missiles. The world is not yet ready to enter upon nuclear disarmament. Indeed, governments are still wondering whether the time has yet come even to summon a disarmament conference of all states. The United States now stands almost alone in questioning openly the value of convening a World Disarmament Conference at this time. The *Annual Report* of the US Arms Control and Disarmament Agency issued in January 1973 carried the following assessment:[37]

> Based on historical experience, the United States believes that negotiating forums of limited size are best able to deal with the complex technical factors inherent in arms control and disarmament issues and provide the best means of achieving meaningful progress. The United States is committed to seek agreements as may be possible at any given time. However, a very large conference of all states would, in all likelihood, not assist in the process. It would not provide a setting for the careful, patient and serious negotiation that had led to each of the arms control achievements of the past few years. Moreover, a World Disarmament Conference, with all the emphasis it would place on questions of image and national prestige, could well detract from the serious negotiations now in progress in other bilateral and multilateral forums.

[37] *12th Annual Report to the Congress*, US Arms Control and Disarmament Agency, p. 24.

# 9

## Arms Control

The fact that total disarmament is perceived as lying beyond man's present reach has not led to despair on the part of governments. All the nuclear powers in varying degrees have manifested some awareness of the need for managing military power wisely and cautiously. Evidence of this has been seen in various crises in Korea, Berlin, Cuba, Vietnam, the Middle East, the Indian subcontinent, and along the Amur-Ussuri Rivers. All five nuclear powers seem at present to shun nuclear war as a means of accomplishing any foreign policy objectives, and they will probably continue to steer clear of a frontal collision with each other. All appear to recognize some interest in "arms control," whether formal or tacit, whether in the shape of unilateral policies of military-technological self-restraint or in the form of negotiated agreements. Up to now, it has not been politically possible for all five nuclear powers to sit down at the same negotiating table. Those that have worked out agreements have learned that modern military technology does not lend itself easily to regulation by the traditional diplomatic device of the written treaty. But some limited agreements have been made—not all of them merely "cosmetic," as those critics of arms control who want more rapid progress toward substantial disarmament have sometimes charged.

The remainder of this study will treat the specific arms control agreements and measures that have been reached, or sought unsuccessfully, since 1959; (a) the Antarctica Treaty; (b) the "Hot Line" Agreement; (c) the Partial Nuclear Test Ban Treaty; (d) a comprehensive nuclear test ban; (e) the Outer Space Treaty; (f) a cutback in the production of materials for nuclear weapons; (g) military budget reductions; (h) the Nonproliferation Treaty; (i) the Seabed Treaty; (j) the Agreement on Measures to Reduce the Risk of the Outbreak of Nuclear War; (k) the prohibition of biological and chemical weapons; and (1) the Strategic Arms Limitation Talks, to which a separate chapter will be devoted.

## The Antarctica Treaty

This Treaty was signed on December 1, 1959, by twelve countries: Argentina, Australia, Belgium, Chile, France, Japan, New Zealand, Norway, South Africa, the USSR, the United Kingdom and the United States. The Treaty declared that Antarctica shall be used for peaceful purposes only; and it demilitarized the region by prohibiting military bases and fortifications, military maneuvers, and the testing of any type of weapons; but it did not prevent the use of military personnel and equipment for scientific research and other peaceful purposes. The Treaty recognized the right of each national signatory to carry out inspections to insure observance by all parties. The United States carried out onsite inspections in Antarctica in 1964, 1967, and 1971, and found no violations.[1]

It may seem ironic to some that the South Pole was the first region in the world to be removed from the "Cold War." Obviously, the region is not considered an area of crucial strategic competition between the superpowers; but there was some fear at the dawn of the nuclear missile age—shared by policymakers in the United States, Australia, Argentina, and Chile—that the Soviet Union might some day attempt to establish a military base or rocket-launching site in

[1] *Documents on Disarmament 1945-1959,* vol. 2, pp. 1550-1557. For the background to the Treaty and its relation to the International Geophysical Year (IGY), see Howard J. Taubenfeld, *A Treaty for Antarctica*, International Conciliation No. 531 (New York: Carnegie Endowment for International Peace, January 1961); *7th Annual Report to the Congress,* US Arms Control and Disarmament Agency (Washington: US Government Printing Office, 1968), p. 36.

Antarctica, or else deploy nuclear-armed submarines in adjacent waters.[2] In terms of arms control, the treaty has often been hailed as a precedent for demilitarizing an area before it became an arena of strategic-military competition. In this sense, it helped to pave the way for a United Nations General Assembly resolution on November 28, 1961, which declared that the African Continent should be treated as a denuclearized zone; the Treaty of Tlatelolco, February 14, 1967, which prohibited nuclear weapons in Latin America; and the Outer Space and Seabed Treaties, which are discussed below.[3]

## The "Hot Line"

The Washington-Moscow "hot line," on which an agreement was reached on June 20, 1963, was installed for purposes of facilitating crisis communications under circumstances such as those surrounding the US-Soviet confrontation over Cuba in October 1962, when in the opinion of some observers war was brought closer by a confusion over the proper sequence of messages from Premier Khrushchev to President Kennedy.[4] During the early years, the "hot line" was used only for the exchange of season's greetings between the two capitals. Then, in the Middle Eastern June 1967 war, this emergency communications link was used to exchange messages of reassurance concerning the desire of each side to avoid direct embroilment. It was again used for a similar purpose in the Middle Eastern crisis of September-October 1970, which arose out of the Syrian-Jordanian confrontation at the height of the Palestinian guerrilla campaign. In the early Fall of 1971, the "hot line," which originally consisted of telegraphic-teleprinter, wire telegraph, and radio telegraph circuits, was technologically updated and replaced by a new system using communications satellites (to become fully operational in 1973). The American circuit is being arranged through Intelsat, the Soviet circuit through the Molniya II system.[5]

---

[2] Taubenfeld, *op. cit.*, pp. 261-262.

[3] For the resolution on Africa, see *Documents on Disarmament 1961*, pp. 647-648; for the Treaty on the Prohibition of Nuclear Weapons in Latin America, see Appendix VIII in *7th Annual Report to the Congress*, US Arms Control and Disarmament Agency, pp. 65-67. Out of 22 countries in the zone, only Cuba refused to sign. The United States voted for a General Assembly resolution supporting the Treaty. *Ibid.*, pp. 33-35. China announced in November 1972 that it would respect the Treaty.

[4] Theodore C. Sorensen, *Kennedy* (New York: Harper and Row, 1965), p. 712. For the text of the agreement, see *Documents on Disarmament 1963*, pp. 236-238.

[5] *11th Annual Report to the Congress*, US Arms Control and Disarmament Agency (Washington: US Government Printing Office, 1972), p. 6.

The value of having in being a communications link capable of rapidly transmitting messages which might clarify superpower intentions at times of acute crisis, and thus of minimizing the risk of unintended war as a result of technical accident, miscalculation, misreading of warning signals, human psychic breakdown, catalytic action by third parties, and related causes is undoubtedly great. There is some danger, not to be completely ignored, that the "hot line" might some day be exploited for purposes of psychopolitical warfare in the midst of an international crisis. One side, for example, might send a chilling message designed to freeze the other in its tracks, by insinuating that a component of its military force has gone beyond its control when in fact it has not, or by suddenly introducing an ambiguous element of heightened threat into a hitherto noncritical confrontation. These will remain possibilities with which the superpowers must learn to live, and for which they must be constantly prepared without becoming paranoid. Obviously, both Washington and Moscow have reached the reasonable conclusion that the dangers accompanying the existence of a "hot line" facility are more manageable, and thus more tolerable, than the dangers of not being able to communicate when the need to do so is desperate in the extreme.

**The Partial Nuclear Test Ban Treaty**

As indicated earlier, the pressures for a nuclear test ban came originally from scientists who were concerned about the adverse genetic effects of radioactive fallout resulting from the testing of nuclear weapons in the atmosphere. Thus, in a sense the Test Ban Treaty may be considered as the first significant effort in modern times to prevent environmental pollution by way of international treaty. The technical problems of verifying a complete test ban had been the subject of considerable diplomatic controversy at Geneva for five years, from 1958 to 1963. (These issues were listed earlier in the section on The Technical Problems of Verification and Inspection.) One of the lessons learned from these years of debate about detection seismology, onsite inspection quotas, and the feasibility of achieving a hundred percent foolproof system was that it is impossible to draw a clear dividing line between the technical judgment and the political judgment of the experts who advise the policymakers, regardless of whether they favor or oppose a particular proposal.[6] As late as April 1963, Soviet Premier Khrushchev reiterated his offer to allow a maximum of two or three onsite inspections annually on Soviet territory; but it seemed unlikely that the comprehensive test ban treaty then being proposed by the United States could receive the required two-thirds vote in the Senate, because too many Senators entertained grave reservations even as to the adequacy of the US proposal for seven onsite inspections annually.[7]

Since both superpowers had recently completed a series of nuclear tests in the atmosphere, the diplomatic effort shifted to a partial test ban that would circumvent all the problems of policing a comprehensive ban by permitting underground testing to continue. The Treaty Banning Nuclear Weapon Tests in the Atmosphere, in Outer Space, and Under Water was announced in a communique of July 25 and signed on August 5, 1963. During the course of the ratification hearings in the Senate, some military and scientific witnesses expressed concern over the possible implications of the treaty for the acquisition of further scientific knowledge in a few crucial areas of military technology—for example, in respect to the penetration capability of missiles, the development of antiballistic missiles, the survival capability of missile sites and systems, and the effects of atmospheric phenomena such as communications blackout (induced by nuclear blast and radiation) upon the operation of offensive and defensive nuclear weapons.[8] But most of the Administration witnesses, including the Joint Chiefs of Staff, while sometimes conceding that the treaty entailed certain military disadvantages, nevertheless recommended ratification on the ground that the advantages would outweigh the disadvantages, especially if the security measures required by the new conditions would be implemented—by improving unilateral detection capabilities, by pursuing an underground testing program, and by maintaining a readiness to resume testing in the prohibited environments in case the Soviets violated the treaty.[9] Secretary of State Dean

[6] See Robert Gilpin, *op. cit.*, pp. 15-18 and ch. 9; and Harold Karen Jacobson and Eric Stein, *Diplomats, Scientists and Politicians: The United States and the Nuclear Test Ban Negotiations* (Ann Arbor: University of Michigan Press, 1966), chs. 6 and 7.
[7] *Ibid.*, pp. 447-449.
[8] *Nuclear Test Ban Treaty*, Hearings Before the Committee on Foreign Relations, US Senate, 88th Congress, 1st Sesson, August 12 to 27, 1963.
[9] *Ibid.* Also *The Nuclear Test Ban Treaty. Report of the Committee on Foreign Relations*, US Senate, September 3, 1963, pp. 10-21. Actually, the US test resumption capability has atrophied. See Abram Chayes, "Bureaucracy: An Ally in Arms Control," *Survival*, vol. 14 (July/August 1972), p. 187.

Rusk also gave assurances that the treaty would in no way limit the authority of the Commander-in-Chief to order the use of nuclear weapons for the defense of the United States and its allies, nor would it alter the diplomatic status of East Germany as a signatory.[10] The Senate approved the treaty by a vote of eighty to nineteen. Eventually, it was adhered to by some 120 states.

The Test Ban Treaty permitted underground testing, provided that it would not cause radioactive debris to be present outside the territorial limits of the state conducting the tests. Both the United States and the Soviet Union have conducted underground tests in substantial numbers, the former more than the latter. On a few occasions, each has protested to the other against radioactive "venting" in violation of the treaty. But neither country has shown any disposition to invoke the withdrawal clause, whether for this reason or for the reason that France and China—nonsignatories—have continued to conduct tests in the atmosphere. Incidentally, domestic opposition within the United States to the underground detonation of a five-megaton warhead of the Spartan antimissile on Amchitka Island in November 1971 was based upon the charge that it would violate the National Environmental Policy Act rather than the Nuclear Test Ban Treaty.[11]

The Test Ban Treaty made weapons tests more inconvenient and more costly for the two superpowers. There is no reason to conclude that it has placed the United States at any particular disadvantage *vis-à-vis* the Soviet Union unless the latter possessed, at the time of the signing, greater knowledge of very large weapon effects—knowledge which could not be replicated by US scientists as a result of extrapolation from smaller subterranean tests.

## Proposed Comprehensive Test Ban

Even since the signing of the Test Ban Treaty, there has been frequent discussion of the need for a comprehensive test ban. Early in 1964, both the United States and the Soviet Union proposed a comprehensive test ban at the ENDC in Geneva. President Johnson

[10] *Ibid.*, pp. 5-6.
[11] *New York Times*, October 31, 1971.

listed such a ban among measures calculated to prevent the proliferation of nuclear weapons.[12] The notion of a comprehensive ban has long been popular among the neutral nations precisely because it would prevent the leading nuclear powers from developing weapons indefinitely. Agreement has been precluded, however, by differences over the question of inspection. The Soviet Union has consistently adhered to the position that national means of detecting and identifying seismic events are sufficient to verify compliance with a ban on underground tests, and that onsite inspection is therefore not needed. The United States has always contended that a comprehensive ban must be subject to adequate verification, that despite improvements in national detection capabilities some seismic events remain unidentifiable, and that hence some onsite inspections would still be necessary. The eight neutral nations at Geneva pressed the idea that underground tests above a certain threshold (usually 4.75 on the Richter scale) should be banned by way of a treaty, while, pending the conclusion of a comprehensive treaty, all other underground tests should be suspended.[13] Sweden took the lead in advancing suggestions for the formation of an international "detection club" and a system of "verification by challenge" (or "verification by invitation"). Under this concept, all nuclear tests would be banned for a trial period, during which time a variety of methods would be relied upon to dispel suspicion concerning the nature of doubtful seismic events. The government of the country where the event had occurred would be expected to volunteer information about it and to enter into an informal dialogue concerning the scientific evidence. If the evidence supplied proved unpersuasive to the suspicious party, the latter would be entitled to withdraw from the agreement.[14]

In April 1969, Sweden introduced in the ENDC a draft treaty banning underground tests. This was based partially upon technical data contained in a 1968 report of the Stockholm International Peace Research Institute (SIPRI), in which a number of scientists contended that the existing Worldwide Standard Seismological Network could not only detect but correctly identify nuclear tests (distinguishing

[12] *Documents on Disarmament 1964*, p. 8.
[13] *Documents on Disarmament 1966*, p. 576.
[14] *Ibid.*, pp. 130-139 and 506-513.

them from earthquakes) down to the level of twenty to sixty kilotons exploded in a hard rock like granite.[15] The US Representative, Adrian Fisher, pointed out that, according to the SIPRI report, nuclear explosions up to tens of kilotons could not be properly identified by teleseismic means, and he noted that such explosions could have significant military value. Tests continue to have utility for maintaining confidence in weapons stockpiles, for proof-testing newly designed weapons based on established principles, for measuring effects, and for carrying out advanced R & D. Since 1963, the United States in most years has conducted 25 to thirty underground tests, and the Soviets about one-third that number.[16]

In the early 1970s, the UN General Assembly and members of the Conference of the Committee on Disarmament (CCD) in Geneva continued to call for a comprehensive test ban that would end underground testing. There was a growing expectation that worldwide seismological capabilities might eventually be improved to the point at which onsite inspections would no longer be required to police such a ban effectively. But in late 1971, a stiff report issued by the Senate Disarmament Subcommittee would not go beyond the cautious conclusion that in view of "enormous advances" made since 1963 in seismic detection methods, "it would seem that a comprehensive test ban resting on seismic verification means alone would provide a high degree of assurance that high-yield violations were not occurring."[17] A nation determined to test clandestinely, at great expense and some risk of detection, could still test weapons in the range of a few kilotons, in large underground cavities, in soft soil, or by waiting for the cover of earthquakes which are frequent in some regions of the world. It is still the case that a comprehensive ban that fails to eliminate grounds for suspicion would operate under a considerable burden, and might eventually collapse under the weight. The US position within the CCD had not changed up to May 1973.

[15] International Institute for Peace and Conflict Research, *Seismic Methods for Monitoring Underground Explosions* (Stockholm: SIPRI, 1968), pp. 13-17. (This report was republished by Almqvist and Wiksell in 1969.)

[16] *Documents on Disarmament 1969*, pp. 162-163. For a full discussion of the proposed comprehensive test ban, see *SIPRI Yearbook 1972*, pp. 420-431 and 523-532.

[17] *New York Times*, November 7, 1971. For a report of US Atomic Energy Commission Project RULISON, a "peaceful uses" explosion designed to serve, among other purposes, those of seismic investigation, see the Statement of Representative Leonard to the CCD, August 4, 1970, in *Documents on Disarmament 1970*, pp. 351-355.

So long as the two superpowers were far apart on the question of national verification *versus* onsite inspection, both could call for a comprehensive ban but neither had to worry too much about its implications for national security, since its achievement was far from imminent. Now, as the development of worldwide seismic capabilities brings a complete ban on underground testing technically within reach of the superpowers, Washington and Moscow may soon have to decide politically whether they really want such a ban. An absolute test ban, effectively verified, would undoubtedly slow down the rate of weapons development. But it is logical to ask whether the two leading nuclear powers are ready to eliminate entirely the possibility of carrying out nuclear testing underground while France and China still reserve the right to test nuclear weapons in the atmosphere. Even if these two latter powers should prove willing to discontinue atmospheric testing, for which they have incurred a certain amount of international displeasure within recent years, they probably are not prepared to stop all testing, and may very well regard a comprehensive test ban as a form of superpower collusion aimed at "disadvantaged" nuclear powers. Finally, the question arises as to whether the US and the Soviet Union, having entered a SALT Phase I agreement which results in a *quantitative* freeze on certain strategic weapons categories, will also wish to rule out any forms of *qualitative* weapons improvements which may in the future require underground testing. Nevertheless, threshold powers and neutral powers can be expected to press increasingly, both in the CCD and in the UN General Assembly, for the superpowers to accept a comprehensive test ban.

**The Outer Space Treaty**

Following the conclusion of the Test Ban Treaty, there was an effort to preserve the "arms control momentum" by negotiating additional agreements. The UN General Assembly adopted a resolution on October 17, 1963, urging all states to "refrain from placing in orbit around the earth any objects carrying nuclear weapons or any kinds of weapons of mass destruction, installing such weapons on celestial bodies, or stationing such weapons in outer space in any other manner."[18] Prior to 1963, when US arms control strategists had discussed the possibility of a prohibition against orbital weapons, they usually had taken it for granted that such a prohibition would have to be linked to a system of global launch surveillance and pre-launch inspection.[19] The UN resolution made no provision for inspection. It merely reflected a feeling, widespread at the time, that the deployment of nuclear weapons in space, even though technologically feasible, did not seem desirable on political or military grounds, and might well prove dangerously difficult to control. Neither the United States nor the Soviet Union appears anxious to allocate resources for an extension of the arms race from earth to space. Instead of insisting upon a form of inspection that was unobtainable from the Soviets and probably not attractive to American military leaders, the United States seemed content to rely upon the strength of a presumed mutuality of interest.

The Treaty Governing the Activities of States in the Exploration and Use of Space was signed on January 27, 1967. It provides, *inter alia,* that outer space (including the moon and other celestial bodies) shall be free for exploration and use by all states equally in accordance with the principles of international law; that outer space is not subject to national appropriation by claim of sovereignty, occupation, or other means; that parties will not place in orbit any objects carrying nuclear weapons or other weapons of mass destruction; that no military installations shall be emplaced on celestial bodies; that parties shall regard astronauts as envoys of mankind in outer space and render them all possible assistance in the event of accident, distress, or emergency landing; and that parties assume international responsibility for their activities conducted in space, including liability for damages.[20] The Treaty provides for unilateral national inspections, but up to mid-1973 no such inspections had been carried out by the United States.

[18] A/RES/1884 (XVIII), October 17, 1963.

[19] See Donald G. Brennan, "Arms and Arms Control in Outer Space," in Lincoln P. Bloomfield, ed., *Outer Space: Prospects for Man and Society*, for the American Assembly (Englewood Cliffs, N.J.: Prentice-Hall, 1962), pp. 147-148.

[20] Text of Treaty in *Documents on Disarmament 1967*, pp. 38-43. At the time the Senate ratified the Treaty on April 25, 1967, 79 countries had signed. *New York Times*, April 26, 1967. As of January 1973, 102 states had signed, and 66 had ratified.

The Outer Space Treaty, like the Antarctica Treaty, was aimed at reserving for "peaceful purposes" part of man's environment that had not yet been militarized. But the Treaty specifies that the use of military personnel for scientific research and other peaceful purposes in space shall not be prohibited. Thus it cannot be said that the treaty has fully "demilitarized" space. Both superpowers have continued to man their space flights with military personnel. They have continued to rely upon reconnaissance satellites for gathering strategic military intelligence. The Treaty has not been interpreted to prohibit such military developments in space as the manned orbiting laboratory (MOL), the testing of multiple warheads (MIRV and MRV), the fractional orbit bombardment system (FOBS), and satellite destroyers.[21] It cannot be said, therefore, that the Treaty has up to now seriously hindered the two leading space powers from carrying out any missions related to national military security that they have deemed necessary. The "peaceful space rocket," like the "peaceful atom," is a Janus capable of showing a more belligerent face.

Since the Outer Space Treaty was signed, additional states—including France, China, and Japan—have become nascent "space powers." Space technology is one of the most difficult of all sectors to regulate by treaty. In the future, as China develops a missile capability, it is possible that both the Soviet Union and the United States, aware that the survivability of existing deterrent forces is being put in doubt by technological gains in satellite reconnaissance, antisubmarine warfare (ASW), multiple warheads, and improved guidance accuracy of missiles, may be tempted to think about achieving a new invulnerability by deploying strategic systems in deep space.[22] At the time the Space Treaty was negotiated, there were some critical comments to the effect that it was not exactly relevant to the here-and-now problems of arms control on the planet Earth, but was directed toward the remote, the futuristic, and the esoteric. Yet it is conceivable that the Outer Space Treaty will take on added im-

---

[21] Neither the US nor the Soviet Union has ever lodged any official protests concerning developments in these weapons sectors as treaty violations.

[22] See Robert Salkeld, *War and Space* (Englewood Cliffs, N. J.: Prentice-Hall, 1970). Wolfram von Raven has written a book on the subject in German, *Die Zwei Gresichter des Mondes. Strategie im Weltraum* (The Two Faces of the Moon: Strategy in Space) (Salzburg: S-N Verlag, 1969). For a discussion of space reconnaissance in world politics, see Neville Brown, "Reconnaissance from Space," *World Today*, vol. 27 (February 1971), 68-76.

portance with the passage of time, and that we shall hear more frequent contentions in the future that one party or another, under the guise of the peaceful exploration of space, is developing technological capabilities that pose a threat to the national security of another.

**Production Cutback**

During the late 1950s, the United States and the other Western powers had worked out a package disarmament agreement in which one element was a cutoff on the production of fissionable materials for weapons purposes.[23] This type of measure naturally became a key item in the draft treaties for General and Complete Disarmament, but because of the impasse over inspection, and probably for other reasons as well, no progress was made on a verified cutoff. Shortly before the opening of the 1964 meeting at Geneva of the ENDC, President Johnson announced in his State of the Union message that the United States would reduce production of fissionable materials for weapons purposes by 25 percent, by closing four of its fourteen plutonium plants. This was followed in April 1964 by simultaneous announcements, coordinated through Geneva, that the US would cut production of plutonium by twenty percent and of enriched uranium by forty percent, while the Soviet Union would halt the scheduled construction of two new atomic reactors for producing plutonium and would also, "during the next few years," reduce substantially the production of uranium-235 for nuclear weapons.[24]

The less precise nature of the Soviet commitment was attributed to the fact that the Soviet Union, which had been producing fissionable material for a shorter time and from a smaller number of plants than the United States, was less able to cut output. The West had no way of being certain that the Soviets had really planned to build two new reactors. Probably US policymakers thought this country was in a position to carry out the declared reductions regardless of what the Soviets did. In any event, a measure originally announced unilaterally by the United States was converted into what looked like reciprocal

[23] *Control and Reduction of Armaments*, p. 7.
[24] *Documents on Disarmament 1964*, pp. 165-168.

arms control gestures by the two superpowers. The move partially undermined the US proposal for a formal agreement on a verified cutoff of the manufacture of all nuclear weapons materials.

In September 1965, Ambassador Arthur J. Goldberg, addressing the General Assembly, reiterated the US call for a verified production cutoff and a transfer of agreed quantities of fissionable materials to peaceful purposes. The United States had earlier suggested such a transfer in the ratio of sixty thousand kilograms of weapons-grade U-235 by the United States to forty thousand by the USSR. Goldberg's new proposal provided for the demonstrated destruction of thousands of nuclear weapons to obtain the materials needed for the transfer;[25] but nothing came of the proposal. Early in 1967, the Johnson Administration, in a budget-minded move, announced that by mid-1967 the Atomic Energy Commission would shut down another large plutonium production reactor at Hanford, bringing to five the number of reactors closed since 1964. This time, the United States made no bid to the Soviets for a reciprocal gesture.[26] Early in 1969, President Nixon reaffirmed the US intention to press for a cutoff agreement. In an effort to solve the verification problems inherent under adversary inspection arrangements, the United States then proposed that the International Atomic Energy Agency be asked to verify the continued shutdown of all facilities for the manufacture of fissionable materials that would be closed. This, if accepted, would place the superpowers under the same safeguards system accepted by the nonnuclear weapon states that adhere to the Nonproliferation Treaty.[27] The Soviet Union has not accepted the proposal.

## Military Budget Reductions

The cutting of military budgets by ten to fifteen percent was proposed by Soviet Delegate S. K. Tsarapkin in January 1964.[28] He argued that this would not entail any lopsided alteration in the military balance, since each state would be able to determine for itself

[25] *5th Annual Report to the Congress*, US Arms Control and Disarmament Agency (Washington: US Government Printing Office, 1966), pp. 9-10.
[26] *New York Times*, January 25, 1967.
[27] *9th Annual Report to the Congress*, US Arms Control and Disarmament Agency, pp. 8-9.
[28] *Documents on Disarmament 1964*, p. 14.

which components of its defense forces would be reduced. Although it looked attractive in theory, both the United States and Britain opposed the suggestion in the absence of further technical studies and agreement on precise methods of policing the measure. As we have seen previously, Western analysts have long been skeptical of control by fiscal inspection alone, in view of the ease with which governments can disguise appropriations or transfer funds from one account to another. When the British pressed for technical studies on the verification of budgetary agreements, the Soviets retorted that back in the days of the League of Nations technical studies, instead of leading to disarmament, were merely a cloak for war preparations, and demanded that the cut should be accepted in principle prior to the inauguration of technical studies.[29]

Nevertheless, in that period it looked as though the two superpowers, despite their inability to negotiate a formal agreement at Geneva, were interested in turning down the arms burner by at least a few degrees and carrying out, informally, modest curtailments in their military budgets. The Soviets announced a 4.3 percent cut in defense spending. Shortly thereafter, the Johnson Administration said that the US arms budget would be sliced from $52 billion to $51 billion by eliminating obsolescent weapons systems, dismantling installations and bases no longer required, and tightening management efficiency in the defense establishment. It was suggested that both powers were willing to see whether they might apply to the budgetary sector what Western writers called "reciprocal unilateral measures" of a "confidence-building" nature, and what the Soviets described as "mutual example." At the end of 1964, both countries once again announced defense cuts, the Soviets from 13.3 to 12.8 billion rubles and the United States from $51 to $49 billion.

During 1965, however, the expansion of the war in Vietnam necessitated extraordinary US military expenditures. In December of that year, the Soviets responded by announcing a five percent increase in defense spending for 1966. In January 1966, the United States un-

[29] ENDC/PV. 166, February 13, 1964, pp. 37-39. A Soviet participant in the Pugwash Conference argued at about the same time that, since budget cuts involve no actual disarmament, international control is unnecessary. See Igor Glagolev, "The Reduction of Military Expenditures," *Disarmament and Arms Control,* vol. 2 (Summer 1964), p. 311.

veiled a defense budget increase from $49 billion to $57.2 billion, of which $10 billion was attributed to the prosecution of the Vietnamese conflict. Actually, this estimate proved to be short of the mark. By December 1966, US forces in the area of Vietnam were approaching a total figure of four hundred thousand, and the government admitted that defense costs in the current fiscal year were running as much as $10 billion higher than had been officially anticipated in the previous January. In December also, the Supreme Soviet heard that the defense program for 1967 would cost 8.2 percent more than in 1966. Then in January 1967, the Johnson Administration proposed a $73 billion defense budget, including $22 billion for the cost of the Vietnam operation. This meant that US spending for strategic arms systems was approximately at the 1964 spending level. How much of the Soviet increase was going to the cost of Vietnam, and how much to finance strategic arms developments in offensive and defensive missile systems, could not be known exactly; but it seemed likely that only a small percentage could be attributed to military aid for Vietnam.[30]

The question of budget cuts for arms control purposes had become somewhat academic in the late 1960s. Between 1965 and 1968, US outlays for military expenditures of all kinds had risen forty percent. Military spending in the Warsaw Pact countries also went up by forty percent in the four-year period from 1965 to 1969. But whereas US military spending (measured in constant 1964 dollars) fell back by seventeen percent during the three years after 1969, Warsaw Pact spending held constant or increased slightly during that same period. Western analysts, in making their estimates, are convinced that there are important items included in US and NATO reports which are excluded from Soviet and Warsaw Pact published figures—R & D expenditure, the cost of civil defense, foreign military aid, military materials stockpiling; the testing, manufacturing, and stockpiling of nuclear weapons, and some investment in arms procurement industries. According to projections made by President Nixon's Office of Management and Budget, it was expected that total national defense outlays would increase from $76.4 billion in 1973 to $81.1

[30] When Congressman Melvin R. Laird released a report estimating Soviet military aid to North Vietnam at about one billion dollars, mainly in the form of SAM missiles, some Administration officials regarded the estimate as a bit high. *New York Times*, March 31, 1967.

billion in 1974 to $85.5 billion in 1975. These increases were attributed primarily to pay and price increases at a time when the United States is moving toward an all-volunteer force. Inflation of defense costs does not pose a comparable problem to Soviet planners.[31]

**The Nonproliferation Treaty**

Several years ago, a Soviet mathematician expressed the danger of nuclear weapons proliferation in the formula R equals $N^2$, in which R stands for the risk of nuclear war and N for the number of nuclear powers. This formula implies a geometric progression in the chances of nuclear war with every increase in the number of nuclear states. The formula fails to take into account significant political factors, including the political quality of governments controlling nuclear weapons and the character of their foreign policies. If Sweden or Switzerland, for example, were to acquire nuclear weapons, it is at least doubtful that the risks of nuclear war would be increased as much as they would be if North Vietnam, Cuba, or Syria were to acquire them. In this sense, if no other, the formula was deficient.

Some analysts have been inclined to go much further in questioning the fundamental assumptions implicit in the notion that increases in the number of nuclear powers are fraught with grave dangers to mankind and that an antiproliferation policy must be assigned the highest priority. It is sometimes pointed out that the acquisition of nuclear weapons may compel a brash, militant, and irresponsible government to start acting with greater prudence, maturity, and restraint. Fred Charles Iklé has questioned both the "statistical theory" and the "catalytic war" theory underlying the argument that the diffusion of nuclear capabilities inevitably increases the probability of global thermonuclear war. He contended that the spread of nuclear weapons might just as well reduce the risks of nuclear war by making major powers less likely to intervene in local conflicts, without necessarily leading to the temptation that a small nuclear power would de-

[31] *The United States Budget in Brief: Fiscal Year 1973*, p. 30. *See also SIPRI Yearbook 1972*, pp. 75-76.

liberately try to provoke a war between the superpowers by simulating an attack from one upon the other.[32] Morton Kaplan, writing in a theoretical vein, has postulated a "unit veto international system," in which all actors possess the capabilities of destroying any other actor even though it cannot prevent its own destruction—a "standoff" system in which each actor is governed by "the negative golden rule of natural law . . . not doing to others what he would not have them do to him."[33] Finally, several critics of the US antiproliferation policy have argued strenuously that, however desirable it may be on certain grounds to prevent the proliferation of nuclear weapons, the effort to do so might give rise to serious political problems with our NATO allies, and will, in the end, prove technologically impossible to accomplish.

Nevertheless, in spite of the suggestions that a world of many nuclear powers might be more stable than a world of few, and that an antiproliferation policy is an exercise in futility, the prevailing point of view within the US government since the late 1950s has been that a world of twelve or fifteen nuclear states would be a more dangerous place in which to live than a world of four or five, because it would pose a greater statistical probability of technical accident, unauthorized use, strategic miscalculation, or uncontrolled escalation from limited to general war, and it would also compound the difficulties of achieving a negotiated international agreement on the limitation of nuclear armaments.

For many years, the United States sought to persuade aspirants to independent national nuclear power that the game was not worth the candle because small deterrents are costly, provocative, and accident-prone, lack credibility, become obsolescent quickly, and render young nuclear powers vulnerable to preventive attack during the early stages. The argument was frequently made that a nuclear weapons program will divert needed resources from development purposes. After aiding Britain in its weapons program, the United States refrained from aid-

[32] Fred Charles Iklé, "Nth Countries and Disarmament," *Bulletin of the Atomic Scientists* (December 1960), 391-94.

[33] Morton A. Kaplan, *System and Process in International Politics* (New York: John Wiley and Sons, 1957), p. 50. See also R. N. Rosencrance, "International Stability and Nuclear Diffusion," in the book he edited, *The Dispersion of Nuclear Weapons* (New York: Columbia University Press, 1964), pp. 293-314.

ing France in the late 1950s, while at the same time the Soviets began to disengage from the Chinese weapons effort. In all probability, both Washington and Moscow expected France and China to persist in their nuclear weapons programs, but hoped that the arguments leveled against the British, French, and Chinese forces as being wasteful and strategically ineffective might serve to dissuade other countries from trying to join the club. As the two superpowers deployed intercontinental missiles, the contention was frequently heard that nuclear weapons alone would not enhance a nation's strategic power status unless they were accompanied by highly sophisticated and very expensive delivery systems. Finally, the smaller powers were often reminded that their role of moral leadership in the world disarmament forum would be greater if they abstained from acquiring nuclear weapons.[34]

Western arms control analysts were aware that, beyond the five existing nuclear powers, at least eleven states possessed the economic and technological resources to produce some Hiroshima-type bombs within a decade: Belgium, Canada, Czechoslovakia, East Germany, India, Israel, Italy, Japan, Sweden, Switzerland, and West Germany.[35] Any country fabricating a crude bomb, based upon a design which by the early 1960s was well known, would be justified in expecting the weapon to explode even without carrying out a testing program.[36]

The arguments in favor of acquiring nuclear weapons can be summed up briefly. *Militarily,* nuclear weapons alone can deter a nuclear-equipped opponent; a smaller power does not need intercontinental delivery systems if it is mainly concerned about a neighboring country rather than a distant superpower; it may merely wish nuclear weapons for tactical defensive purposes to prevent the foe from massing his armies or to deny him access to easy avenues of approach. *Economically,* while nuclear weapons programs undoubt-

[34] See Paul M. Doty, "The Role of the Smaller Powers" in Brennan, ed., *op. cit.*, pp. 304-314; and Morton H. Halperin, "A Ban on the Proliferation of Nuclear Weapons," in Evan Luard, ed., *First Steps to Disarmament* (New York: Basic Books, 1965), pp. 132-160.

[35] *The Nth Country Problem and Arms Control, A* Statement by a Special Project Committee of the N.P.A. (Washington: National Planning Association, 1960). This report names all the countries listed except Israel, whose capabilities are discussed in Leonard Beaton and John Maddox, *The Spread of Nuclear Weapons* (New York: Praeger, 1962), pp. 168-181.

[36] Arnold Kramish, *The Peaceful Atom in Foreign Policy* (New York: Harper and Row, 1963), p. 23.

edly divert scarce scientific-engineering talent from immediate development purposes, in the long run they can contribute to the growth of the technological base; the initial investment required is no longer prohibitive for a country that already possesses a civilian reactor program; and eventually the acquisition of nuclear weapons might permit savings through reductions in the size of the conventional armed forces. *Politically and strategically,* nuclear weapons provide an ultimate guarantee of a country's independence; by giving a state a finger on the nuclear trigger, they foreclose strongarmed tactics by more powerful states, and crisis deals by the superpowers at the expense of that country; they are a source of prestige within an alliance, within a region, and the world at large, and provide one with a ticket to summit conferences. Nationalists in many states are inclined to agree with the Gaullist axiom that a proud nation cannot rely upon another government for its defense. As for the argument that entrance into the nuclear club renders a country vulnerable to preventive attack in the early stages, aspirants to *n*th power status can point to the experience of Numbers Two, Three, Four, and Five, for none of which did mere acquisition, when combined with a strategy of restraint, prove to be a *casus belli.*

Recognizing that the case *for* acquisition might prove stronger than the case *against* in some countries, the United States and the Soviet Union began in 1964 to work toward a nonproliferation treaty of a kind that had been under discussion in the United Nations for at least two years. In December 1961, Ireland had introduced a resolution calling for an international agreement under which the nuclear states would bind themselves not to transfer nuclear weapons or their control to nonnuclear states, and the latter would bind themselves not to manufacture or otherwise acquire control of such weapons.[37]

Negotiations for the Nonproliferation Treaty lasted for more than four years, in the context of a world debate over the following questions: Is a formal treaty really necessary, insofar as the five nuclear powers may already be in tacit agreement that it is not in their interest to dilute the currency of nuclear prestige by helping to create other nuclear powers? Should nonnuclear states renounce their option

[37] A/RES/1665 (XVI), December 1965.

of acquiring a nuclear military capability before they have reason to believe that the nuclear powers will make substantial progress toward disarmament? Would not a formal treaty place all the burdens upon the nonnuclear rather than the nuclear states, since the three nuclear states likely to sign would be doing little more than protecting their privileged position, while all the sacrifices would be imposed upon those not yet possessing nuclear weapons? In other words, would the treaty represent no more than an effort by the armed to disarm the unarmed? Can the nuclear powers give credible security guarantees to the nonnuclear countries? Would the Nonproliferation Treaty in any way jeopardize the freedom of such countries as West Germany, Japan, India, and Brazil to exploit the atom's peaceful uses, or would the international inspection which the treaty requires entail dangers of industrial espionage? Finally, given the whole history of the Nonproliferation Treaty—especially in relation to the once-proposed and later-shelved NATO multilateral force, and also to the future role of Euratom—is the treaty likely to have an adverse effect upon European integration and the cohesiveness of the Atlantic Alliance?

All the foregoing questions were by no means satisfactorily answered before the Nonproliferation Treaty was opened for signature on July 1, 1968.[38] Generally speaking, the misgivings of most of the states concerned over the implications of the treaty for their future development of peaceful reactor technology were attenuated before they signed. Nonnuclear states were guaranteed that potential benefits from peaceful nuclear explosions (for example, to excavate canals, harbors, or lakes, to divert rivers, and to make deep deposits of oil and minerals commercially exploitable) would be made available to them on a nondiscriminatory and low cost basis. Each nonnuclear signatory accepts the safeguards system of the IAEA to ensure that fissionable materials are not diverted to weapons manufacture. Provision was made for the members of the European Community to concert their negotiations with IAEA (and thus preserve the interests and prerogatives of Euratom). Less satisfactory was the negative result of efforts by nonnuclear states to obtain a specific security

[38] *Documents on Disarmament*, 1968, pp. 461-465. For the background of the negotiations, see James E. Dougherty, "The Non-Proliferation Treaty," *Russian Review*, vol. 25 (January 1966), pp. 10-23; and "The Treaty and the Nonnuclear States," *loc. cit.*

guarantee from the nuclear powers. The attempt to extend such a guarantee by treaty provision was considered to be not credible for unforeseen future circumstances. The nuclear powers relied instead upon a UN Security Council resolution which declared that actual or threatened nuclear aggression against a nonnuclear weapon state would "create a situation in which the Security Council, and above all its nuclear weapon state permanent members, would have to act immediately in accordance with their obligations under the United Nations Charter."[39] (Whether the seating of Communist China in the UN will enhance or detract from the credibility of such a guarantee in the Security Council, where the veto prevails, remains to be seen.) Article VI of the Treaty committed each party to pursue negotiations in good faith toward the cessation of the arms race at an early date, toward nuclear disarmament and a GCD treaty under strict and effective international control. This provision furnished one of the motives of the United States and the Soviet Union to enter the SALT talks.

The Nonproliferation Treaty, described by President Johnson as "the most important international agreement since the beginning of the nuclear age" up to that time, was approved by the US Senate on March 13, 1969, by a vote of 83 to fifteen.[40] As of early 1973, 103 states had signed. But, as we have seen, several states have not signed the Treaty (Argentina, Brazil, China, France, India, Israel, Pakistan, South Africa, and Spain). Those that have signed, but not yet ratified, include Belgium, the Federal Republic of Germany, Italy, Japan, the Netherlands, Turkey, and Switzerland.

The Safeguards Committee of the International Atomic Energy Agency has designed means of ensuring that fissionable materials in nonnuclear signatory countries will not be diverted from peaceful uses to the production of nuclear weapons. This involves a system of controls based on reports, record-keeping, inspections and other techniques monitoring the international flow of fissionable materials at

[39] UN Security Council Resolution 255, June 19, 1968. *Documents on Disarmament 1968*, p. 444.
[40] *New York Times*, March 14, 1969. See Young, *op. cit.*; and Frank Barnaby, "Limits on the Nuclear Club," reprinted from *New Scientist*, March 19, 1970, in *Survival*, vol. 12 (May 1970).

selected strategic points.[41] The IAEA and Euratom concluded their negotiations during 1972, thereby paving the way for the ratification of the Treaty by the members of the European Community. The Vienna Agency has also been conducting negotiations with the United States and Japan. Article VIII of the Nonproliferation Treaty provides that five years after the entry into force of the Treaty (which occurred on March 5, 1970) a conference of all parties shall be held at Geneva to review the operation of the Treaty and to assure that its purposes are actually being realized. Some signatories might postpone final ratification pending the outcome of that conference.

## The Seabed Treaty

The year 1967 witnessed the emergence of an international interest in the concept of extending arms control to another environment that had not yet been militarized—the ocean floor. Naval strategists were beginning to speculate about the desirability and feasibility, now that land-based missile systems were again becoming vulnerable as multiple warheads appeared, of shifting strategic capabilities to the sea. The Delegate of Malta to the General Assembly, Arvid Pardo, was one of the first diplomats to call attention to the growing possibility that antiballistic missile systems might be deployed on oceanic mountain ranges to counter multiple warhead missiles aimed at land targets. He urged the major powers to recognize the futility of attempting to achieve a temporary military advantage by locating weapons installations on the ocean floor beyond the continental shelf (since efforts to protect these from espionage would probably sooner or later lead to curtailment of lawful traditional activities on the superjacent sea). He called for a treaty which would reserve the seabed and the ocean floor beyond the limits of national jurisdiction exclusively for peaceful purposes.[42] In the same year, 1967, the US Arms Control and Disarmament Agency was studying the possibility of an arms control agreement that would prohibit the emplacement of nuclear weapons or other weapons of mass destruction on the seabed.[43] Such an agree-

[41] See *The Structure and Content of Agreements Between the Agency and States Required in Connection with the Treaty on the Non-Proliferation of Nuclear Weapons,* International Atomic Energy Agency, INFCIRC/153, May 1971.
[42] Statement of November 1, 1967. *Documents on Disarmament 1967,* pp. 547-554.
[43] *7th Annual Report to the Congress,* US Arms Control and Disarmament Agency, p. 38.

ment, like the Treaties on Antarctica and Outer Space, was to be based on the assumption that it is easier to exclude weapons from an environment to which they have not yet been introduced than to limit or remove them where they already exist.

Interest in the seabed continued to grow for the next two years. The negotiations that began in the General Assembly and finally issued in a draft treaty prepared by the superpowers involved several issues: the right of all nations to benefit from the peaceful exploitation of the oceans—the common heritage of mankind; whether national military activities on the seabed should be limited to territorial waters or extended to the continental shelf; the relationship between an arms control measure for the seabed and the existing international law of the sea; whether the term "peaceful uses" is compatible with some military activities; whether the treaty should fully demilitarize or merely denuclearize the ocean floor; whether the agreement should prohibit (as originally proposed by the USSR) bottom-mounted submarine surveillance systems which the US deems essential to its defense; and how compliance with a seabed treaty would be verified. The United States and the Soviet Union on October 7, 1969, tabled a joint Draft Treaty on the Prohibition of the Emplacement of Nuclear Weapons and Other Weapons of Mass Destruction on the Seabed and the Ocean Floor and the Subsoil Thereof. After additional amendments, the Treaty was opened for signature on February 11, 1971. The United States signed on that day and ratified on May 18, 1972. As of early 1973, the treaty had been signed by 88 states and ratified by 42 states.

The Treaty prohibits the emplacement of nuclear weapons and other weapons of mass destruction beyond a twelve-mile coastal "seabed zone." None of the Treaty's provisions are to be interpreted as prejudicing the position of any party in respect to still unresolved issues of the law of the sea. In a rather complex article on verification, each party is given the right to verify, through observation, and by itself, with other parties, or through the United Nations, to make sure that others are living up to their treaty obligations, so long as they do not interfere with legitimate seabed activities.[44]

[44] Treaty text in *10th Annual Report to the Congress*, US Arms Control and Disarmament Agency (Washington: US Government Printing Office, 1971), pp. 37-40.

The Seabed Treaty denuclearized the ocean floor; it did not fully demilitarize it. Moreover, it deals only with the control of mass destruction weapons, not the whole gamut of issues posed by the technological-economic exploitation of ocean resources by the nations of the world and the effort to prevent pollution of the ocean environment. Several governments supported the Treaty with little enthusiasm, thinking it was too limited in scope. The debate over the Treaty brought to light the curious fact that some of the nonnuclear states, particularly those that have not ratified the Nonproliferation Treaty, seemed for the first time to be more concerned than the United States over the question of adequately verifying compliance with an arms control measure.[45] Some European observers were disposed to dismiss the Seabed Treaty as a "cosmetic agreement" designed to make the superpowers look as if they were making progress toward disarmament when they really were not.[46] The Chinese Communists denounced the Treaty as a joint effort by the superpowers to preserve their dominant oceanic positions by giving legal respectability to their nuclear-armed submarines and by enabling them to build military bases on the seabed under the guise of conventional installations.[47] Although the ocean floor now seems a rather esoteric arms control environment, the Seabed Treaty, like the Outer Space Treaty, may grow in importance during the years ahead.

## Reducing the Risk of the Outbreak of Nuclear War

Ever since the latter 1950s, when strategists and arms control planners began worrying seriously about the dangers of strategic instability and surprise attack, as well as the implications of fast-reacting and vulnerable weapons systems, they also started to become concerned about "accidental war" or "unintended war." In 1960, Herman Kahn placed "unpremeditated war" at the top of his list of possible ways in which nuclear war might occur. Kahn, along with Thomas C. Schelling, Hedley Bull, J. David Singer and other writers,

[45] See Elizabeth Young, "Ocean Policy and Arms Control," *World Today*, vol. 26 (September 1970), pp. 401-407.

[46] For a sample of the view that the Seabed Treaty is not a contribution to the disarmament process, see Jane Klein, "L'utilisation militaire des fonds marins et le désarmement," *Politique Etrangère*. vol. 35 (1970), pp. 405-438.

[47] *Hsinhua* (New China News Agency) release, Peking, October 22, 1969. *Survey of China Mainland Press*, No. 4526, October 29, 1969.

realized that the shiftover from bombers to missiles would raise the international level of strategic "nervousness" by increasing the strategic disadvantages attendant upon waiting to absorb a first strike before retaliating. They saw that a government in the age of nuclear missiles would be under heavy pressure to launch its weapons as soon as it suspected that an outbreak of war was imminent—to "strike back first," as it were—even though the information at its disposal was scanty, ambiguous, and not entirely credible. There was in the late 1950s and early 1960s a considerable amount of discussion concerning misinterpreted radar signals (perhaps the result of meteors, or geese on the screen), the faulty operation of a piece of electronic equipment, the mistaken issuance of attack orders, the behavior of a deranged officer, and the accidental detonation of a nuclear weapon.[48]

For several years, the Soviets appeared less concerned than Western analysts over the possibility of accidental war. One plausible explanation is that Soviet writers in this field publish only a fraction of the output of their Western counterparts, and are not notorious for communicating exactly what is on their minds. Thus, they may have been more concerned than they seemed. Another possible explanation springs from ideology. Instances can be found in the early 1960s in which Soviet commentators went out of their way to ridicule American theories of accidental war. Those who subscribe fully to the Marxist view of history do not readily accept the notion that a nuclear war—the most cataclysmic event in history—might occur purely by chance rather than through the interplay of titanic social forces, especially the aggressive policies of capitalist imperialism.[49]

There is reason to believe, however, that the Soviets never lightly dismissed the danger of accidental war. In 1958, Andrei Gromyko scored the "provocative" military policies of the United States under which an atomic war might result from the slightest mistake on the

[48] Herman Kahn, "The Arms Race and Some of its Hazards," in Brennan, ed., *op. cit.*, p. 91; Thomas C. Schelling, "Meteors, Mischief and War," *Bulletin of the Atomic Scientists*, vol. 16 (September 1960), pp. 292-300; Singer, *Deterrence, Arms Control and Disarmament*, ch. 4, "Fear, Ambivalence and Unintended War;" and Bull, *op. cit.*, ch. 10.

[49] See V. Berezhkov, "The 'Automobile Accident' Theory of War," *New Times* (Moscow), April 18, 1962. The author denied that there was a danger of accidental war, and accused Western writers of stressing the danger of accident merely to cloak the imperialists' designs for surprise attack.

part of an American technician.[50] Undoubtedly, Soviet planners have read with great interest of "fail-safe" systems, "two-key" systems, "permissive action link" systems, and other administrative, political, and technical safeguards designed by US authorities to reduce the changes of uncontrollable events. From time to time, the Soviets have shown theoretical interest in measures designed to reduce fears of surprise attack. Lincoln P. Bloomfield has suggested that Soviet interest in plans for disengagement or denuclearization in Central Europe were at least partially motivated by a desire to minimize the risks of accidental war in that region.[51] Following the Cuban missile crisis, the Soviets agreed, as we have seen, to the establishment of a "hot line" to facilitate emergency communications between the superpowers. A famous compendium of Soviet military writings published in the early 1960s acknowledged the danger of accidental outbreak of war, but added that this danger requires the greatest vigilance on the part of the Soviet armed forces "and the enormous wisdom and sagacity of our national political and military leadership so that a war is not allowed to start for any such accidental reasons."[52] Implicit in this statement is a sensible recognition of the fact that the danger of unintended war can be reduced in two ways: by minimizing the chances that accidents will happen; and by further minimizing the chances that accidents, if they do happen, will lead to an actual political decision for war. It is reasonable to conclude that the Soviets are interested in making the international military-strategic environment in which they operate as safe as possible against the contingency of unintended war, and are willing to participate in formal measures toward this objective, provided that such measures involve no specific disadvantages or liabilities from the Soviet point of view (such as the acceptance of on-site inspectors).

On September 30, 1971, the United States and the Soviet Union concluded a formal Agreement on Measures to Reduce the Risk of Outbreak of Nuclear War. The parties undertook (1) to improve existing organizational and technical arrangements to guard against

[50] *New York Times*, April 19, 1958. See also Alexander Dallin and others, *The Soviet Union, Arms Control and Disarmament*, pp. 93-94.
[51] Lincoln P. Bloomfield and others, *Khrushchev and the Arms Race*, p. 150.
[52] *Soviet Military Strategy*, p. 289.

the accidental or unauthorized use of nuclear weapons; (2) to notify each other immediately in the event of an accidental, unauthorized, or any other unexplained incident involving a possible detonation of a nuclear weapon which could create a risk of outbreak of nuclear war; (3) to make every effort, in the event of such an incident, to render the weapon harmless or to destroy it without its causing damage; (4) to notify each other immediately in the event of detection by missile warning systems of unidentified objects, or at any signs of interference with communications facilities, if such occurrences could create a risk of nuclear war; (5) to notify each other of planned missile launches extending beyond the national territory in the direction of the other party; (6) otherwise to reduce the possibility of actions being misinterpreted when there may be risks of nuclear war as a result of unexplained nuclear incidents.[53] Since the agreement also provided for consultations on implementing its provisions, it clearly formalizes and institutionalizes understandings about superpower behavior that may have been tacitly in effect for several years. Within two weeks of the conclusion of this agreement, US and Soviet military representatives gathered in Moscow to start discussing ways of reducing the dangers stemming from mutual military surveillance on the world's waterway, and to lower the risks involved in what has become known as the game of "chicken-of-the-sea" by devising some new maritime-aerial "rules of the road."[54] An agreement designed to prevent incidents at sea from escalating to dangerous proportions was signed in Moscow in May 1972.

## The Prohibition of Biological and Chemical Weapons

In modern times, no form of warfare has aroused greater popular revulsion than the use of chemical and biological weapons. The experiences of soldiers in World War I who suffered from the choking and blinding effects of the greenish-yellow gas clouds that glided ominously over the trenches became deeply impressed upon the public consciousness in Western countries. During the interwar period, chemical warfare seemed to many the cruelest form yet de-

[53] Text of Agreement in *New York Times*, October 1, 1971.
[54] *New York Times*, October 10, 1971.

vised of "man's inhumanity to man." As for biological weapons, a civilization that places a high premium on health and the conquest of disease is bound to loathe the very idea of "germ warfare," for it conjures up from the depths of man's psyche (and historic memory) the dread of uncontrollable plague. Perhaps it is understandable that many people should still regard chemical and biological agents as more odious even than nuclear weapons.

There have been repeated attempts in this century to outlaw biological and chemical (B/C) warfare weapons. The Washington Treaty of February 6, 1922 (discussed earlier), prohibited the use in war of "asphyxiating, poisonous, or other gases." The United States ratified this treaty; but its coming into effect was contingent upon ratification by all signatories, and France failed to ratify. Later, the Geneva Protocol of June 17, 1925, added to the Draft Convention in International Trade in Arms and Ammunition and in Implements of War, repeated the language of the Washington Treaty and extended the prohibition to "the use of bacteriological methods of warfare." The Geneva Protocol was eventually adhered to by more than ninety states. Although it was signed by the United States, it was not approved by the Senate. It languished in committee until 1947, when it was withdrawn along with other obsolete treaties by President Truman because purely declaratory disarmament treaties were falling into disfavor in a period of growing interest in effective controls as essential concomitants of disarmament agreements. (For the later history of US ratification, see below.)

It should be noted that nearly forty adherents to the Geneva Protocol appended formal reservations maintaining the right to use the proscribed weapons against an enemy that used them first. Since the weapons could be used legally in reprisal, several signatory countries continued their programs of research, manufacturing, and stockpiling.

The United States did not consider itself obligated in the strict legal sense to refrain from using the weapons named in the Geneva Protocol, because this country never ratified any legal instrument prohibiting their use that ever became effective as a part of international law, and because customary law in this field was considered much too nebulous to be binding.[55] For all practical purposes, however, the executive branch of the US government acted as if it adhered to the Geneva Protocol. American Presidents have always been outspokenly opposed to the use of lethal B/C weapons; but prior to President Nixon, none denied the necessity of maintaining a full range of national capabilities in this field, particularly for the purpose of deterring other nations from using them against American forces in wartime. In 1943, for example, President Roosevelt condemned gas warfare as inhumane and gas weapons as "outlawed by the general opinion of civilized mankind." He then added: "I state categorically that we shall under no circumstances resort to the use of such weapons unless they are first used by our enemies."[56]

During the Korean War, the Soviets launched an intemperate propaganda campaign against the United States, hurling unproved accusations of "germ warfare." The Soviets at that time were seeking to reap full advantage from the fact that the US had not adhered to the Geneva Protocol.[57] The US Representative in the UN Disarmament Commission, Benjamin V. Cohen, asserted that the Geneva Protocol was inadequate because it was merely declaratory. He noted that Italy had accepted the Protocol, but Mussolini was not prevented thereby from using poisonous gas in Ethiopia; and that Hitler was deterred by fear of reprisal rather than by the Protocol. Cohen added that the USSR, after signing the Protocol, continued research and preparations in respect to the use of chemical and bacteriological weapons—for which precautionary measures the US did not criticize the USSR. He reiterated the US insistence, for B/C as well as other types of mass destruction weapons, upon "an effective and continuous system of disclosure and verification" relating to "the progressive curtailment of production, the progressive dismantling of plants, and the progressive destruction of stockpiles of bacteriological weapons and related appliances."[58]

[55] See the materials cited in ch. 4, fn. 9, above.
[56] *New York Times*, June 9, 1943.
[57] See Waldemar Jollos, "Propaganda and Bacteriological Warfare," *Swiss Review of World Affairs*, vol. 2 (May 1952), pp. 6-8; and Wesley R. Fishel and Herbert Garfinkel, "The Germ Warfare Charge in Communist Atrocity Propaganda," in Grace E. Potter and William R. Steinhoff, eds., *Papers of the Michigan Academy of Science, Arts and Letters*, vol. 39 (Ann Arbor: University of Michigan Press, 1954), pp. 445-458.
[58] Statement on Bacteriological Warfare by Deputy US Representative Cohen to the Disarmament Commission, August 15, 1952. *Documents on Disarmament 1945-1959*, vol. 2, p. 380.

Throughout the nuclear era, most of the analytic effort in strategic and arms control literature has focused upon the problem of nuclear weapons, not B/C weapons. Before we can fully understand the challenge of controlling B/C weapons, we must try to assess, even though in a sketchy fashion, the military and other arguments for and against such weapons. Most strategic analysts usually contend that a nation should seek to maximize its choice in weapons selection in order to achieve the widest possible flexibility for dealing with threats to its security. Hence, they see B/C weapons as strengthening the deterrent against attack, since such weapons compel a would-be aggressor, in his strategic and tactical planning, to take into account additional complex weapons systems, and thus compound the uncertainty of his calculations. Under certain circumstances, the use of nonlethal B/C weapons might in the opinion of some military analysts be highly desirable as an alternative to the use of nuclear weapons.

More specifically, it has been argued that B/C weapons offer a wide range of selectivity both in impact on target and in method of delivery. They may be difficult to identify for purposes of rapid defense reactions. The threat of their use can prevent the enemy from massing his forces. B/C weapons that have no persistent contaminating effects are preferable to nuclear weapons because they permit occupation of an area soon after attack. Nonlethal B/C weapons produce no permanently deleterious effects upon human beings. The lightweight character of many B/C weapons can simplify the logistics problems, especially of airlifted forces. In the event of localized aggression that the West is unable to contain by conventional methods, the employment of B/C weapons might be sufficient to prevent the aggressor from achieving his military objective without having to resort to tactical nuclear weapons, which involve a risk of escalation to general nuclear war.

But every weapons system has liabilities as well as assets. To be fully effective, chemical and biological weapons have to be employed over large areas. Thus, it is difficult to use them and to maintain the distinction between military targets and civilian populations in the vicinity. Although these weapons may be light in weight, many of them require special storage conditions and careful handling. They are antipersonnel rather than antiequipment weapons, and may prove ineffectual against a foe who is more interested in conserving hardware than manpower. Their use may hinge upon highly favorable meteorological conditions if a boomerang effect upon the user and other friendly forces is to be precluded. Biological weapons especially may pose a problem of spatio-temporal control—that is, their use may lead to the dissemination of organisms far beyond the battle zone, perhaps causing damage to one's own or friendly forces and populations. These organisms could go on reproducing pathological offspring long after the military engagement has ended. If both belligerents have prepared their forces for defense against B/C warfare, such warfare may have no decisive military significance but will merely shift most of the damage to civilian populations. The use of these weapons, especially in their more odious forms, is likely to give rise to adverse psychopolitical reactions that may well prove more enduringly detrimental to the user's political interests than a limited or temporary military setback would be.

In the final analysis, there is no reason to conclude that B/C weapons could ever prove decisive in a tactical or strategic military context. In certain cases, they might be more "humane" than nuclear bombs or napalm. But chemical weapons alone have never won a major battle; while biological weapons have never been tested on a large scale, and their ultimate consequences are unpredictable. Thus the skeptic cautions against making any exaggerated claims for the effectiveness of B/C weapons. He also notes that these weapons are cheaper and thus more readily available than nuclear weapons to the great majority of nations of the world. Since the less advantaged nations often borrow the technology of the more advanced, the skeptic suggests that it is in the interest of the latter to stress research and development for defensive rather than offensive purposes.[59]

So far as planning for disarmament and arms control is concerned, B/C weapons are extremely difficult to regulate under verifi-

[59] For representative arguments concerning the military, strategic, and political advantages or disadvantages of using B/C weapons, see the following: B. H. Liddell Hart, "Is Gas a Better Defense than Atomic Weapons?" *Survival,* vol. 1 (September 1959); Brig. Gen. J. H. Rothschild, "Germs and Gas: The Weapons Nobody Dares Talk About," *Harper's* (June 1959); *Research in CBR,* Report of the Committee on Science and Astronautics, 86th Congress, August 10, 1959; Brook Chisholm, "Biological Warfare: Demand for Answers," *Bulletin of the Atomic Scientists,* vol. 15 (May 1959), p. 210; Walter Schneir, "The Campaign to Make Chemical Warfare Respectable," *Reporter,* October 1, 1959.

able agreements. The technology of toxological warfare is available to almost all states, large or small. B/C weapons are relatively cheap. Their production is easy to hide, since it requires none of the huge industrial establishments that are the *sine qua non* of nuclear weapons programs. Research of this type of weaponry can be carried on almost anywhere—in university laboratories, hospitals, agricultural experiment stations, breweries, or the basements of private homes. Thus, many opportunities exist to disguise expenditures for CBW preparations under such headings as public health services, materials testing, agricultural and medical research, conservation, weather studies, and other categories difficult to monitor through fiscal controls, registration of scientific personnel, materials accounting, or physical inspection. A decade or so ago, it was thought that the large areas required for testing biological weapons, and the magnitude of the precautions needed to make sure that pathogenic organisms do not spread beyond the proving grounds, might make the inspection problem a bit easier. The problem now is that enough is known about the operational characteristics of a variety of B/C weapons to reduce the necessity of testing except for defense purposes. Effective technical delivery systems already exist in abundance (for example, missiles, aircraft, submarines) and could scarcely be prevented except by a ban on all forms of transport, civil and military. We should not forget that B/C weapons can be made inconspicuous enough to be carried by saboteurs, or light enough to be wafted across a country by balloons. Small wonder that the Fifth Pugwash Conference in 1959 reached the somewhat pessimistic conclusion that "however difficult the international control of atomic weapons may be, the international control of biological and chemical weapons by any system of inspection seems incomparably more difficult."[60]

Both the Soviet and US proposals for general and complete disarmament called specifically for prohibiting the production of chemical and biological weapons. In the late 1950s and early 1960s, American GCD proposals were somewhat more cautious than Soviet

[60] Statement of the Fifth Pugwash Conference, "On Biological and Chemical Warfare," *Bulletin of the Atomic Scientists*, vol. 15 (October 1959). See also Vincent Groupé, "On the Feasibility of Control of Biological Warfare," in Seymour Melman, ed., *Inspection for Disarmament*, pp. 185-190; and James E. Dougherty, *B/C Weapons and Arms Control*, Background Paper for the Third Strategy for Peace Conference, Airlie, Virginia, October 1922, 1961, pp. 38-59.

proposals, inasmuch as the former called for studies in the earlier stages of GCD to determine the feasibility of reducing stockpiles at various specified rates. Nothing, of course, came from the GCD proposals. At the end of 1967, the Arms Control and Disarmament Agency published the following conclusion concerning B/C weapons: "The development and production of such weapons is so relatively easy that the design of a practical verification system has presented almost intractable problems."[61] During the same year, the International Red Cross issued a statement confirming the use of poison gas in the Yemen, and the United States condemned the use of lethal gas as "clearly contrary to international law." The Arms Control and Disarmament Agency continued to study B/C inspection techniques and concepts. The UN Secretary General was authorized to prepare a study of the possible effects of using B/C weapons. Great Britain submitted a working paper to the ENDC proposing a new Convention for the Prohibition of Microbiological Methods of Warfare, not to supercede but to supplement the 1925 Geneva Protocol. The United States supported the British initiative, while the Soviets took the position that there was no need for a new convention, provided that all nations would adhere to and strictly observe the existing Protocol.

The incoming Nixon Administration recognized the need for a review and clarification of US policy in this area. At least through the 1950s, US agencies had often pointed out that this country, strictly speaking, was not bound by the Geneva Protocol. Beginning in the mid-1960s, the United States formally pledged itself to adhere to the principles of the Protocol. President Nixon ordered a comprehensive study of US policy within the National Security Council. As a result of the study, the President on November 25, 1969, announced several policy decisions on chemical and biological warfare programs: (1) The United States reaffirmed its oft-repeated renunciation of the first use of lethal chemical weapons, and extended this renunciation to the first use of incapacitating chemicals. (2) The President would resubmit the Geneva Protocol to the Senate for approval. (3) Since biological weapons have massive, unpredictable, and potentially un-

[61] *7th Annual Report to the Congress*, US Arms Control and Disarmament Agency, p. 38.

controllable consequences (including global epidemics and impairment of the health of future generations), the United States renounced the use of lethal biological agents and weapons, and all other methods of biological warfare, even in retaliation. (4) The United States would confine its biological research to defensive measures such as immunization and safety measures. (5) The Department of Defense would make recommendations as to the disposal of existing stocks of bacteriological weapons. (6) The United States would associate itself with the principles and objectives of the United Kingdom draft convention, which would ban all methods of biological warfare. (7) The US intelligence community would continue to watch carefully the nature and extent of the biological programs of other nations.[62]

President Nixon's announcement left some questions unanswered. One of the most important concerned the status of toxins. These are poisonous chemical substances which are produced by living organisms and which produce effects commonly described as disease. Although they are not contagious, they can cause severe illness and even death if ingested or inhaled. One of the most powerful is botulinum, which produces the generally fatal disease, botulism. Since the President's message had made no reference to toxins, their status became a matter of controversy. Were they biological agents, thus to be renounced absolutely, or chemical agents, and thus subject only to the no-first-use limitation? On February 14, 1970, the White House announced that toxins would be included in the total ban on the use of biological agents.[63]

On August 19, 1970, the President resubmitted the Geneva Protocol of 1925 to the Senate for approval, accompanied by a report from the Secretary of State noting that 39 nations (including the USSR, Britain, and France) have previously attached reservations to their adherence, stipulating that the Protocol is considered binding only with respect to parties (not to nonsignatories) and only to the extent that the other parties abide by its provisions. The Secretary of State proposed that the Senate give consent to ratification, subject

---

[62] Statement by the President Announcing Policy Decisions on Chemical and Biological Warfare Programs, November 25, 1969. *9th Annual Report to the Congress*, US Arms Control and Disarmament Agency, Appendix IV, pp. 45-46. US biological warfare facilities have since been converted to environmental and health missions.
[63] *New York Times*. February 15. 1970.

to the following more limited reservation (which applies only to chemical weapons, since the use of biological weapons has been renounced by the United States even in retaliation):[64]

> That the said Protocol shall cease to be binding on the government of the United States with respect to the use in war of asphyxiating, poisonous, or other gases, and to all analogous liquids, materials, or devices, in regard to an enemy state if such state or any of its allies fails to respect the prohibition laid down in the Protocol.

The United States continued to support the draft convention for a ban on the production and stockpiling of biological weapons proposed by Great Britain in 1969. The Soviet Union and a majority of the countries in the UN General Assembly were for some time opposed to decoupling biological from chemical weapons in a disarmament treaty. The United States, having already subscribed to a policy of unilateral disarmament in respect to biological weapons, argued that it would be relatively simple to reach early agreement on a treaty banning biological weapons alone, whereas a ban on chemical weaponry would pose more complex problems. A chemical weapons prohibition, for example, would require effective verification. The United States was also unwilling to accept a total ban on chemical weapons if this were to include herbicides (which were used in Vietnam) and tear gases (which were used in the United States and other countries for riot-control purposes). These same difficulties were causing a delay in Senate approval of the Geneva Protocol. Up to mid-1973, the Protocol had not been ratified.

Eventually, the Soviet Union agreed to a separate treaty on biological weapons. A Draft Convention on the Prohibition of Biological Warfare and of the Production of Biological Weapons was approved by the General Assembly on December 16, 1971, by an overwhelming vote, with no abstentions. The Convention was opened for sig-

[64] *10th Annual Report to the Congress*, US Arms Control and Disarmament Agency, pp. 12-13. See also *Chemical-Biological Warfare: U. S. Policies and International Effects*, Report of the Subcommittee on National Security Policy and Scientific Developments of the Committee on Foreign Affairs, House of Representatives, May 16, 1970; Philip A. Karber, "The Nixon Policy on CBW," *Bulletin of the Atomic Scientists*, vol. 28 (January 1972); and Jozef Goldblat, "Biological Disarmament," *ibid.* (April 1972).

nature on April 10, 1972, and by January 31, 1973, it had been signed by 105 nations.[65] Under its terms, each party is required to destroy or divert to peaceful purposes (after its entry into force) all stocks of bacteriological weapons, agents, and toxins. All uses, including defensive uses, of biological weapons, agents, or toxins is prohibited. But research is not banned, and the production of certain quantities of biological agents and toxins may be continued for purposes of disease prevention and the development of protective equipment and devices. Appropriate military training for protective purposes is also permitted. Undoubtedly, there will be considerable room for argument in the future as to whether particular types of development, production, stockpiling, and retention are "justified" under the terms of the Convention. If any party finds that another party is acting in breach of its obligations, the former may lodge a complaint with the Security Council of the United Nations which may, subject to the veto provisions of the Charter, initiate an investigation.[66]

The Stockholm International Peace Research Institute, which has a particular interest and expertise in this field, has spoken favorably of the agreement in so far as it reflects, more than previous arms control measures, the views of smaller countries; because it will help to prevent the spread of biological weapons to countries not already possessing them; and because it outlaws the development of biological agents militarily more attractive than existing ones. But the Institute deplores the fact that in this Convention, the traditional linkage of biological and chemical weapons under international law has been severed. Priority has thereby been accorded to agents which are judged too uncontrollable and unpredictable to possess much military utility. "Biological disarmament," concludes the Institute, "is a marginal disarmament measure compared to the banning of chemical weapons."[67] Yet the fact remains that in this Convention, the superpowers lend their support to the principle of uninspected, total disarmament in the realm of biological weaponry.

[65] *Arms Control and Disarmament Agreements 1959-1972* (Washington: US Arms Control and Disarmament Agency, June 1, 1972), p. 107. *12th Annual Report to the Congress*, US Arms Control and Disarmament Agency, Appendix I.

[66] The text of the Convention as commended for signature by the UN General Assembly may be found in the *11th Annual Report to the Congress*, US Arms Control and Disarmament Agency, pp. 46-49. See also the analysis of the Convention in *World Armaments and Disarmament, SIPRI Yearbook 1972*, pp. 501-513.

[67] *Ibid.*, p. 513.

# 10

## Strategic Arms Limitation Talks

The Strategic Arms Limitation Talks (SALT) carried on in Helsinki and Vienna since late 1969 constitute the most important effort yet made to achieve a diplomatic agreement on the international distribution of military power between the Soviet Union and the United States. We should be clear at the outset that what Washington and Moscow were negotiating up to May 1972 was not substantial disarmament, or any actual arms reduction for that matter, but merely a quantitative freeze on the deployment of strategic offensive and defensive delivery vehicles. Phase II of SALT might get into the question of significant armaments reductions—but this is not yet certain.

President Johnson first proposed a verified freeze on the nature and number of strategic nuclear offensive and defensive vehicles in January 1964.[1] This proposal was based upon the common sense conviction that there can be no genuine disarmament until after strategic weapons production and deployment have been brought to a real and not just a pretended halt. The buildup of armaments can

[1] *Documents on Disarmament 1964*, pp. 7-9 and 17-21.

scarcely be reversed before it has been halted, any more than an automobile can shift the direction of its movement from forward to backward without at some moment being at a zero-velocity position. The concept of the freeze is based upon the assumption that it would be futile to undertake the dismantling of missiles if there were reason to think that similar weapons of equal or greater magnitude were still being manufactured and set on their launching pads.

From the very beginning, US arms control planners realized that there were several crucial questions to be answered: (1) Is it possible for the two leading nuclear powers, given their different mixes of weapons systems and their different geostrategic requirements, to devise a mutually satisfactory formula for establishing a freeze at some sort of stable quantitative-qualitative balance that would enable each side to feel reasonably confident that it was not being placed at an unfair disadvantage? (2) In view of the constantly changing nature of modern military technology, is it realistic to expect a static freeze, or is it necessary to think of the freeze in dynamic terms that would permit symmetrical-equitable development (qualitative if not quantitative) on each side? (3) Should the purpose of the freeze be to put a halt to the development of superpower military technology, and thus gradually to degrade the margin of strategic superiority which the superpowers enjoy over other states? Or should it be rather to stabilize and ratify the emerging condition of crude strategic parity (however hard that may be to define) between the United States and the Soviet Union, while prudently coordinating the perpetuation of their favorable situation *vis-à-vis* other states—especially China—until they have entered the arms control dialogue? (4) Coming down to the more mundane specifics of negotiation, is it possible to arrive at an agreed definition of "strategic" as distinct from "tactical" delivery vehicles? (5) Which types of freeze agreements are more readily verifiable, and which less? (6) For purposes of freezing, can offensive strategic systems be separated, or must they be linked? (7) Can the strategic freeze be negotiated segmentally, or must it be approached as comprehensively as possible? Much of the six-year prehistory of SALT, from initial proposal to the start of actual negotiations, and of the history of the Helsinki-Vienna negotiations from late 1969 until the May 1972 Agreements, was devoted to the effort to answer these difficult questions.

Why did the Soviet Union and the United States become involved in the SALT negotiations? There was a variety of motives, of course, not necessarily similar or of equal intensity on both sides. First of all, they were expected by the nonnuclear parties to the Nonproliferation Treaty to negotiate arms limitations. Both nations had to ponder the "economics of futility"—the indefinite and costly expansion of nuclear missile capabilities that produce a reciprocal canceling effect. They both seemed to realize the possibility that if the SALT were to collapse, competition in military research, development, and deployment might well be stepped up in a familiar action-reaction process that would not really improve either side's ability to deter attack, much less permit either side to achieve military superiority in a meaningful sense.

Both nations were beset by uncertainties, internal and external. As previously indicated, the internal problems seemed greater for the United States. But the Soviets undoubtedly experienced internal uncertainties and strains, including the disaffection of some scientists and writers, the Jewish problem, the beginnings of the alienation of youth, and the arguments over optimum allocation of resources. Soviet leaders undoubtedly felt economic pressures to limit spending for strategic arms—pressures for increased investment in agriculture and consumer industries, for narrowing the "technological gap" with the West in nondefense sectors, and for shifting defense priorities away from missiles to ground forces and the fleet. (But it should be noted that the Soviets are generally under less domestic political pressure to reallocate economic resources from military to nonmilitary purposes than is the United States government.)[2]

When we shift attention from internal to external motivating factors, we can see that the Soviets must carefully watch the United States, Germany, and China. They retain a healthy respect for the total productive capabilities of the American economic-technological system. They knew in the late 1960s that once the Safeguard ABM and radar technology had been developed for a few missile sites, it

---

[2] For analyses of the various pressures upon Soviet decisionmakers, see the paper by Thomas W. Wolfe "Soviet Approaches to SALT." *Problems of Communism* (September/October 1970). See also Lawrence T. Caldwell, *Soviet Attitudes to SALT* (London: Institute for Strategic Studies, Adelphi Papers No. 75, February 1971). Caldwell describes the pressures in terms of "modernist" versus "orthodox" positions with respect to SALT in the USSR.

could be extended nationwide rather quickly in the absence of a ban. As for Germany—always on the minds of Russian leaders—Moscow was engaged in an intensive diplomatic effort to secure a permanent acceptance of Europe's postwar frontiers, and SALT fitted into such a strategy very well. At present, Soviet elites—whether rightly or mistakenly—appear to perceive a greater future security threat from China than American elites perceive from the direction of the Soviet Union. Thus, the Soviets have found themselves in a highly ambiguous situation with respect to SALT. On the one hand, the Chinese danger has prompted the leadership in Moscow to seek detente and come to terms with the West. On the other hand, the same danger has set and will continue to set rigid parameters on the ability of the Soviets to reach agreement in SALT, especially if an arms freeze is expected to generate pressures for arms reduction.[3]

It was necessary to consider SALT broadly, not merely as a diplomatic-dialectical exercise in numerical and technological gamesmanship, but as a more comprehensive effort on the part of the superpowers to understand and manipulate the relationship between strategic armaments and the outstanding problems of international politics. Phase I of SALT, therefore, had to be structured as part of the total international problem on which the two superpowers wished to conduct negotiations. Knowledgeable analysts accepted a number of basic propositions pertinent to the success of SALT: (1) Each side was expected to speak frankly about what it found most worrisome in the political-military-technological postures of the other. (2) Both had to recognize that local conflicts in which they were deeply engaged (for example, in Southeast Asia or in the Middle East) might flare out of control and culminate in a disastrous confrontation. (3) Progress in the SALT negotiations was not completely dependent upon the achievement of finally satisfactory solutions to US-Soviet political differences in critical areas of the world; but some "linkages" had to be made, and it was unrealistic to expect SALT to proceed serenely at the level of technical negotiations without reference to the world political climate. (4) The strategic situation in

[3] For a fuller discussion of US and Soviet motivations in SALT, see James E. Dougherty, "Arms Control in the 1970's," *Orbis*, vol. 15 (Spring 1971); and "The SALT and the Future of International Politics," in William R. Kintner and Robert L. Pfaltzgraff, Jr., eds., *op. cit.*

Europe and the alliance systems of the two superpowers would have to be taken into account sooner or later in working out the SALT equations. (5) Whatever arms limitations would be agreed upon would have to lie within the unilateral verification capabilities of the nations involved, and thus the initial agreements would have to exclude warheads (MIRV and MRV), since these could not be detected by satellite reconnaissance. (6) It was clear that the timing of an initial SALT agreement was delicate and crucial; if it came too soon, the Soviets would want to exclude submarine-based missiles (a category in which they still trailed the United States in the early 1970s); while if the agreement was delayed too long, the United States was expected to grow increasingly concerned over the continued rapid deployment of Soviet land-based ICBMs.[4]

The conduct of strategic arms negotiations has been based upon the widespread assumption that a crude parity of assured strategic sufficiency (that is, a survivable capability to inflict unacceptable damage in retaliation) now exists as between the United States and the Soviet Union. This parity is thought to consist of several fluctuating and compensating asymmetries. In other words, at any given time the United States holds superiority in some areas and the Soviets in others. From time to time, there may be mild disturbances in the strategic equilibrium. But generally speaking, the equilibrium is a highly complex one involving numerous factors—different numbers of bombers; land-based missiles and sea-based missiles, all of varying ranges; different numbers of deliverable warheads of varying yields; different total "throw weights" (measured in megatons); differences in hardening and dispersal, firing reliability, guidance accuracy, reentry speeds, defense capabilities, penetration aids, detonation altitudes, and other weapons design characteristics; and differences in warning systems, intelligence, military doctrines, offensive and defensive weapons mixes, command and control systems, and so forth. Few would deny that several uncertainties inhere in the present military-technological situation. But it can be argued that even some of the uncertainties have more of a stabilizing than a destabilizing effect.

[4] These points represent the author's summation of the Fourth International Arms Control Symposium, held in Philadelphia in October 1969. See "What Shape Might a Strategic Arms Agreement Take?" *War/Peace Report*, no. 11, (December 1969).

Military analysts continue to worry, as they must, about the numbers game, the possibility of decisive breakthroughs, and about the "worst possible case" in which *our* systems fail to perform well while *theirs* work perfectly. It is difficult to imagine, however, that the political leaders in Washington or Moscow seriously fear a first strike deliberately planned by their counterparts in the other capital, simply because the risks of retaliatory disaster are too frightful and unpredictable.[5]

The assumption of superpower "parity" is important because this is the first time in the history of the nuclear era that such a condition has been thought to exist. The United States reached its present levels of missile deployment in the mid-1960s, and has held steady on the number of offensive ICBMs ever since (but not on the number of warheads). For about five years, from 1965 to 1970, it seemed as if US decisionmakers were "marking time," as it were, waiting for the Soviets to "catch up" to the point where serious arms negotiations could begin. During the three years from 1969 to 1972, the Soviets were "coming abreast" at a disturbingly rapid rate on land and sea. They surpassed the United States in the number of landbased ICBM's by more than fifty percent, and they had either operational or under construction a number of submarine-launched missiles comparable to that of the US.[6] The United States moved to reinsure its security position by scheduling the deployment of the Safeguard ABM system around a few (three or four) missile sites and by arming its landbased Minuteman missiles and three quarters of its submarine missiles with multiple-warhead weapons.[7] US defense experts expressed the belief that the Soviets could readily develop six-warhead clusters instead of the three-warhead clusters originally expected for each Soviet SS-9 missile, and that this development would pose a threat to the US Minuteman force.[8]

Some critics of multiple warheads (MIRV and MRV) viewed these as such a "destabilizing" technological development that they

[5] McGeorge Bundy, "To Cap the Volcano," *Foreign Affairs*, vol. 48 (October 1969), p. 9.
[6] See *World Armaments and Disarmament, SIPRI Yearbook 1969/70* (Stockholm: Almqvist and Wiksell, 1970), pp. 36-58; *The Military Balance 1971-1972* (London: Institute for Strategic Studies, September 1971), pp. 1-2. See also *New York Times*, October 11 and 20, 1971.
[7] *Ibid.*, February 27 and October 3, 1971.
[8] *Ibid.*, February 9, 1971. But as of Spring 1972, Defense Secretary Laird and other US defense officials were saying that the Soviets were actually deploying three rather than six warheads on their ICBMs. It was estimated by some that about 85 Soviet SS-11s would be fitted with three nuclear warheads each by mid-1972. *Washington Post*, March 7, 1972.

assigned the highest priority to banning them, despite the fact that such a ban is not verifiable. Herbert Scoville, for example, who is a former official of the Arms Control and Disarmament Agency, conceded that even onsite inspection of a MIRV ban would not be reliable; yet he argued that the risks from an unlimited MIRV race outweigh the risks from possible violations of a MIRV ban. He held that MIRV control can be achieved by imposing a ban on the testing and production as well as the development of MIRV.[9] The weakness of this position is that it may have had a good deal of validity six or seven years ago, before the United States and the Soviet Union began to fire missiles for the testing of multiple warheads. We should not forget that it was Defense Secretary Robert McNamara's aversion to ABM, and his conviction that it would always be cheaper to saturate defensive systems with additional offensive warheads, which led the US government to press the development of MIRV both to dissuade the Soviets from developing Galosh antimissile missiles and to neutralize advocates of ABM in this country. It is highly probable that both the United States and the Soviet Union know enough by now about the performance of multiple warheads to conclude that it is in their interest to deploy them even if their testing in the future should be prohibited by agreement. A ban on the testing of multiple warheads is verifiable, and thus it would make some sense in its own right if in the opinion of weapons experts it would inhibit the achievement of greater on-target accuracy for multiple warheads. But a ban on testing, which is verifiable, cannot be regarded as a safeguard for a ban on deployment, which is not verifiable.

In any event, by the early 1970s it was too late for a ban on the deployment of MIRV. Many US weapons have, we know, already been MIRVed. An agreement to prohibit further deployment could not provide for the undeployment of those MIRVs already deployed. But such an agreement would create strong political inhibitions against the further deployment of MIRV in US weapons systems, without creating symmetrical inhibitions in the USSR. The Soviets could go on for years arming most of their missiles with multiple warheads, and even increasing the number of warheads in every missile. If MIRV is destablizing when both sides are free to deploy it,

[9] *Ibid.*, series of two articles, February 8 and 9, 1971.

it is potentially much more destabilizing if only one side remains politically uninhibited from deploying it indefinitely into the future. Thus an unpoliceable ban on MIRV would violate the fundamental principle, accepted in the McCloy-Zorin Agreement, that no arms limitation measure should place either side at an unfair disadvantage with respect to national security.

One of the persistent problems of SALT pertained to the definition of "strategic" weapons. We might be tempted initially to define a "strategic weapon" as one which can reach the territory of the other superpower, but this gives rise to difficulties. The Soviets have frequently sought to include within this category the five hundred US planes based in NATO Europe and aboard Sixth Fleet carriers in the Mediterranean—planes which, according to the US vocabulary, are deployed for the "tactical" defense of Western Europe. The United States has taken the positon that if NATO-assigned aircraft are to be counted in on the ground that they are capable of reaching targets in the Soviet Union, then the seven hundred medium- and intermediate-range missiles located in western Russia and targeted on Western Europe must also be included.[10] In other words, if the two superpowers are engaged in strategic arms negotiations, and both of them regard the situation in Europe as one of strategic importance, then forward-based systems (FBS) and their counterparts must eventually be taken into account in SALT calculations. Europe is a region whose peace depends upon intricate and subtle linkages. Nuclear weapons in Europe are related to conventional force levels in Europe, and both are related to strategic nuclear weapons systems deployed outside Europe. Defense Secretary Melvin Laird held that the proper forum for discussing the possible reduction of US fighter-bombers deployed within range of the USSR is not SALT but a conference on mutual balanced force reductions (MBFR) in Europe, composed of NATO and the Warsaw Pact.[11] More will be said on this point subsequently.

As soon as SALT got under way, a central focus of debate was the question whether the United States should be willing to negotiate a

---

[10] *New York Times,* December 24, 1970.
[11] *Ibid.,* February 5, 1971.

separate agreement to ban ABM as demanded by the Soviets, or hold out for an agreement encompassing both offensive and defensive missiles. Advocates of the separate agreement argued that a ban on ABM would help to pave the way for a subsequent limitation on offensive deployments. The Nixon Administration, in this writer's opinion, was well-advised to take the position that the offense-defense problem is a single problem and should be negotiated as such. First of all, it was the Soviet deployment of large numbers of SS-9s and the threat of deploying other large ICBMs, capable of hurling three to six warheads at Minuteman silos, which reduced the invulnerability of the US land-based missile force and increased the US motivation to deploy a Safeguard system around selected Minuteman sites. Secondly, an ABM-only agreement would be more likely to diminish than to augment the Soviet incentive to negotiate a limitation on offensive missile systems. Third, a combined defense-offense agreement would be, compared to an ABM-only agreement, both strategically more significant (because it would halt both ongoing and planned deployments) and politically more viable (because it would reduce apprehensions in the United States as well as in the Soviet Union). Thus, the fact of the offense-defense linkage announced in Washington and Moscow on May 20, 1971,[12] was more important than the precise final form of the ABM limit—whether zero-ABM deployment (never very likely), equal ABM deployment around the two national capitals only (politically awkward in the US), or an ABM freeze at an agreed low level (to protect both capitals and a small portion of the ICBM forces). There was no problem in assigning to ABM a priority in the negotiations, so long as the final agreement would include both ABM and ICBMs. But there was reason to be concerned over the possibility, referred to in the joint SALT communique early in 1972, that there would be a formal treaty limiting ABM, combined with an "interim agreement" on offensive weapons, pending a subsequent solution to the problem of submarine-based missiles, unless the duration of the treaty would be clearly dependent upon the achievement in the near future of an equally binding treaty covering offensive weapons.[13]

[12] *Ibid.*, May 21, 1971. For an official statement of President Nixon's position on the offense-defense linkage, see *U. S. Foreign Policy for the 1970's*. A Report to the Congress by Richard Nixon, President of the United States, February 9, 1972, pp. 173-174.

[13] *New York Times*, February 5, 1972.

A certain amount of gamesmanship is inevitable in strategic arms negotiations. Each side at times manifested suspicion that its rival was trying to use SALT to gain or to perpetuate a unilateral military advantage. Each side oscillated between optimistic and pessimistic estimates of the prospects for agreement. At one time, the Soviets slowed down or halted the deployment of SS-9s; and at another time, they resumed construction related to very large missiles. Similarly, the United States would announce a decision to extend the deployment of Safeguard around certain Minuteman sites, or to defer such extension, at least partially, pending the outcome of SALT. In this way, each played upon the deployment option which it knew was most worrisome to the other. Thus, both superpowers combined the opposite processes of building "bargaining chips" one day and making overt gestures the next calculated to show their desire for agreement. Each side wished to keep the negotiations going. Neither wished to give away anything substantial without obtaining something from the other. Both sought to obtain the best possible terms in whatever bargain they would finally reach.

There was no reason to believe that the assumption of approximate parity would last very long in the absence of a SALT agreement. The third edition of *Jane's Weapons Systems*, published in late 1971, carried this conclusion: "Russia now has the initiative in weapons technology. Whereas for a long time it was assumed—with considerable justification—that the NATO countries had a clear lead in the development of sophisticated weapons, it is now clear that the USSR has extinguished that lead and is now outstripping the West."[14] For three years, US defense and arms control planners wondered whether the Soviets would be content to level off at crude parity, or whether they might try to sustain and increase their recent momentum in an effort to achieve the kind of strategic superiority which the United States has for all practical purposes renounced. Such superiority, even if not intended for surprise-attack purposes, could be exploited to the Soviets' advantage in critical political-military confrontations, especially in the sensitive NATO area.

[14] *Ibid.*, November 21, 1971.

Those who are skeptical of SALT's prospects for success often contend that while American writers frequently speak of "parity," no such concept can be found in Soviet strategic literature. From this they go on to argue that it could prove disastrously unwise for the United States to hold itself in check while the Soviets come on with a rush. But it has been precisely the central US purpose in SALT to find out whether the Soviet political leaders are ready to accept the notion of parity and to impose it upon the Soviet military. The Soviets could not enter upon a Phase I SALT agreement and continue to deploy land-based missiles. But given the present Soviet lead in land-based missiles, the United States sought a Phase I agreement while still enjoying both a substantial advantage in respect to the total number of warheads and the freedom to expand its sea-based deterrent, if need be, to ensure the prolongation of parity. Walter Slocombe has noted that one of the principal advantages to be derived from a SALT agreement is that it would reduce the danger that "parity is merely a prelude to substantial American inferiority"—an inferiority with "great potential for creating continued and politically disturbing anxiety."[15]

Some thirty months after the Helsinki-Vienna negotiations began, the United States and the Soviet Union signed an ABM Treaty, an Interim Agreement on strategic offensive weapons, and a related Protocol at Moscow on May 26, 1972. The signing marked the climax of the Summit Conference between President Nixon and General Secretary Brezhnev. The ABM Treaty is of unlimited duration (although subject to review at five-year intervals). The Interim Agreement and accompanying Protocol are for five years, unless replaced earlier by a formal treaty covering offensive weapons.[16]

Under the ABM Treaty, the two superpowers renounce the option of deploying a nationwide defense system based on existing ABM technology—that is, the Safeguard and Galosh systems which depend upon phased-array radars and involve both short-range and long-range interception. Each side is permitted to deploy a total of two

[15] Slocombe, *op. cit.*, p. 18.
[16] Texts in *New York Times*, May 29, 1972. Subsequently published in *Arms Control and Disarmament Agreements 1959-1972*, pp. 108-119.

hundred ABM's—a hundred around the national capital and a hundred around a missile site geographically far enough away from the capital to make it difficult to use the two sites together as a base for a future national defense network. According to the "Agreed Interpretations" made public later, the distance separating the centers of the two permitted sites was set at "no less than 1,300 kilometers."[17]

Up to the time the Treaty was concluded, the Soviets were known to have deployed ABMs only around Moscow. The United States had not deployed missile defenses around Washington, but had been constructing two Safeguard sites—one at Grand Forks Air Force Base, North Dakota, and one at Malmstrom Air Force Base, Montana. The latter project was immediately discontinued by order of Defense Secretary Melvin Laird.[18]

The ABM Treaty contains other prohibitions, corollary yet significant. Neither party may (1) keep more than fifteen ABM launchers at test ranges; (2) develop, test, or deploy ABM systems or components which are sea-based, air-based, or mobile land-based; (3) develop, test, or deploy ABM launchers capable of launching multiple missiles or of being rapidly reloaded; (4) upgrade existing antiaircraft defense systems to the level of an ABM capability, or test them in an ABM mode; (5) deploy, in the future, radars for early warning of strategic ballistic missile attack except at locations along the periphery of its national territory and oriented outward; (6) store ABMs in excess of the number allowed to each side; (7) transfer ABMs to other states, or deploy them outside its national territory. Article VII specifically states, however, that apart from the limitations spelled out in the Treaty, modernization and replacement of ABM systems or their components may be carried out.

In the "Agreed Interpretations," the parties further concurred that if ABM systems based on "other physical principles" (an obvious reference to laser and perhaps other technologies) should be created in the future, they will discuss such developments under those provisions pertaining to the standing consultative commission

[17] *New York Times*, June 14, 1972.
[18] *Ibid.*, May 28, 1972.

(treated below) and the review of the Treaty at five-year intervals. But the ABM Treaty as it stands does not prohibit research and development in new missile defense technologies, nor does it prohibit the deployment of new and more effective ABMs as replacements for existing ones under the Treaty. Moreover, although the Treaty strictly speaking prohibits the deployment of all antimissile technologies, whether actual or potential, except as provided for in the agreement, nevertheless it specifies that if a new principle of defense should emerge (such as one based upon lasers), further discussions would be necessary in order to work out specific limitations upon its deployment.

The ABM Treaty does not provide for onsite inspection. Article XII states that each party shall use national technical means of verification to assure compliance by the other party, in a manner consistent with generally recognized principles of international law. In the same article, each pledges not to interfere with the legitimate verifying activities of the other. This means, among other things, that neither party should take advantage of its undoubted capability to interfere with the operations of the other country's reconnaissance satellites.

The signatories agree to establish a standing consultative commission to handle questions and problems likely to arise in connection with the implementation of the Treaty, specifically concerning compliance with obligations assumed, unintended interference with national verification activities, possible changes in the strategic situation which might have a bearing on provisions of the Treaty, procedures and dates for the destruction or dismantling of ABM systems in excess of the permitted numbers, proposals for increasing the viability of the Treaty and for negotiating further measures aimed at limiting strategic arms. The presumption is that if two states find it to their advantage to enter such an agreement and wish to keep it from being repudiated, they will also perceive an interest in satisfying each other that they are living up to their part of the bargain.

Thus, when one side becomes suspicious of a development within the other country, and raises a question as to its compatibility with the terms of the Treaty, under normal circumstances the party challenged will be motivated to supply "positive evidence" by way of explanation in order to show that the event, activity, or object does not indicate a violation of the Treaty. Either side, for example, might in the future become worried that the other is trying to upgrade its surface-to-air (SAM) missiles and give them an ABM capability, or that the other is deploying large phased-array radars (in excess of three million watts) ostensibly for the purpose of tracking objects in outer space or for use as technical means of national verification, but actually for the purpose of preparing a national missile-defense network. Such suspicions, if they do arise, might prove very difficult to dispel unless the party whose intentions are suspect voluntarily invites onsite inspection. If in the final analysis the suspicious party cannot be satisfied, and if it becomes convinced that it is being placed at an unfair disadvantage, this would create an abnormal situation and probably pose a serious crisis for the continued viability of the Treaty.

The kind of mutuality of interest implied in the foregoing discussion is not the same as "the fear of offending world public opinion" which used to be cited many years ago as a possible bulwark against violating arms agreements. The Soviet leaders have shown more than once that when national military security is thought to be at stake, they do not care much for world public opinion. But they do have to pay attention to the opinion of US political and military policymakers, and *vice versa.* We can expect that, when both sides feel their freedom to deploy strategic weapons to be limited by a diplomatic agreement, they will intensify their surveillance efforts. Shortly after the agreements were signed, the US government announced that it would establish a special group to start monitoring Soviet compliance with the agreement as of July 1, 1972, so as to avoid a repetition of the embarrassment which the United States experienced in the late summer of 1970, when it was unprepared to cope promptly with reports that Soviet missiles in Egypt were being moved in violation of the ceasefire agreement.

By this ABM Treaty, the United States renounces the nationwide deployment of an antimissile defense system (Safeguard) which is generally assumed to be technologically superior to that of the Soviets (Galosh). In recent years, the leadership of neither one of the superpowers has seemed to be completely convinced (to the point of enthusiasm) as to the efficacy of missile defense—that is, of ABM's decisive significance in a nuclear exchange. In the United States, a debate had raged over this point for at least twelve years—sometimes a confusing debate, it must be admitted, inasmuch as the opponents of ABM often seemed unable to make up their minds whether it was laughably unworkable from a technical standpoint or frightfully destabilizing from a strategic standpoint. Soviet spokesmen, for their part, had stopped boasting (after Khrushchev) about possessing a capability "to hit a fly in space." Neither Washington nor Moscow seemed too anxious to undertake a major new round in strategic arms competition by deploying a nationwide defense system which would use existing ABM technology.

Soviet military planners had more reason than their US counterparts to be uncomfortable at the prospect that the other side might deploy on a large scale, and within a relatively short period of time, an ABM system of respectable credibility. But the Soviets probably realized that the Nixon Administration might run into domestic political difficulty if it tried to achieve the deployment of Safeguard throughout the national territory. It is never easy, of course, to determine what might have happened, but the Soviets could not predict with certainty what the American reaction would have been if SALT had collapsed in failure. President Nixon, speaking at a press conference on June 29, 1972, indicated that both the Soviet Union and the United States were prepared to spend large sums for the deployment of large numbers of additional strategic weapons in the absence of an agreement.[10]

Whereas the ABM Treaty embodies a form of arms limitation to which the Soviets assigned the higher priority, the Interim Agreement and the Protocol deal with a subject on which US policymakers were more anxious to obtain agreement—namely, a freeze on ICBMs. But while the ABM Treaty is of unlimited duration (unless one party should invoke the escape clause of "supreme interest"), the Interim Agreement limiting strategic offensive arms is to remain in

[10] *Ibid.*, June 30, 1972.

force for a period of five years "unless replaced earlier by an agreement on more complete measures limiting strategic offensive arms." Both sides declare it to be their objective to conduct active follow-on negotiations toward concluding such an agreement as soon as possible. Presumably, if they should prove unable to reach agreement for a permanent treaty on offensive weapons within the five-year period, the present Interim Agreement could be extended by mutual consent. Otherwise it would expire, with the result that the two parties would be bound to observe an ABM Treaty but not bound to observe limitations on the further deployment of land-based or sea-based ICBMs. That was precisely the situation which the US government sought to avoid in originally linking defensive and offensive weapons systems for purposes of negotiation. Naturally, one can argue that if the Interim Agreement should expire, and if the Soviets were to resume the deployment of ICBMs, the United States could then invoke the "supreme interest" clause of the ABM Treaty. This will be a difficult thing for the American political system to do; there may be a heated debate, first over the facts of the situation and then over the necessity of such a drastic reaction. Perhaps the problem will never arise. But the possibility that an arms control measure such as the ABM Treaty will someday come under the strain of reexamination and the danger of reversal is now somewhat greater than it would have been had the final effectiveness of the ABM Treaty been clearly contingent upon the coming into force of a treaty limiting offensive weapons. Whether the conclusion of the ABM Treaty will increase or decrease the motivation of the Soviet Union to negotiate a treaty on offensive weapons remains to be seen.

The Interim Agreement pertains only to US and Soviet fixed land-based ICBMs and submarine-launched ballistic missiles (SLBMs.) It places no limitations on mobile land-based missiles, strategic bombers, US forward-based systems (FBS) in Europe, the Mediterranean, Southeast Asia, and the Far East, or on Soviet IR-MRBMs in western Russia which are targeted on Western Europe. The provisions of the Interim Agreement are as follows:

> *Article I.* The parties undertake not to start construction of additional fixed land-based intercontinental ballistic missile (ICBM) launchers after July 1, 1972.

> *Article II.* The parties undertake not to convert land-based launchers for light ICBMs, or for ICBMs of older types deployed prior to 1964, into land-based launchers for heavy ICBMs of types deployed after that time.
>
> *Article III.* The parties undertake to limit submarine-launched ballistic missile (SLBM) launchers and modern ballistic missile submarines to the numbers operational and under construction on the date of signature of this interim agreement, and in addition launchers and submarines constructed under procedures established by the parties as replacements for an equal number of ICBM launchers of older type deployed prior to 1964 or for launchers on older submarines.

Article IV allows for modernization and replacement of strategic offensive missiles and launchers covered by the Interim Agreement. Article V deals with national technical means of verification in terms identical with those in the ABM Treaty. In Article VI, the parties agree to use the standing consultative commission set up under the ABM Treaty for purposes of implementing the Interim Agreement. Articles VII and VIII deal with the pursuit of further negotiated agreements, the coming into force of the Interim Agreement, and the right to withdraw if supreme interests are jeopardized.

The Protocol stipulates that the United States may have no more than 710 ballistic missile launchers on submarines (SLBMs) and no more than 44 modern ballistic missile submarines. The Soviet Union is limited to 950 launchers on 62 modern submarines. Since at present the US possesses 41 missile submarines and the Soviets 42 (in operation or under construction), the increase in the number of SLBMs (for the US from 656 to 710, and for the Soviets from 750 to 950) will be achieved by replacing equal numbers of ballistic missile launchers of older types deployed prior to 1964 or on older submarines. We can infer from the Protocol, therefore, that the United States intends to convert its 54 land-based Titan missiles into three new modern submarines, each armed with eighteen missiles, and that the Soviets expect to convert 210 of their older land-based missiles (SS-7s and SS-8s) into SLBMs on twenty additional modern submarines not yet operational or under construction. Thus the

Interim Agreement reflects an awareness by the superpowers of the growing vulnerability of land-based missile forces in the era of MIRV and increasing warhead accuracy, and hence of the growing importance of sea-based deterrence. This fact will undoubtedly attract a greater amount of attention in strategic and arms control literature during the coming years, and might figure prominently in negotiations for the next phase of SALT.

US spokesmen in recent years had often asserted that the Helsinki-Vienna negotiations were based upon the assumption that the SALT would serve to codify overall US-Soviet strategic parity. Actually, the Interim Agreement assigns numerical superiority in ICBMs and SLBMs to the Soviet Union. After all the permissible conversions from land-based to sea-based missiles have been made, the USSR will have 1,408 ICBMs to 1,000 for the United States (a margin of about forty percent), and 950 to 710 SLBMs (a margin of some 34 percent). At the present time, the United States is thought to be in a position to forfeit such a numerical advantage in launchers to the Soviets because the former possesses certain compensating advantages—in bomber technology, forward-based systems, MIRV technology, missile submarine technology, and the total number of warheads presently available to each side—reported to be 5,700 for the US and 2,500 for the Soviet Union.[20]

Although little is publicly known in Western quarters about the current state of Soviet MIRV (as distinct from MRV) technology, US planners must assume that the Soviets can eventually master the technology of independently targetable warheads if they wish to do so. Moreover, Western strategic analysisits take it for granted that the USSR already possesses at least a four-to-one advantage over the United States in the total "throw weight" of missiles, measured in

[20] *Ibid.*, May 27, 1972. The United States began to replace Minuteman I with Minuteman III missiles in June 1970. Minuteman III, which carries three MIRV warheads, each of approximately 200 kilotons, has greater survivability and penetrability, longer range and higher accuracy. The US also began to deploy Poseidon missiles in place of A-3 missiles on 31 nuclear submarines. Since each submarine carries sixteen missiles and each Poseidon missile will carry an average of ten 50-kiloton warheads, the planned deployment involves a total of 4,960 warheads. If all planned MIRV programs are carried through, the United States will have nearly 8,000 strategic missile warheads deliverable by 1975—not counting several thousand warheads that will be deliverable by strategic bombers and forward-based tactical aircraft. See *World Armaments and Disarmament, SIPRI Yearbook 1972*, pp. 5-8 and 13. See also *The Military Balance 1972-73* (London: Institute for Strategic Studies, September 1972), Appendix I, "SALT and the Strategic Balance," pp. 83-86.

megatonnage. If the Soviets should be determined to replace larger warheads with smaller multiple warheads, they could eventually surpass the United States in the total number of warheads deployed, since the United States will be prevented by the present Agreement from achieving any substantial increase in its total payload capacity.[21] In this particular dimension, the Interim Agreement provides the Soviet Union with greater "room for expansion" than it does the United States. On March 21, 1973, the *New York Times* carried a report from Administration military analysts that the Soviets had conducted their first successful test of a computer aboard a new ICBM. This could mark a significant advance both toward increased accuracy of the SS-11 type of missile and toward the development of accurate MIRVs.

There is no reason, however, to assume that all of the significant technological advances in the post-SALT period will be made by the Soviet Union. Few knowledgeable analysts really expect the SALT I Agreements, which limit only a few crude quantitative variables and even fewer qualitative variables in the realm of strategic weaponry, to bring military-technological competition between the superpowers to a halt. Rather, the agreements are likely to have the effect of shifting the competition from the quantitative to the qualitative dimension. The variables frozen by SALT I—numbers of launchers and missiles, and the weight of the pre-1964 missiles—will not be the only important variables, or even necessarily the most crucial ones, during the coming decade. Research and develpment can be expected to continue on both sides. Both sides will seek to improve the invulnerability of their land-based missiles through hardening or "superhardening," the accuracy of their missile guidance systems, and multiple warhead and SLBM technology. In all of these areas, it is generally held that the United States already leads the Soviet Union. Defense Secretary Laird, testifying before the Senate Armed Services Committee on the SALT Agreements, said that he could support their ratification only if the Congress at the same time author-

[21] See the statement by Senator Henry M. Jackson, Chairman of the Subcommittee on Strategic Arms Limitation Talks of the Senate Armed Services Committee, *Congressional Record*, June 1, 1972. It should be noted that, according to the "Agreed Interpretations," during the period of the Interim Agreement, the process of modernization and replacement will involve no significant increase in the dimensions of land-based ICBM silo launchers—that is, no more than ten to fifteen percent of present dimensions.

ized the Department of Defense to proceed with the development of new strategic weapons systems permitted under the SALT accords—especially the B-1 heavy bomber and the Trident submarine.[22] The B-1, a supersonic manned intercontinental bomber, is planned to replace the B-52s and FB-111s before the end of the current decade. The Trident submarine would become the basis of an Undersea Long-Range Missile System (ULMS) to replace the Poseidon system. The ULMS missile, using high energy propellants, would have a much longer range than Poseidon, and would greatly increase the oceanic area in which the US sea-based deterrent force could be dispersed, concealed, and protected. Administration statements about new strategic weapons systems were probably calculated to serve at least two purposes: (1) to reassure those who were apprehensive that the SALT I Agreements might come to have adverse effects upon US security; and (2) to lay the basis for a post-SALT I defense program which would motivate the Soviet leaders to negotiate seriously toward a permananet limitation on strategic offensive weapons.

Despite the numerical discrepancies with respect to the total number of launchers permitted each side, the SALT I Agreements probably do codify overall strategic parity, and need not place the United States at an unfair disadvantage, provided that the US government pursues a comprehensive R & D program as it has all through the era of arms control agreements, and maintains a prudent, nonprovocative readiness to deploy new weapons systems as these may be necessary to preserve the effectiveness and credibility of the US strategic deterrent.[23]

Reactions to the SALT I Agreements were mixed. Henry Kissinger called them "without precedent . . . in all relevant modern history," since never before "have the world's two most powerful nations, divided by ideology, history, and conflicting interests, placed their central armaments under formally agreed limitation and restraint."[24] Bernard T. Feld was torn between the impulse to cry "bravo" and

[22] *New York Times,* June 21, 1972.
[23] For a discussion of the scope of the US-Soviet R & D effort, see Milton Leitenberg, "The Present State of the World's Arms Race," *Bulletin of the Atomic Scientists* (January 1972), pp. 15-21.
[24] Congressional briefing by Dr. Henry A. Kissinger, Office of the White House Press Secretary, June 15, 1972, p. 1.

the desire to shout "fraud." He noted that the Agreements would avert a costly and futile race in ABM systems and halt the upward spiral in the deployed numbers of land-based and sea-based missiles. But he lamented the fact that the Agreements had not been reached earlier; that they fell short of a total ban on ABMs; that they failed to provide for a ban on MIRVs or for a comprehensive nuclear test ban; and that they "may actually encourage a shifting of the arms race from the quantitative to the qualitative."[25] George W. Rathjens commented in a similar vein, and critized the Nixon Administration for submitting the SALT Agreements to the Congress in the context of simultaneous requests for the funding of new strategic weapons programs, particularly the B-1 bomber and the Trident submarine.[26] Donald G. Brennan roundly scored the SALT accords because they bind the signatories not to defend themselves against each other or against any other party, and commit both sides to a strategic posture of "mutual assured destruction" for which the appropriate acronym, says Brennan, is MAD.[27] In Brennan's view, such a posture might have to be reluctantly tolerated if there were absolutely no alternative; but to deem it desirable and to make it the preferred goal of arms control negotiations is nothing short of bizarre.

The US Senate overwhelmingly approved the ABM Treaty by a vote of 88 to two on August 3, 1972.[28] Consideration of the agreement limiting offensive weapons, however, was delayed by a move on the part of Senator Henry M. Jackson, apparently with some ambiguous support from the White House, to offer a substitute resolution that would put pressure on the Soviet Union, during the life of the five-year agreement, not to take even permissible steps to strengthen its arsenal that would pose a threat to the survivability of US strategic forces. The Jackson Amendment would also call upon the President to achieve a follow-on offensive weapons agreement with the Soviets that would assure aggregate numerical equality, taking throw-weight into account.[29] Actually, the Interim Agreement

[25] Bernard T. Feld, "Looking to SALT-II," *Bulletin of the Atomic Scientists*, vol. 38 (June 1972), pp. 2-3.
[26] George W. Rathjens, "The SALT Agreements: An Appraisal," *ibid.*, vol. 28 (November 1972), pp. 8-10.
[27] Donald G. Brennan, in "Strategic Forum: the SALT Agreements," *Survival*, vol. 14 (September/October 1972), pp. 216-219.
[28] *New York Times*, August 4, 1972.
[29] *Ibid.*, August 4, 8 and 11, 1972.

was an executive agreement which did not require formal approval by the Senate, but President Nixon nevertheless sought a joint Senate-House resolution approving it. The House passed its equivalent of the Jackson Amendment in August, and the Senate in mid-September approved the Interim Agreement with the proviso that any future US-Soviet treaty limiting offensive arms must be based on the principle of numerical equality.[30]

SALT II negotiations began in Geneva in November 1972, with both parties probing. In the new talks, the United States will probably place primary emphasis upon the effort to negotiate a comprehensive treaty on strategic offensive weapons systems. The Soviet Union will probably insist that a comprehensive treaty must include strategic bombers and forward-based systems capable of delivering attacks against Soviet territory. Some arms control planners would like to see a ceiling on the total number of MIRVs made a part of SALT II, but this will remain unlikely unless there is some dramatic breakthrough in the technology of national verification capabilities. Neither side is really interested in subscribing to limitations that it cannot unilaterally monitor to its own satisfaction.

As suggested earlier, the SALT I accords will increase the importance of sea-based deterrence; for even if each side, as a result of MIRV technology, improved accuracy of missile and warhead guidance systems, and the low-level limit on ABM systems, could theoretically wipe out the adversary's land-based ICBMs in a surprise first strike, neither side is able to neutralize the retaliatory threat posed by the other's submarine-launched ballistic missiles. Herbert Scoville, Jr., notes that antisubmarine warfare (ASW) technology "is so far behind that it could not possibly threaten the submarine deterrent, if it can threaten it at all, until far in the future."[31] To preserve indefinitely the invulnerability of SLBMs, Scoville proposes that future SALT negotiations include consideration of arms control agreements to curb developments in the area of ASW—comparable to the agreement to curb ABM on land. This, he says, could involve

[30] *Ibid.*, September 15, 1972.
[31] Herbert Scoville, Jr., "Missile Submarines and National Security," *Scientific American*, vol. 226 (June 1972), p. 16.

a ban on acoustic detection systems as well as submarine-tracking ships and aircraft in specified oceanic areas.[32] Scoville admits that such a ban would be extremely difficult to control. Quite aside from the policing problem, which would be formidable to say the least, ASW does not constitute a single unified technology, but a "mixed bag" that cuts across a large number of general military purposes, and which involves nuclear and conventional, strategic and tactical applications. NATO planners, who have long recognized the crucial importance of ASW technology for an alliance heavily dependent upon maritime supply lines, and who have become increasingly concerned in recent years over the growth of Soviet naval capabilities, will carefully scrutinize proposals for self-denying limitations in anti-submarine defense.

Undoubtedly, some arms control analysts are hopeful that SALT II will produce agreements for the substantial reduction of strategic weapons levels. But as we have seen before, the Soviets have shown few signs of being seriously interested in the destruction or dismantling of weapons already in existence. They will, of course, get some practice in this area if they phase out old land-based missiles in favor of more modern sea-based missiles. But as they keep their eye on the growth potential of China's nuclear arsenal, the Soviet leaders will probably wish to preserve the largest possible margin of superiority over the PRC as long as they can do so. They might even attempt to argue that, given their geostrategic position, they cannot be content to settle permanently for strategic parity with the United States, but must move toward a "two-power standard" as the British did at the turn of this century. It would be irresponsible in the extreme for any future US leadership to acquiesce in such a specious Soviet argument, because it is impossible to foretell whether and when the USSR and the PRC might move toward rapprochement in their relations with each other. The history of international politics in the twentieth century provides ample evidence that nations are capable of such fundamental reversals of orientation. It would be the height of foolishness to base national security policy upon the conviction that it could not happen.

[32] Herbert Scoville, Jr., "Beyond SALT ONE," *Foreign Affairs,* vol. 50 (April 1972), pp. 492-494.

Rather than move toward strategic weapons reductions, the Soviets may prefer to focus upon negotiations for redeployments of existing military forces for the purpose of lowering international tensions and promoting detente, especially in Europe. Under this hypothesis, SALT II would be linked to mutual balanced force reductions (MBFR) and the phasing out of forward-based systems in Europe. MBFR is a subject of considerably greater political-military complexity than the strategic weapons systems that were the subject of SALT I negotiations, if for no other reason than the fact that MBFR would require agreement among a fairly large number of NATO and Warsaw Pact governments. It might very well involve the conduct of intricate, simultaneous negotiations at several levels and in different places. There might be bilateral US-Soviet talks in SALT II; bilateral contacts between individual NATO and Warsaw Pact governments; discussions between individuals or groups representing the two alliance systems; and discussions within a 33-nation European Security Conference. Exploratory talks on force reductions in Central Europe got under way in Vienna on the last day of January 1973.[33] If there is to be one central negotiating forum for MBFR, certainly there will be several "echo chambers," and the process might well last for several years.

MBFR poses problems of considerable complexity. The French fear that if the withdrawal of forces should be limited initially to the United States and the Soviet Union, West Germany's Bundeswehr would then become the dominant military force in Central Europe. Naturally, all of the countries with troops in Central Europe will wish to be represented as full participants, and some peripheral countries (in NATO, for example, Norway, Denmark, Italy, Greece, and Turkey) will also want a voice in alliance decisions that affect their future security and which might lead to economic savings in the realm of defense. NATO members at some distance from the Central European front will undoubtedly want assurances that Soviet troops pulled back from the central sector will not be immediately redeployed on the northern and southeastern flanks (for example, near

[33] *New York Times*, February 1, 1973. A disagreement developed almost immediately over the parties to the negotiations. The West wanted Hungary to participate as a full-fledged member; the Soviets insisted that Hungary take part on a limited basis as being outside the area of negotiation of force reductions in Central Europe. The West finally conceded on this point. *Ibid.*, May 15, 1973.

the borders of Norway and Turkey), thereby shifting the locus of the security threat.

Most NATO strategists remain convinced that a purely one-for-one reduction in the NATO and Warsaw Pact areas would be disadvantageous to the West, unless perhaps it was certain that the unit being withdrawn by the Soviets would be redeployed on the Chinese border. (In September 1972, it was reported that the Soviets had recently added three mechanized divisions to its buildup along the Chinese border, bringing to 49 the number of divisions known to be in that sector, compared to fifteen in 1968.)[34] In the event that there would be no necessity to redeploy all of the withdrawn Soviet divisions to the Far East, the question confronting NATO planners is whether the Soviets can be persuaded to make larger numerical cuts than the United States, or demobilize part of the forces pulled back, or accept restrictions on and surveillance of force deployments and movements that would add to the time needed to reinforce units in the Warsaw Pact area, while simultaneously increasing NATO's warning time and reinforcement capability.

Another major set of questions pertains to the kinds of trade-offs that might be arranged—for example, NATO's quick reaction aircraft for Warsaw Pact tanks, or NATO's tactical nuclear weapons for Soviet IR-MRBMs in western Russia. Each weapons system redeployment to be discussed would pose its own constellation of military, political, and perhaps economic subtleties, and this will influence the determination of where in the interlocking structure of European East-West negotiations the discussions should take place, and among which parties. In any event, the Soviets probably look upon MBFR as a means of controlling the rate and mode of change in the European political-military environment more effectively than would be the case if the United States were to carry out unilateral withdrawals. In Soviet eyes, the latter might produce some unforeseen and undesirable consequences (for example, increased political pressure for the USSR to reduce its military presence in Eastern Europe before the Kremlin is ready to do so). What NATO planners must be concerned about is the danger that the Soviets will be able

[34] *Ibid.*, September 10, 1972.

to use MBFR and European security negotiations as a means of gaining leverage over the NATO military planning process, and of exploiting the disagreements that are more easily perceptible in an alliance of liberal democratic states. It will be important for the NATO countries, therefore, to develop as unified a strategy as possible to guide their conduct in the years of bargaining that lie ahead.[35]

The implications of SALT for European security and deterrence are still ambiguous. The general European reaction has been favorable, despite an uneasiness and uncertainty as to what the accords might portend for the future.[36] The nuclear-conventional balance of local forces in Europe has always been closely related in the thinking of strategic analysts to the nuclear equation outside of Europe proper. Perhaps the "codification of parity" between the United States and the Soviet Union will make the local balance of forces in Europe more important than ever, and thus make the actual imbalance of Warsaw Pact and NATO forces (which has been disadvantageous to the latter) less politically tolerable to the West Europeans than it has been in the past, when American strategic superiority was taken more for granted. Spreading through the minds of many well-informed West Europeans is the disturbing thought that, even though it will probably remain unthinkable for the Soviets to use their gross numerical superiority for the purpose of carrying out an actual military attack against Western Europe, nevertheless the Soviets might be able to project an image of military superiority in order to acquire greater political leverage over West European governments. This specter, combined with the possibility that the Mansfield type of thinking might eventually prevail in the formulation of US foreign policy, leads some Europeans to speak ominously of "the Finlandization of Europe"—as future possibility, not present reality.

[35] For a fuller discussion of problems associated with MBFR, see Christoph Bertram, *Mutual Force Reduction in Europe: The Political Aspects* (London: Institute for Strategic Studies, Adelphi Papers No. 84, 1972); Walter F. Hahn, "Nuclear Balance in Europe," *Foreign Affairs*, vol. 50 (April 1972), pp. 501-516; *The Military Balance 1972-73*, Appendix II, "The Theatre Balance between NATO and the Warsaw Pact," pp. 86-92. For a Soviet interpretation of MBFR problems, see Yu. Kostko, "Mutual Force Reductions in Europe," *Survival*, vol. 14 (September/October 1972), pp. 236-238. For a subtle analysis by a Belgian delegate to the North Atlantic Council, see Albert Willot, "Mutual and Balanced Force Reductions in Europe," *NATO Review*, no. 1 (1973), pp. 5-9.

[36] It is difficult to estimate the potential impact of SALT I upon European security because it is difficult to assess the overall effects of SALT upon the general global strategic equation. See William R. Kintner and Robert L. Pfaltzgraff, Jr., "Assessing the Moscow SALT Agreements," *Orbis*, vol. 16 (Summer 1972), pp. 341-360. In a similar vein, it is difficult to predict just what effect the application of the Nixon Doctrine will eventually have in Europe. See Walter F. Hahn, "The Nixon Doctrine: Design and Dilemmas," *ibid.*, pp. 361-376.

There are only two principal routes, either singly or in combination, by which the West Europeans could attempt to compensate for a drawing down of the American military presence in Europe. The first involves a substantial increase in European conventional forces. Proposals to this effect have never been popular in the past; and they are not likely to attract much support in the future, for the simple reason that the Europeans are much more interested in deterrence than in defense. This leaves as the other principal alternative the creation of a joint European nuclear deterrent force, probably growing out of an Anglo-French *entente nucleaire*. The concept has been discussed frequently since the early 1960s, and might seem more logical now that Britain is a member of the European Economic Community. Since British and French nuclear weapons and missiles are not covered by the SALT I Agreements, the British and French governments could, if they wished, coordinate their moves on the development of a sea-based deterrent force, toward which the former would contribute the warhead technology and the latter the missile propulsion. Some European strategic analysts might look in such a direction as a means of offsetting the Warsaw Pact's conventional force advantage, superior reinforcement capability, and Soviet MRBM-IRBM forces located in western Russia. Technologically, the West Europeans have better reason than the Chinese to regard a low-level ABM agreement between the superpowers as favorable to the possibility of creating a credible deterrent force.

Technologically speaking, there is no reason why the West Europeans could not create their own independent nuclear deterrent force, invested with at least a minimal credibility. But such a force would be very costly. There are few signs at present that the governments of Western Europe are seriously interested in trying to mobilize public support for the political and financial measures necessary to establish a European nuclear force. Despite the significant progress that has been made toward economic integration during the past two decades. Western Europe is still a long way from the kind of common foreign and defense policies that a joint deterrent would presuppose. In other words, there could be serious disagreements over the political-military control and use of such a force. The question of how Germany as a member of the Community would participate in the management of a European deterrent force would be highly controversial, and would generate another intensive dialogue among the Big Four comparable to that sparked a decade ago by the ill-fated proposal for the NATO Multilateral Force.

Certainly the Soviets would be adamantly opposed to the formation of a politically and strategically significant nuclear power on their immediate western flank. The French and the British governments would be wary of a West German role in a Community nuclear force, as would the government of Willy Brandt. Much will depend upon the policy of the United States, which can facilitate or hamper the development of European nuclear deterrence by granting or withholding authorization for the transfer from the UK to France of certain types of information pertaining to nuclear weapons previously transmitted from Washington to London. Since Article IX of the ABM Treaty forbids either party to transfer to other states ABM systems or components, the Soviet Union might argue that any future transfer of information concerning warhead and other nuclear weapons information contravenes this provision. (In a unilateral statement of April 18, 1972, the United States asserted that this article sets no precedent with respect to the transfer of strategic offensive arms, which may require a different solution.) Because of these and other complications, the British government, while ready to cooperate on defense matters to the extent that its Community partners (especially France) urge, probably will not take the initiative in pressing for a course of action aimed at anything beyond a European defense program that will remain closely coupled to the US strategic deterrent. British political-strategic analysts are well aware that if, on the one hand, the SALT I Agreements in some ways make the European allies of the US at least mildly interested in the prospects for a European nuclear effort, those same Agreements viewed in combination with the German-Eastern treaties, the Berlin Accord, and the stepped-up diplomatic activity relating to a European Security Conference, will probably cause a continued decline in public support for defense expenditures in Europe.

The effects of SALT I will, of course, be felt far beyond the European region. Brief mention must be made of the way in which other states, both nuclear and nonnuclear, are likely to assess the significance of the Moscow Agreements for their own future nuclear weapons and arms control policies. As we have seen earlier, a decision by India or Israel or Japan to go nuclear or to continue to abstain from nuclear weapons probably will not be determined primarily by estimating the outcome of SALT I; but foreign capitals can be expected to take the latter into account in assessing the changes within the international enviroment to which they must constantly adjust. Much will depend upon the manner in which the socalled threshold states perceive the emerging "multipolar balance" that is now commonly assumed to be replacing the older "bipolar balance," as the world moves from an era of Cold War confrontation toward a neo-Metternichian era of flexible negotiation. How will the threshold states attempt to take advantage of the new framework, occasionally characterized as "the waltz of the powers," in order to pursue their own national security and foreign policy objectives? What pitfalls and dangers might the threshold states discern in an international system in which the rigid alignments of former days seem in process of becoming "unstuck," especially in view of the superpowers' reluctance, as Stanley Hoffmann puts it, "to allow themselves to be dragged into partly alien causes and to let confrontations by proxies turn into direct clashes."[37]

Nearly a decade has passed since China joined the ranks of the nuclear powers in 1964, and there has been no addition to the list up to the present time. India and Israel are two of the most critical nonsigners of the Nonproliferation Treaty. Japan is one of the most important signers but nonratifiers. (West Germany and its original partners in the European Economic Community all refrained from ratifying the Nonproliferation Treaty until after agreements had been worked out between the members of Euratom and the International Atomic Energy Agency for the implementation of Treaty safeguards.[38]) India's success in the Bangladesh war, combined with the Treaty of Peace, Friendship, and Cooperation with the Soviet Union, has helped to revive India's sense of confidence in its ability to accomplish its basic security and foreign policy objectives, at least at

[37] Stanley Hoffmann, "Weighing the Balance of Power," *Foreign Affairs*, vol. 50 (July 1972), p. 618.
[38] See *The Structure and Content of Agreements between the Agency and States Required in Connection with the Treaty on the Non-Proliferation of Nuclear Weapons.*

the present time, without acquiring a nuclear force.[39] For Israel, the state of Soviet-US strategic rivalry in the Middle East continues to be important. For the time being, the withdrawal of the Soviet presence from Egypt has reduced the tensions and pressures under which the Israelis have lived; but the incentive to acquire and maintain a nuclear weapons capability for possible use as a last resort (even if not publicly announced in advance of an extremely grave security crisis) will endure for a country in Israel's circumstances until a stable peace has been established in the area. Japan, given its geographical position, the US-Japan Mutual Defense Treaty, and the still relatively low level of Chinese strategic nuclear delivery capabilities in a multipolar world, is probably under less pressure at the present time to "go nuclear" than either India or Israel. The Japanese, writes Richard Ellingworth, "are likely to put more faith in a nonmilitary overseas defense policy which would use money rather than arms as a means of persuasion."[40] In other words, so long as the Japanese are able to exert their influence on the world scene by exploiting their position as the world's third greatest economic power, and so long as the Japanese government can expect to obtain strategic support in a critical situation from the United States and perhaps from the Soviet Union as well, Tokyo may find the advantages of remaining nonnuclear more attractive than those of embarking upon the nuclear route.

But the future of the Nonproliferation Treaty remains doubtful. If any one of the principal threshold states decides to become a public nuclear power, the whole fabric of nonproliferation may begin to unravel. Certainly all three countries mentioned above are "close to" or "not very far from" the bomb. George H. Quester concludes: "Stemming the spread of nuclear weapons may not be hopeless, but it also may not ever be definitively accomplishable."[41] President Nixon's recent policies toward Moscow and Peking, the achievement of a peace settlement in Southeast Asia, and the emerging political climate of multilateral balance may all have subtle, indirect effects in

[39] The self-confidence is evident in the tone of the article by Indira Gandhi, "India and the World," *Foreign Affairs*, vol. 51 (October 1972), pp. 65-77.
[40] Richard Ellingworth, *Japanese Economic Policies and Security* (London: Institute for Strategic Studies, Adelphi Papers No. 90, October 1972), p. 3.
[41] George H. Quester, "Some Conceptual Problems in Nuclear Proliferation," *American Political Science Review*, vol. 76 (June 1972), p. 497.

New Delhi, Tel Aviv, and Tokyo that will compensate for what might otherwise be regarded as a certain disappointment that SALT I did not make more substantial progress toward the nuclear disarmament of the superpowers. It is still a debatable question, however, whether India really wants to see the Soviet Union reduce its strategic capabilities, or whether Japan and other countries want to see the United States reduce its forces and global commitments, or whether several countries in the world do not perceive very real advantages in preserving the precarious equilibrium now prevailing in the world.

China's policy will be a major factor. Will Peking continue to pursue the relatively restrained course which it has pursued in recent years—most markedly at the time of the Bangladesh crisis on the Indian subcontinent? China at the moment is wooing the new government of Premier Tanaka in Japan, and the Chinese government has noticeably muted its criticism of the US-Japan Mutual Defense Treaty since Nixon's Peking visit. But it is difficult to predict whether, as China's nuclear and missile capabilities grow during the next decade, Peking will become more militant around the Eurasian periphery, demanding the return of Taiwan, supporting Pakistan in a future conflict with India, aiding guerrilla movements in the Philippines, Southeast Asia, and the Middle East (where Peking might seek to spoil a Soviet-American accommodation if this should come within reach). Peking can be expected to strive toward a maximization of its nuclear deterrent capability against the USSR. In this connection, it should be noted that the ABM Treaty limits the superpowers to a "thin defense" which will not increase beyond 200 missiles so long as the Treaty is observed, and thus it gives China a fixed goal at which to aim in its effort to achieve some sort of credibility for its nuclear deterrent. Meanwhile, China denies aiming at superpower status.

In late 1972, China supported a resolution in the UN General Assembly's Political Committee to examine the prospects for a world disarmament conference. The Soviet Union enthusiastically backed the resolution, which passed overwhelmingly by 111 affirmative votes and only the United States abstaining. The United States took the position that a universal disarmament conference—presumably one attended by delegates from 136 states—would not be a forum for serious negotiations, but rather would wind up as a mere propaganda exercise, costly yet unproductive. After voting for the proposal, which called for a 35-member committee to study the opinions of governments on a world disarmament conference, the Chinese delegation declared that the Peking government would not actually participate in the committee but would exchange views with it. The Chinese made it clear that they were still opposed to the convocation of a world conference unless the nuclear powers would first accept Peking's conditions, which include the dismantling of all foreign bases and pulling back all troops from foreign soil.[42] If China's preconditions should prevail in a future General Assembly, as a result of the votes of middle and smaller powers (mainly from the Third World), then the conference would have to be postponed indefinitely, until after the complete withdrawal of US and Soviet forces from Western and Eastern Europe, respectively—something not yet even envisaged in MBFR negotiations—or else it would go forward with most of the nuclear powers and their principal allies absent. In the same session of the General Assembly, the United States and the Soviet Union both found themselves in the minority on a resolution calling for a comprehensive test ban, that is, one prohibiting underground tests as well as those in the atmosphere, outer space, or under the oceans.[43] Australia, New Zealand, and other Asian countries pressed successfully for a resolution calling for an end to nuclear testing in the atmosphere over the Pacific.[44] In February 1973, French sources announced that, following one more megaton-range detonation in the Pacific atmosphere, France would shift to underground testing.[45] Thus if France should enter the arms control community along with the US, the UK, and the USSR, this development would probably serve to strengthen the case against an underground test ban in the near future.

The foregoing developments are mentioned not because they are necessarily of great or enduring importance, but because they serve to illustrate some of the subtle complexities of the contemporary armaments impasse in the international diplomatic forum. In that forum, things are not always what they seem. Not every government

[42] *New York Times*, November 26, 1972. For the US position, see p. 129 above.
[43] *Ibid.*
[44] *Ibid.*
[45] *Washington Post*, February 10, 1973.

that votes for a committee to explore the prospects for a disarmament conference wants or expects such a conference to be convened; numerous obstacles can be counted upon to intervene between the initial overture and the final crescendo, several scenes later. Not every government that wants a conference to be convened either desires or expects it to lead to disarmament. Some governments may be interested in having a conference for its potential value as a propaganda sounding board or an arena of political warfare. Some may be interested merely in creating an additional opportunity to enhance by ever so little their almost infinitesimal bargaining power within the international system. Nearly all governments are sophisticated enough to be convinced that so long as the political communities of the world continue to behave as they characteristically have behaved throughout the history of the nation-state system, they are not likely to renounce their reliance upon military power as an instrument of achieving their security through the process of deterrence and equilibration. Thus does disarmament remain a persistent yet elusive theme in the foreign policies of states, like a recurring ballad refrain by an ancient bard who sang of the day when swords would be turned into plowshares.

## Selected Bibliography

Beaton, Leonard. *The Reform of Power: A Proposal for an International Security System* (New York: Viking, 1972).

Bechhoefer, Bernhard G. *Postwar Negotiations for Arms Control* (Washington: Brookings, 1961).

Biddle, W. F. *Weapons Technology and Arms Control* (New York: Praeger, 1972).

Bloomfield, Lincoln P., Clemens, Walter C., Jr., and Griffiths, Franklyn. *Khrushchev and the Arms Race* (Cambridge: MIT Press, 1966).

Bramson, Leon, and Goethals, George W., eds. *War: Studies from Psychology, Sociology, Anthropology,* revised edition (New York: Basic Books, 1968).

Brennan, Donald G., ed. *Arms Control, Disarmament and National Security* (New York: Braziller, 1961).

Buchan, Alastair, ed. *A World of Nuclear Powers?* (Englewood Cliffs, N.J.: Prentice-Hall, 1966).

Buchan, Alastair, and Windsor, Philip. *Arms and Stability in Europe* (New York: Praeger, 1963).

Bull, Hedley. *The Control of the Arms Race* (New York: Praeger, 1961).

Clemens, Walter C., Jr. *The Arms Race and Sino-Soviet Relations* (Stanford: Hoover Institution on War, Revolution and Peace, 1968).

Dallin, Alexander, and others. *The Soviet Union, Arms Control and Disarmament* (New York: School of International Affairs, Columbia University, 1964).

Dougherty, James E. *Arms Control and Disarmament: The Critical Issues* (Washington: Center for Strategic Studies, Georgetown University, 1966).

Dougherty, James E., and Lehman, J. F., Jr., eds. *Arms Control for the Late Sixties* (Princeton: Van Nostrand, 1967).

Halperin, Morton H., ed. *Sino-Soviet Relations and Arms Control* (Cambridge: MIT Press, 1967).

Iklé, Fred Charles. *How Nations Negotiate* (New York: Harper and Row, 1964).

Kintner, William R., and Pfaltzgraff, Robert L., Jr., eds. SALT: *Implications for Arms Control in the 1970s* (Pittsburgh: University of Pittsburgh Press, 1973).

Luard, Evan, ed. *First Steps to Disarmament* (New York: Basic Books, 1965).

Schelling, Thomas C. *Arms and Influence* (New Haven: Yale University Press, 1966).

The reader is also referred to *Documents on Disarmament* published annually by the US Arms Control and Disarmament Agency, as well as the Agency's Annual Report to the Congress, transmitted at the end of January each year. Periodicals which frequently carry articles on arms control and related matters are *Foreign Affairs, Orbis, Survival, World Politics, Bulletin of Atomic Scientists*, and *Journal of Conflict Resolution.*

**National Strategy Information Center, Inc.**

**Strategy Papers**

Edited by Frank N. Trager and William Henderson
With the assistance of Dorothy E. Nicolosi

*Nuclear Weapons and the Atlantic Alliance* by Wynfred Joshua, May 1973

*How to Think About Arms Control and Disarmament* by James E. Dougherty, May 1973

*The Military Indoctrination of Soviet Youth* by Leon Gouré, January 1973

*The Asian Alliance: Japan and United States Policy* by Franz Michael and Gaston J. Sigur, October 1972

*Iran, The Arabian Peninsula, and the Indian Ocean* by R. M. Burrell and Alvin J. Cottrell, September 1972

*Soviet Naval Power: Challenge for the 1970s* by Norman Polmar, April 1972

*How Can We Negotiate with the Communists?* by Gerald L. Steibel, March 1972

*Soviet Political Warfare Techniques, Espionage and Propaganda in the 1970s* by Lyman B. Kirkpatrick, Jr., and Howland H. Sargeant, January 1972

*The Soviet Presence in the Eastern Mediterranean* by Lawrence L. Whitten, September 1971

*The Military* Un*balance*
*Is the U.S. Becoming a Second-Class Power?* June 1971

*The Future of South Vietnam* by Brigadier F. P. Serong, February 1971 (Out of print)

*Strategy and National Interests: Reflections for the Future* by Bernard Brodie, January 1971

*The Mekong River: A Challenge in Peaceful Development for Southeast Asia* by Eugene R. Black, December 1970

*Problems of Strategy in the Pacific and Indian Oceans* by George G. Thomson, October 1970

*Soviet Penetration into the Middle East* by Wynfred Joshua, July 1970. Revised edition, October 1971

*Australian Security Policies and Problems* by Justus M. van der Kroef, May 1970

*Detente: Dilemma or Disaster?* by Gerald L. Steibel, July 1969

*The Prudent Case for Safeguard* by William R. Kintner, June 1969

*Forthcoming*

*The People's Liberation Army: Communist China's Armed Forces* by Angus M. Fraser

*On Research and Development and the Prospects for International Security* by Frederick Seitz and Rodney W. Nichols

*The Horn of Africa* by J. Bowyer Bell, Jr.

*The Soviet Presence in Latin America* by James D. Theberge

*The Development of Strategic Weapons* by Norman Polmar

*Contemporary Soviet Defense Policy* by Benjamin S. Lambeth

*Raw Material Supply in a Multipolar World* by Yuan-li Wu.